Nourishing
the
Seed

DESTINY IMAGE BOOKS BY BOB MUMFORD

Agape Road

Mysterious Seed

Nourishing the Seed

Learning to Please God as a Father

BOB MUMFORD

DESTINY IMAGE® PUBLISHERS, INC.

P.O. Box 310, Shippensburg, PA 17257-0310

"Promoting Inspired Lives."

This book and all other Destiny Image, Revival Press, MercyPlace, Fresh Bread, Destiny Image Fiction, and Treasure House books are available at Christian bookstores and distributors worldwide.

For a U.S. bookstore nearest you, call 1-800-722-6774.

For more information on foreign distributors, call 717-532-3040.

Reach us on the Internet: www.destinyimage.com.

ISBN 13 TP: 978-0-7684-4138-3

ISBN 13 Ebook: 978-0-7684-8823-4

For Worldwide Distribution, Printed in the U.S.A.

1 2 3 4 5 6 7 8 / 16 15 14 13 12

Dedication

To our daughter Keren Alene Kilgore whose authentic love for her Lord, combined with her passion for truth, goes far beyond the call of duty. This book could not have been born without her writing and editing skills. Knowing the heart of my message, she made sense of my disorganized phrases and brought clarity to the content. Through this effort, we all discovered that Father God is not a sheriff, but chooses to reveal Himself as a wise and careful farmer, cultivating and nourishing the mysterious Seed of His Kingdom in all of us.

Endorsements

Bob Mumford has a more mature, extended, unfettered grip on the dynamics of *Agape* love than anybody alive. I heartily and happily commend this work to you and everyone! *Agape* love.

Jack Taylor, president
Dimensions Ministries
Melbourne, FL

My friend and brother, Bob Mumford, is a man who has agonized in the garden of revelation to bring us an understanding of the love of the Father. This love gives the soul cleansing and an ever-increasing revelation of the eternal, incorruptible Seed planted in us at the new birth and called forth by Father to grow and mature. Bob's journey has had its rewards, pains, revelations, and years of persevering in search of the Seed that, when sown in our hearts and lives, will produce oaks of righteousness. Over the many years that I've known him, he has never taken the easy road but has persevered in the acquisition of truth. Bob has a heart after God that is a rare and exquisite gift causing him to always embrace reality—resulting in change and intimacy with the Father.

Herman Kanis, friend

I love Bob. I love our times of conversation where we explore possibilities in the Spirit. To be honest, if Bob wrote a grocery list, I would buy it. I love his heart and his renewed mind.

Here's the thing: We do not become a new person by changing our behavior. We discover the person we already are in Jesus and behave accordingly. *Nourishing the Seed* is an excellent book to really get to grips with the new self. God is not dealing with our old nature; it's dead. He seeks rather to establish our righteousness and our new creation capacity to be as wonderful as Jesus.

Graham Cooke
www.brilliantbookhouse.com

For when He was invested with honor and glory from God the Father and a voice was borne to Him by the [splendid] Majestic Glory [in the bright cloud that overshadowed Him, saying], This is My beloved Son in Whom I am well pleased and delight.

(2 Peter 1:17)

Contents

Part II Becoming Father Pleasers

Part III Fatherhood

Part X Freedom and Mental Health

Part XI Unshakable

Part XII Reality and Unreality

Foreword

In 1942, God the Father ransomed and adopted a sweaty, 12-year-old "Jersey boy" named Bob Mumford. A *mysterious seed* was implanted in him, and he was predestined to become both a pioneer and ambassador of the Kingdom of God. After leaving the United States Navy in 1954, the *seed germinated* and mightily emerged as he zealously answered that call. Like a heat-seeking missile, Bob has pursued, proclaimed, and imparted the message of the Kingdom for nearly six decades. Faithfully *nourishing the seed* in His son, Father matured and transformed Bob into a spiritual papa through whom many of us could discover and participate in the precious inheritance of abundant Kingdom life.

Bob Mumford is both my natural and spiritual father, and it has been an honor to watch this transformation take place. Words simply fail to describe the exceeding value of the contents of this book. Understanding the regenerative *Seed* of *Agape* has served as an unshakable foundation for everything Father has called me to "build" as a husband, father, pastor, missionary, and Bible teacher. *Nourishing the Seed* has been especially valuable to me as a father and steward of 23 formerly orphaned Ukrainian and Ugandan children whom Father entrusted to me over the past ten years.

We have seen this *Seed* implanted in our children, who were ransomed from circumstances of darkness in orphanages, refugee camps, and slums, and watched it grow over time transforming sons and daughters into true givers and mature *Father pleasers*. A certain verse has been very meaningful in this process:

So it will be...that [the enemy's] *burden will be removed from your shoulders and his yoke from your neck, and the yoke will be broken because of fatness* (Isaiah 10:27).

The yoke of abuse, deception, misplaced affections, witchcraft, and even the *Eros* nature is broken because the Seed of Christ growing mightily in these children has simply *outgrown* the enemy's leash and claim on them! These sons and daughters are set free, made new, and become acculturated into Father's family.

It is much more than principle contained here; these are living words—the tested, proven ways of the Lord that come to bear upon our practical, day-to-day life, language, and relationships, both in our large family household in Uganda, and in the ministry and family of Lifechangers. I am confident that you will find them just as practical in your own life. *Nourishing the Seed* truly expedites our own growth in the image and likeness of God; it also equips us to feed and water the *Seed* in those whom Father has entrusted into our care.

ERIC MUMFORD, MDIV
PRESIDENT, LIFECHANGERS

Preface

A s A BRAND NEW Christian, I was just home from the Navy and was visiting a neighboring church, when an unusually sophisticated, white-haired man stood to say, "The Lord has been my healer and faithful provider for 63 years." This man, then 85 years old, was still healthy, fresh, open, and malleable, and to me it felt like he was putty in the hands of the Lord. As a new believer, I had never seen anything quite like it. He had obviously discovered the secret to living life as an overcomer. I found a hunger burning in my heart to emulate that life.

Now, at 80 years of age, I am that white-haired man, and I want to share with you something of what I have learned about how to be vibrant, alive, and full of the joy of the Holy Spirit when you are 85. The Lord has my permission to come tomorrow—but suppose it's another 50 years? For many of us, this journey is longer than we first realized.

I am a papa. If I had all my children and grandchildren in a room and had opportunity to speak to them, I would talk about how to be a Father pleaser. John 8:29: *"He who sent Me is with Me; He has not left Me alone, for I always do the things that are pleasing to Him,"* is my life verse, and it has taken me almost a lifetime to learn it. It is not enough to know what to do; it is important to know how to do it. After 56 years walking with the Lord and having as many failures as successes, I was ready to embrace a new way of seeing the New Testament. All of us learn by trial and error—too many trials and quite a few errors; but nevertheless we learn.

Nourishing the Seed is the result of my unfolding journey of walking with the Lord for over 55 years, and learning to love what Father loves.

Like *Mysterious Seed*, I am passing on more nuggets from the bag of Seed that Father has given me. The DNA of the acorn enables it to become all that God the Father intended: a huge, symmetrical, and fully formed oak tree. The Father's Seed in us comes to maturity in the same way. Our two objectives in this book are: first, to understand *Agape* as the mysterious Kingdom Seed that must be cultivated and nourished in order to grow and produce fruit in our lives; and second, to address the issues that keep that from happening.

Jesus said, *"If it were not so, I would have told you"* (John 14:2). There are no cons, tricks, or gimmicks in the New Testament; it is straightforward and forthright. Jesus always put the cost up front. The church tells us about wanting to take us to a beautiful land with butterflies, and we end up in Vietnam. Jesus says right up-front that if we follow Him, we will need to carry our own cross. He then continues, *"I go to prepare a place for you"* (John 14:2). In Father's house there is a place for everyone. If this were not true, He would have told us. This uncomplicated, up-front statement, full of clarity and purpose, has given me a fresh confidence in the essence, words, and central purpose of the New Testament. It allows us the freedom to approach the New Testament as intentional Father pleasers, knowing that He who sent us is with us. Being a Father pleaser is the key to enjoying an abiding, unbroken relationship with God. If the purpose were not that of learning to please the Father, Jesus would have told us. Notice the next statement, which is almost a repeat, *"He has not left Me alone, because I always do the things that are pleasing to Him"* (John 8:29).

Hebrews 13:5 says, *"I will never desert you, nor will I ever forsake you."* His faithfulness to us is not dependent upon our acting in a manner that is always pleasing. However, the eventual, intended, and defined purpose is that of learning to please our Father, and Jesus Christ has been assigned to help us get there.

BOB MUMFORD
SEPTEMBER, 2012

PART I

The Necessity of *Agape*

The Mysterious Seed

God's kingdom is like seed thrown on a field by a man who then goes to bed and forgets about it. The seed sprouts and grows—he has no idea how it happens. The earth does it all without his help: first a green stem of grass, then a bud, then the ripened grain (Mark 4:26-29 MSG).

THE MYSTERY OF THE Kingdom can be seen in the parable of the sower. Mark tells a beautiful story of how Kingdom fruit does not emerge fully mature. This mysterious Seed contains all that is necessary to produce fruit. It germinates, and we do not really know how the growth occurs—but it grows and produces fruit by itself. We can cultivate, water, and nourish, but we cannot make the fruit grow. Every farmer knows the futility of trying to force a seed to grow. He also knows it is not possible to plant watermelon seeds today and get watermelons tomorrow. The farmer quickly learns not to give himself a spiritual hernia trying to make the seed grow or to reap a crop before it is ready. The end result is a harvest of fruit that is pleasing to the farmer.

The Seed reproduces after its kind. Apple trees produce apples, and peach trees produce peaches. The source of the Eternal Seed is not from the earth, nor is its origin mortal, as in human sperm, but from One who is immortal by the ever-living Word of God. Coming in Seed form, *Agape* is required to mature, or be perfected, so that it can find expression and release. When the Kingdom Seed of *Agape* begins to grow, it brings forth characteristics of the Kingdom—it produces God's *Agape* as fruit after its kind. This is Paul's reasoning to the believers in Galatia: If we depart from Christ, the fruit or manifestation will be fleshly behavior (see Gal. 5:19-21). If we abide in Christ, and water, nourish, and cultivate that Eternal Seed, the fruit will be *Agape* (see Gal. 5:22-23). Many Greek expositors explain Galatians 5:22 as the fruit of the Spirit being *Agape*, out of which there appears joy, peace, longsuffering, kindness, godliness, faithfulness, meekness, and self-control.

God Himself is *Agape* (see 1 John 4:8). His love is covenantally faithful, unconditional, and self-giving. *Agape* is God's absolute by which He judges all things, and it is His nature—His DNA, or His communicable attributes that are imparted to His own. The mysterious, Eternal Seed of *Agape* is ultimate reality. *Agape will never go away* because love never disappears. If I am manufacturing love, it will disappear. If love is the real thing, it will stand, continue, and never disappear because God **is** *Agape*. In Paul's well-known words in First Corinthians 13:13 (AMP): *"And so faith, hope, Agape abide."*

Thoughts and Questions

- In what ways have you tried to force the Seed to grow?

- How has *Agape* found expression or release in your life?

- Explain why the fruit of the Spirit (see Gal. 5:22) comes out of *Agape*.

Reading 2

The Nature of *Agape*

Love never disappears (1 Corinthians 13:8, MOF).

IN ORDER TO UNDERSTAND the importance of the Seed, we must have a grasp of *Agape* and *Eros*. We will look at *Agape* first and *Eros* afterwards.

Agape (Strong's No. 26) is a Greek word for "love." *Agape* is an exercise of the divine will in deliberate choice, made without assignable cause—save that which lies in the nature of God Himself (see Deut. 7:7-8). It is a quality of life and is used as both a noun and a verb derivative. *Agape* unfolds in three progressive steps, none of which can be omitted:

Love God with all of my heart, soul, mind, and strength (see Mark 12:30).

Love myself because God has given me value and worth by pouring His own love into me while I was yet a sinner (see Rom. 5:8).

Love others, even my enemies, in the same manner and degree that He has loved me and gave Himself for me (see Matt. 5:43-48).

God Himself is *Agape* (see 1 John 4:8). His love—covenantally faithful, unconditional, and self-giving—is depicted as a straight arrow. *Agape* is ultimate reality. In First Corinthians 13, the famous chapter on love, we can see several aspects of the nature of *Agape*:

Agape creates community. It brings us to *being* rather than *doing*. We can know all mysteries and all knowledge, but if we do not *have* love, we are nothing (see 1 Cor. 13:3). The reason we are nothing is because it is *Agape* that gives us identity, revealing us to ourselves and to each other. Because *Agape* is relational, we would have to say, "It is God's *Agape*, given to me freely in the person of Christ, which imparts to me value and identity." Apart from Christ's act, we would remain dead and incapable of the *Agape* responses that God desires. God has given us *His* capacity to love, but that capacity must be brought to its full end so that we can love as He loves.

Agape loves without being self-referential. We can even give all our possessions to feed the poor and still be self-referential, expecting to get something from God in return. God's *Agape* goes out to a hurting world without seeking anything in return, and it comes to us from God as Father without personal advantage or selfish gain.

Agape is the single cohesive factor for the entire Body of Christ and the social fabric of the universe. It is by the instrumental means of *Agape* that the Body builds itself up in love (see Eph. 4:16).

Thoughts and Questions

- From personal experience, how would you interpret the statement "If I do not have love, I am nothing"?

- How does putting *Agape* into action affect your relationships?

- What are the three progressive stages in which *Agape* grows?

READING 3

The Nature of *Eros*

But if your eye is unsound, your whole body will be full of
darkness. If then the very light in you [your conscience] is darkened,
how dense is that darkness! (Matthew 6:23 AMP).

*E*ROS IS A GREEK word, but it is not used in the New Testament because
of its sexual corruption. The essential meaning of *Eros* is the desire or
intention to possess, acquire, or control. *Eros* does not seek to be accepted
by its object, but to gain possession of it. *Eros* has an appetite or yearning
desire that is aroused by the attractive qualities of its object. *Eros,* in Greek
philosophy, came to mean that which is loved for the purpose of personal
satisfaction. It is from this posture that the word *Eros* took on its sexual
and ultimately pornographic connotation. The word is not primarily sexual,
but has more to do with living for our own personal advantage. One of the
Greek words for "evil" in the New Testament is *poneros* (Strong's No. 4190),
from which we get the word pornography. Essentially, *poneros* is a love that
is bought and sold, which is no love at all. *Porne* (Strong's No. 4204), a
related word, is the link that joins *Eros* and original sin. Moffatt translates *porne*, the King James word for evil, as selfishness. Because the New
Testament uses *porne* for its description of evil, it is saying something like,
"all evil is love for God that has been twisted and sold for something else."
Paul explained evil as fallen man exchanging God's glory for his or her own
desires (see Rom. 1:23).

Eros is the mother of all sins. It can be recognized because it is *always*
self-referential. It is not only self-centered, but it becomes self-consuming,
turning increasingly inward upon itself in a tighter and tighter spiral. *Eros*
is a highly refined form of self-interest and self-seeking. It is a love that has

become so distorted that its only purpose is to meet its own needs. When Jesus referred to religion that turned us in upon ourselves, He said, *"How great is that darkness"* (Matt. 6:22-23 KJV). He was talking about selfishness that leads to a form of darkness that has deadening results. Jesus challenged *Eros*-motivated religion with these words, *"But blessed are your eyes, because they see; and your ears, because they hear"* (Matt. 13:16).

The nature of evil is selling or sharing our love, which belongs to God, in an illegal manner. God jealously asks for all our love—heart, soul, mind, and strength—to the limit of our capacity because He knows it is the *one force* that releases us from ourselves and exerts the capacity to keep us from evil. We do indeed become what we love. We are faced with the inexorable truth that no one can set us free from that which we still love—especially an illegal love for ourselves!

Thoughts and Questions

- In what ways have you seen *Eros* functioning with the intention to possess, acquire, or control?

- Explain why *Eros* is always self-referential.

- Why does God ask for all our love – heart, soul, mind, and strength?

ENDNOTES

1. Anders Nygren, *Agape and Eros* (Philadelphia: Westminster Press), viii-xvi.

2. William Barclay, *Flesh and Spirit: An Examination of Galatians 5:9-23* (Nashville: Abingdon Press / SCM Press LTD, 1962), 23.

READING 4

Agape—the Perfect Bond of Unity

And above all these [put on] love [Agape] and enfold yourselves
with the bond of perfectness [which binds everything together
completely in ideal harmony] (Colossians 3:14 AMP).

*S*UMMUM *BONUM* IS A Latin phrase meaning the highest good above which there is no other good. To focus on an issue above which there is nothing higher is quite appealing. Too often, however, we discover that we have put second or third things first, resulting in confusion and added complexity. So, what is the highest good in all of creation? Most of us would say God. Some would say Christ. But *God is Agape* (see 1 John 4:8), and Christ is God incarnate—*Agape* in human form. God's intention in Christ's incarnation was not to reveal His thoughts or plans, but to reveal Himself to each of us. We are the loved ones responding to the One who is doing the loving.

The English word *love* simply does not communicate all that is contained within the concept of *Agape*. In the King James Version, the word *love* is painfully translated "charity," which has caused some serious confusion over the years. The word *Agape* must begin to find its place in our vocabulary because it fully expresses the nature and personality of God the Father, who wishes to be known by His *communicable* attributes: compassionate, gracious, slow to anger, merciful, truthful, covenantally faithful, and forgiving. Father wants to share these seven hidden attributes with us—and the only word that contains them all is *Agape*. These attributes were given to us in Christ's incarnate person at our new birth as the mysterious and Eternal Seed. When Christ is formed within us, these attributes or character traits begin to grow in us. This mysterious Seed, when cultivated, nourished, and brought to fruitfulness, allows the character of Christ to be replicated in us, resulting in the fruit of the Spirit.

Paul gives us the steps to *Agape* in Colossians 3:10 AMP. First we clothe ourselves with *"the new* [spiritual self]," which involves laying aside our old self; then we find ourselves being *"renewed and remolded into* [fuller and more perfect knowledge upon] *knowledge after the image (the likeness) of Him Who created it."* Finally, the end result—a new self, created in the image of God. Only through this process can we put on love, which is the perfect bond of unity (see Col. 3:14.) This sequence is an intentional process with growth and maturity as the goal. Growth in the New Testament is identified as *Agape* being brought to its intended purpose *(telios).*

Agape is not a means to a goal; it *is* the goal. *Agape* is what this Christian life is all about. *Above Agape there isn't anything else* because Father **is** *Agape* and He wants us to find intimacy and fellowship with Him. Like Christ, we are becoming one in purpose, action, and motive with the Father. This is what Paul meant when he said to

> *earnestly desire and zealously cultivate the greatest and best gifts and graces* (the higher gifts and the choicest graces). *And yet I will show you a still more excellent way [one that is better by far and the highest of them all—love]* (1 Corinthians 12:31 AMP).

Thoughts and Questions

🐏 Why is *Agape* needed in our vocabulary?

🐏 Describe your experience with the three incremental steps to *Agape* in Colossians 3:10.

🐏 Why is *Agape* the *summum bonum* (the highest good)?

READING 5

Motivated by *Agape*

No one's ever seen or heard anything like this, never so much
as imagined anything quite like it—what God has arranged
for those who [Agape] him (1 Corinthians 2:9 MSG).

I N ORDER TO UNDERSTAND that *Agape* has to do with behavior, we need
to look at the manner in which Father cares for His family. When I first
discovered this theme, I felt like Albert Einstein when he came upon the
theory of relativity. Einstein said that *the supreme goal of all theory is to make
the irreducible basic elements as simple and as few as possible without having to
surrender the adequate representation of a single datum of experience. Agape* is
that irreducible basic element in the life of the believer and in the constitu-
tion of the redeemed community. In all of its forms, *Agape* is used some 320
times in the New Testament, and each of its uses is *behavioral.* Ephesians
mentions several of them:

- *"...holy and blameless before Him...in [Agape]"* (1:4).

- *"...your Agape for all the saints"* (1:15).

- *"...because of His great Agape with which He Agaped us"* (2:4).

- *"...rooted and grounded in Agape"* (3:17).

- *"...to know the Agape of Christ which surpasses knowledge"* (3:19).

- *"...showing tolerance for one another in Agape"* (4:2).

- *"...speaking the truth in Agape"* (4:15).

- *"Christ...causes the growth of the body for the building up of itself up in Agape"* (4:15-16).

- *"...walk in Agape"* (5:2).

- *"...and [Agape] with faith, from God the Father"* (6:23).

Jesus said,

> *"You shall love [Agape] the Lord your God with all your heart, and with all your soul, and with and all your mind...[and] love [Agape] your neighbor as yourself. On these two commandments depend the whole Law and the Prophets"* (Matthew 22:37, 39-40).

This boils everything down to an irreducible basic element for the believer, the community, and its leadership: *Agape* is behavioral. This is why Paul could say, "The whole law is fulfilled in *one word...Agape!"* (Gal. 5:14).

Jesus' job description is to lead us into an intimate love relationship with God. At the same time, God the Father is reaching out for us through His Son Jesus Christ. Ponder for a moment an inconceivable thought—God Himself passionately desires an intimate relationship with each of us! The path that leads to an open connection with God is called the *Agape* road. It is a path of love that He laid out to bring us to Himself, one that Jesus pioneered during His earthly life. He invites us to journey this path to knowing and loving God as Father—but the choice is ours. It is important to understand that Heaven is not the goal. If you are a Christian and you die, you have to go to Heaven; there is no place else to go! The goal is knowing the Father Himself.

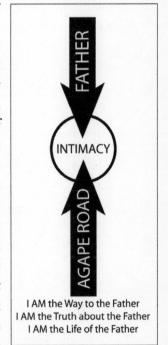

FATHER

INTIMACY

AGAPE ROAD

I AM the Way to the Father
I AM the Truth about the Father
I AM the Life of the Father

When we choose to follow Jesus and we give our hearts to Him, we *do* experience some intimacy with God. However, it is often sporadic and inconsistent. Jesus bases His relationship with us, and our relationship with Him on *Agape*, knowing that if we *Agape* Him, we will discover both the freedom and the willingness to do what He asks. It is our *Agape* for Him that motivates us to change our behavior and abide even when it is to our personal disadvantage to do so. *Agape* allows us to deny our own preferences, even if it involves personal suffering and discomfort.

Thoughts and Questions

🐝 In what ways is *Agape* the *irreducible basic element* of all of life?

🐝 Describe some of the *Agape* behaviors used in Ephesians.

🐝 How can you see *Agape* becoming more behavioral in your own life?

Agape Is Behavioral

And you shall love the Lord your God out of and with your whole heart and out of and with all your soul (your life) *and out of and with all your mind* (with your faculty of thought and your moral understanding) *and out of and with all your strength. This is the first and principal commandment* (Mark 12:30 AMP).

LIKE MANY OF US, my Christian life began with an intense struggle to identify in some working manner the quintessence of the Christian life. At the halfway point of my journey, around 30 years, I became heart-sick and weary of everything and everybody, including myself. I did not feel the vibrancy and joy that I had seen years earlier in that older, white-haired man. I felt foolish and somewhat hostile. In an angry voice I asked God, "What do You want from me!?" His immediate response, in a quiet, fatherly voice was, "I want you to love Me." I went to the Scriptures and reread the commandment: *"And you shall love the Lord your God with all your heart, and with all your soul, and with all your mind, and with all your strength"* (Mark 12:30). Finally, in the midst of an emotional battle, I locked in on an essential truth: The entire Christian life should be—and was always intended to be—centered on learning how to be a Father-pleaser. If we set our goal to please the Father, a thousand problems will be resolved right off the bat, and many of our prayers will suddenly seem superfluous. A lot of the bits and pieces with which we struggle will simply disappear because our whole life has now become centered on learning to please the Father.

So, for the last 25 years, I have been trying to understand, biblicize, and be able to teach how loving God and pleasing Him affects our behavior. If I love God in the manner in which He asks, why would that change my behavior? We all know that behavior is one of the hardest things to change.

You can believe all kinds of things, but *acting* differently is a new challenge; yet biblically, it is the central and intended purpose of God's redemptive plan. This is the meaning and essence of the word Kingdom—we are now responding behaviorally to His governmental purpose!

In Matthew 3:17 Father said, "*This is My beloved Son, in whom I am well-pleased.*" Again in Matthew 12:18, He said, "*Behold, My Servant whom I have chosen; My Beloved in whom My soul is well-pleased.*" It is evident that Father is really pleased with Jesus. Then I linked the word *well-pleasing* to another Scripture: First Corinthians 10:5 states, "*Nevertheless, with most of them God was not well-pleased.*" Father was pleased with Jesus but not pleased with Israel and I saw the Kingdom of God—the terms *Agape* and *Kingdom* are synonymous. Pleasing God is behavioral, and God is *Agape*; therefore, His Kingdom is ruled behaviorally by our motivation to learn to love God with all of our heart, soul, mind, and strength.

When we center our whole being on pleasing the Father, it radically affects our ethical and moral behavior. When the grocery clerk handed me too much change, I said, "Excuse me, you gave me $2 too much." She looked at me as if I had come from Mars. I said, "I'm a Father-pleaser, and my Father wouldn't be pleased if I cheated you out of $2." She was impacted, but I wasn't trying to be spiritual; it was about pleasing the Father. We are now learning the practical lessons of the fear of God. To be as honest as possible results in experiencing Father's pleasure. He is eager for us to discover this as a Kingdom lifestyle.

Thoughts and Questions

🎺 Why do you think problems are solved and prayers seem superfluous when we set our goal to please the Father?

🎺 Explain why the terms *Agape* and *Kingdom* are synonymous.

🎺 Why would honesty result in Father's pleasure?

READING 7

Correction by *Agape*

But now faith, hope, love, abide these three; but the greatest of these is love (1 Corinthians 13:13).

EVERY TIME THERE ARE pivotal personal or doctrinal crises in the Scriptures, *Agape* is the corrective measure that strongly encourages us to continue walking in *Agape* so that we do not lose our Kingdom inheritance. Remember, *Agape* is behavioral, not a new doctrinal theory. I have never seen anyone converted by a proof text. This is why *Agape* rather than the law is used to correct and admonish—because God's Word is not a bullet but a seed. Following are some biblical examples that use *Agape* for serious corrective measures in the New Testament.

In response to many problems, including incest, sectarianism, lawsuits, immorality, and fornication in the Corinthian church, Paul used *Agape* to correct and redirect them back to the *Agape* road. He taught them how the Body of Christ should function and explained the *Agape* character traits of the resurrected Christ. Then he said, *"But now faith, hope, love, abide these three; but the greatest of these is love"* (1 Cor. 13:13).

With a simple concordance, we could examine each of the Gospels and the Epistles to see how His Bride was corrected when she missed the *Agape* road. The Galatian Christians had moved from Christ back to the law, or works of the flesh, and Paul told them that because of this, they would have a lot of problems. After addressing problems such as idolatry, jealousy, anger, and envy, Paul used *Agape* as the corrective measure by saying, *"But... [Agape] is: joy, peace, patience, kindness, goodness, faithfulness, gentleness, and self-control"* (Gal. 5:22-23). *Agape* is what brought the whole Galatian church back to the *Agape* road.

Because the church in Colossae was on a main trade route, it was heavily influenced by ungodly cultures, including Oriental mysticism. In his writings, Paul corrected the false teachings, which were a mixture of pagan occultism, Jewish legalism, and Christianity. He encouraged the believers to keep seeking the things above where Christ is seated (see Col. 3:1), to watch what they say, and *"regardless of what else you put on, wear love"* (Col. 3:14 MSG). Paul instructed the Colossians in the truth of *Agape* because above *Agape* there is nothing else; it is the consummate revelation of God.

Each time a community missed the *Agape* road, it was the apostles' burden to correct and redirect its members back to *Agape*. Paul knew that the law could not redirect them, only *Agape* as the fruit of the Spirit could do so. Paul's *irreducible basic element and* Kingdom corrective was: "Above all, wear *Agape*."

Thoughts and Questions

🦌 Since *Agape* is behavioral, not doctrinal, explain why it is used as a corrective measure.

🦌 How did Paul use *Agape* to put the Galatian church back on the *Agape* road?

🦌 What are some other instances in the Scriptures where *Agape* is used as a corrective measure?

Lying Against *Agape*

But if you have bitter jealousy (envy) *and contention* (rivalry,
selfish ambition) *in your hearts, do not pride yourselves on it and
thus be in defiance of and false to the Truth* (James 3:14 AMP).

MOST OF US THINK of spiritual warfare as the realm of the supernatural, demons, and satan. However, our concept needs to be modified because spiritual warfare also belongs squarely within the *conflict created by our relinquishing our seat with Christ in heavenly places* (see Eph. 2:6). Which would you consider to be a more prevalent problem in the Church in general: human selfishness or demonic activity? Selfishness is much more prevalent, although it is true that the demonic enters and exacerbates our selfishness. In that selfish posture, we have one purpose—that of advancing our own agenda, implementing our own control, or simply yielding to the need to be right.

God is *Agape* and *Agape* is Truth. Only *Agape* is able to cause us to surrender, repent, and value others as better than ourselves. James was addressing several groups of Christians when he said, *"Do not be arrogant and so lie against the truth"* (James 3:14). The context here tells us that something had gone very wrong, and a strange, unexpected mixture of *Eros* and *Agape* had occurred within the fellowship. James points out that selfish ambition can progress until it is actually demonic; but its origin was purely in selfish ambition.

The phrase "selfish ambition" in Greek is *eritheia* (Strong's No. 2052). It is a very strong, bitter word translated as "strife, contention, partisanship, and fractiousness"—basically *a desire to put oneself forward*. When selfish ambition is ruling our mind, heart, and emotions, it consequently becomes our decision maker! Selfish ambition has the capacity to make a liar out of us. In our determination to be right, we will run, hide, and shift blame. We are capable of almost any action, once selfish ambition sets in. It creates a climate of political and emotional confusion by making sure we win, falsely guaranteeing that we will emerge as the leader and defend our right to a recognized title. From a Kingdom perspective, we have won the skirmish and lost the battle.

Lying against the truth is no small issue. In the Book of Romans, the issue is selfish ambition manifested as refusal or *disobeying* the truth. Selfish ambition (*eritheia*) is used seven times in the Greek, and is often translated "contention and strife" (see Rom. 2:8; 2 Cor. 12:20; Gal. 5:20; Phil. 1:15, 2:3; James 3:14, 16). Take some time to look at the Scriptures. In each of them, the source of the conflict is *"seeking after our own interests, not those of Christ Jesus"* (Phil. 2:21). While we are competent to recognize it in others, each of us needs to recognize the selfish ambition that is *within ourselves*.

Agape does not seek its own and manifests primarily within us toward God and then out to others: Love the Lord your God with all your heart, soul, mind and strength, and your neighbor as yourself (see Mark 12:30-31). Father puts these together so that we cannot walk in deception and lie against *Agape*.

Thoughts and Questions

- Describe your understanding of spiritual warfare.

- In what ways does selfish ambition cause us to lie against the truth?

- Why does Father tell us to love God *and* our neighbor?

READING 9

Agape, Our Basis of Judgment

Because He has fixed a day when He will judge the world
righteously (justly) by a Man Whom He has destined and
appointed for that task...(Acts 17:31 AMP).

ALL FUTURE JUDGMENT—OF NATIONS, churches, and individuals—will be based on a person, on one Man who has been destined and appointed for this task. We will be *measured by the Man*, Christ Jesus, Who is *Agape* incarnate. His life, ministry, character, and person were demonstrations of the hidden attributes of God the Father. This is why Jesus could say, "He who has seen Me has seen the Father!" (John 14:9).

The thought of future judgment often causes fear and anxiety because we do not know what to expect or how to get ready, but First John tells us what the Day of Judgment will be like:

> *And we know* (understand, recognize, are conscious of, by observation and by experience) *and believe* (adhere to and put faith in and rely on) *the Agape God cherishes for us. God is Agape, and he who dwells* (abides) *and continues in Agape dwells and continues in God, and God dwells and continues in him. In this [union and communion with Him] Agape is brought to completion [maturity] and attains perfection with us, that we may have confidence for the day of judgment [with assurance and boldness to face Him], because as He is, so are we in this world* (1 John 4:16-17 AMP).

The Day of Judgment is not mysterious or frightening because our confidence is in the Man, Christ Jesus. We are not judged by unknown rules or mysterious, esoteric principles, not even by Moses' Ten Commands but by the presence or absence of *Agape* in our lives. Did we follow Jesus and act like Him by doing good, helping those who are in need, feeding the hungry and healing those who were hurting? Whenever we did one of these things to someone overlooked or ignored, Jesus said that we did it to Him (see Matt. 25:34-40). If we give someone a cup of cold water in Jesus' name (an act of *Agape*), we never lose our reward because *giving out of the love of God becomes an eternal act.* Our basic concern should be another's best interest. Following Jesus means practicing *Agape* toward God, ourselves, and those whom Father puts in our paths in daily life. *Agape* that does not function or manifest is useless. We can have confidence in the Day of Judgment by doing what Jesus asks of us—functioning in *Agape*.

Agape prevents us from relating to others in a utilitarian manner. When we seek to do good rather than harm to our neighbor, an *Agape* conversion has taken place in our life. This involves the incorruptible Seed taking root and growing in human hearts, drawing us to change direction from *Eros* to *Agape* thus, we become a new creation.

Thoughts and Questions

🐾 What is the basis on which you will be judged?

🐾 Explain why judgment is behavioral rather than doctrinal.

🐾 What is the result of an *Agape* conversion?

Reading 10

Agape as the Absolute Necessity

If I have [sufficient] faith so that I can remove mountains, but have not
Agape (God's love in me) I am nothing (a useless nobody)
(1 Corinthians 13:2 AMP).

First Corinthians 13 is a most unusual passage, unlike any other in the Scriptures. The question in these verses is: who loves whom? Who is the object and who is the subject of this *Agape?* The ambiguity, variety of meaning, and possible forms of application is called *polyschemia* in Greek. There are three themes in Paul's writing that are aspects of God hiding Himself. Even Paul's ambiguity makes the multiple meanings of *Agape* rich and profound. If we take the mystery out, we have lost God. The three themes that apply the nature of *Agape* are:

1. *Agape is absolute necessity.* In the absence of *Agape*, nothing works as it should.

2. *Agape is functioning reality.* Apart from *Agape*, all words and actions lose their value and effectiveness.

3. *Agape is permanent.* While all other things will pass away, *Agape* is eternal because *Agape* is uncreated.

In this well-known and transitional passage, Paul celebrates *Agape* as the more excellent way. He shows us that everything God is and does is woven together in *Agape*. Like the harness fastened to the Clydesdale horses guiding the wagon, Paul sees *Agape* as the reins that control or govern our desires. *Agape* is the steering wheel for the Christian life. It is *Agape* that controls and governs us, not human willpower. If anyone loves God, he is known by Him (see 1 Cor. 8:3), so *Agape* becomes the *absolute* by which a Christian is identified.

Agape, then, is *more than a virtue*. *Agape* is God's own DNA manifested in the Man, Christ Jesus, by whom we will be measured in future judgment. In light of this, Paul reveals *Agape* as necessary in two distinct ways:

1. *Agape* is received by revelation and is absolutely necessary (see 1 Cor. 13:1-3). It unifies, heals wounds, and does not condemn. *Agape* is absolute necessity because it alone allows us to give up our egos and brings us to *being* rather than to *having; Agape* is what gives us identity. Because it is relational, one could say, "I love, therefore I am" (see 1 Cor. 8:3). *Agape* creates security, identity, and belonging, resulting in community. It is the ultimate foundation for everyone and everything, because *Agape* is God (see 1 John 4:8).

2. *Agape* is intrinsic in beauty and dignity (see 1 Cor. 13:4-7). When Paul said that *Agape* builds community, the key word he used is *edify*. Whenever *Agape* is working, it is designed to edify and build up both personally and corporately. It is the beauty and dignity of *Agape* that prevents our personality from being transformed into something religious.

Agape is inexhaustible and ineffable because God is *Agape*. God is not faith or hope—He is *Agape*. The entire experience of following Jesus could be summarized by saying that God first loved us and we are now learning how to return that love back to Him in as pure a form as we are able.

THOUGHTS & QUESTIONS

- In what ways is *Agape* a steering wheel for your life?

- How does *Agape* create security, identity, and belonging, resulting in community?

- Describe a situation in your life where *Agape* was the key to victory.

READING 11

Functioning in *Agape*

Love never fails [never fades out or becomes obsolete or comes to an end] (1 Corinthians 13:8 AMP).

IN FIRST CORINTHIANS 13:4-8, Paul takes *Agape* to an autonomous height and actually *personifies* it. The reason Paul wrote about *Agape* this way is because he was describing a person, not a commodity—these phrases describe the character of Jesus, Himself. What will we look like when Christ is fully formed in us? What is so *real* about the word *Agape*? The answers lie in the Eternal Seed. Christ comes to us in the new birth as the Eternal Seed which is *Agape*. *Agape* is maximum virtue, for it is God's own nature that has been made incarnate. When this Seed is received, protected, cultivated, and nourished in our lives, it brings forth fruit after its kind. We begin to see Christ's character replicated in us. When this happens we have embraced the real Christ and are walking in the real Kingdom.

Rather than shopworn religious phrases, these are descriptions of the very person of our Lord Jesus Christ. These are the manners in which Father intends to encounter a hurting world. We need to personally own each of these aspects of *Agape*:

Agape is very patient

It is very kind

Agape knows no jealousy

Agape makes no parade

Gives itself no airs

It is never rude

Never selfish

Never irritated

Never resentful

Agape is never glad when others do wrong

Agape is gladdened by goodness

Always slow to expose others

Always eager to believe the best

Always hopeful

Always patient

Agape never disappears

Each of these attributes is applicable to us because God uses the "all things" of life to replicate them in our walk with Jesus. *Agape* represents the greatest good for humanity, for it is God's own person coming to us in the form of Christ incarnate. When He is honored, *Agape* is the result. *Agape* is the greatest expression of life. It does not exist unless it is revealed or manifested on the level of daily experience (see 1 John 3:18). Christ in you, the hope of glory!

Thoughts and Questions

- In what ways can you see *Agape* personified in the person of Christ in First Corinthians 13?

- Which of these characteristics have been shown to you personally by others?

- Which of these characteristics are you struggling to reflect in your own life?

Reading 12

Agape as Permanence

Love never fails [never fades out or becomes obsolete or comes to an end] (1 Corinthians 13:8 AMP).

I F *AGAPE* IS THE only *permanent* life force and never ends, *why* haven't we seen the issue more clearly? God is *Agape*; therefore, the incarnation is God manifested in human flesh as the Son of God. *Agape* is uncreated, eternal, and unshakable. While all else is shaken and done away with, *Agape* is the final, eternal, and unending revelation of God's own person. It will never go away. *Agape* is permanence, so nothing can separate us from the love (*Agape*) of God given to us in the person of our Lord Jesus Christ.

When we have been victorious, it is God's *Agape* manifesting because *Agape* is the source of all victory (see Rom. 8:37). When we fail, it is God's *Agape* that covers the failure. Only God's *Agape* is indefectible, always young, and always faithful. God, Who is *Agape*, will never go away because love never disappears. If we try to manufacture it or fail to tap into the eternal source, what we think is *Agape* will fail. If it is the real thing, it will stand.

Martyrdom has always been of personal interest to me. I remember reading about a man condemned to die for his faith. He was in prison for about three weeks before execution, experiencing an absence of the presence of the Lord. He repeatedly asked the Lord *why* he was feeling forsaken. The Lord, it seemed, never answered. On the morning the guards came to get him for execution, he stepped into the hall, and the manifest presence of the *Agape* of God came down over his physical person. That was all he had been waiting for, and he walked through martyrdom in the real presence and palpable joy of the Lord. Only God's *Agape* is *indefectible*—it does not disappear, come to an end, wear out, fade away, or evaporate. *Agape* is resilient; it keeps reappearing because it is the nature of God, the source of all eternal hope.

Agape is the incorruptible Seed that continually seeks opportunity and occasion to bear Kingdom fruit in us. Faith and hope serve us well, but God is not faith, nor is He hope—God is *Agape* and *Agape* never disappears.

Thoughts and Questions

🌱 In what ways have you experienced *Agape* as the only permanent thing?

🌱 How does *Agape* function in failure and victory?

🌱 Why does *Agape* keep reappearing?

READING 13

Three Negative Uses of *Agape*

*Men loved [Agaped] the darkness rather than the
Light, for their deeds were evil* (John 3:19).

THE CONTENT OF THE word *Agape* is very strong, suggesting irreversible commitment and unyielding faithfulness to that which we love. In light of this, it is shocking to see this beautiful and unique word used in a negative manner. There are several examples in the Scriptures, but we will look at just three of them.

John addresses the issue of men "*loving the darkness rather than the Light, for their deeds were evil.*" Due to the original Fall of Man, we do not just *have* darkness—*we are darkness.* Like fish whose heritage is water, darkness is natural, desirable, and comfortable to us. We were born in *Eros* so this is where we are most contented. Into this darkness comes the Light of God, and suddenly we can see the Kingdom. We are overwhelmed with the idea of transformation being a real possibility and our future being different. With the new hope of the Kingdom as a result of our having been born from above, we enter the strange but real conflict of Light (*Agape*), which brings forth the fruit of the Kingdom and dismantles the aspects of darkness to which we have been inexorably bound. The question is: What or whom do I love more than I love myself? Like the tequila advertising slogan, "Jose Cuervo, I love you," the word *Agape* can be used in a common, worldly way. We have a problem if we apply the content of *Agape* as unreserved love and commitment to the effects of tequila and love (*Agape*) it in the same manner and with the same faithfulness that we should be giving to God. When we love something more than God, we are walking in darkness and cannot distinguish what the real issues are—so our world ends up in confusion. The pull toward darkness is real, natural and, at times, very strong. It is our love (*Agape*) for the Light that takes us into God and His Kingdom of Light.

> *Do not love [Agape] the world nor the things in the world. If anyone loves [Agapes] the world, the love [Agape] of the Father is not in him* (1 John 2:15).

Like loving darkness, we can also love the world system and its attractions. Wrong attachment to the world system is a displacement of our deepest affections. To love (*Agape*) God with all our heart, soul, mind, and strength is to have no illegal love left for the world system or its pleasures. James forcibly says the same thing: *"Flirting with the world every chance you get, you end up enemies of God and his way"* (James 4:4 MSG).

"Let love (Agape) *be without hypocrisy."* Another version says *"Love from the center of who you are; don't fake it"* (Rom. 12:9 MSG). This godly and practical apostle knows how easy it is to fake it and how hard it is to be authentic and real. Hypocrisy is the congenital disease of the remnants of our old nature in the entire Body of Christ.

While the word *Agape* is sometimes used in a negative sense in the Scriptures, each reference has to do with loving ourselves more than God. The labor of yielding the fruit of *Agape* is long and difficult, but ultimately rewarding.

Thoughts and Questions

- How have you used the word *Agape* in common, worldly ways?

- Why is wrong attachment to the world system a displacement of our deepest affections?

- Describe a time when you chose to fake it rather than to be real. What was the result?

The *Agape* Solution to
Three Unsolvable Problems

If I am a Father, where is My honor? (Malachi 1:6).

WHEN OUR LIVES ARE not centered on the Kingdom, we experience three distinct and observable problems. Because each of these is internal, God's answer is the insemination of His *Agape* in the new birth.

The first is *unnatural resistance*. Most of us have resisted God on more than one occasion. I remember the Lord instructing me to do something and my immediate response was an unnatural resistance to what He was telling me. During years of successful ministry around the globe, I often experienced unnatural resistance, resulting in conflict. One day I said to God, "I don't care what it costs; I'm asking You to resolve this internal resistance in me!" That started me on a 20-year journey in which the *Agape* of the Father began to transform my internal person. When we learn to *Agape God with all our heart, soul, mind, and strength*, the alienation between us and God begins to dissolve, and unnatural resistance or fear of what He may ask of us is also lessened or removed.

The second problem is *internal contradiction*. Even for Paul this was virtually an unsolvable problem: I decide to do good, but I don't really do it; I decide not to do bad, but then I do it anyway (see Rom. 7:19). Internal contradiction is common the world over. The solution is to *Agape ourselves* because God's love is what gives each of us value. Our love for God and for our own person causes the war inside us to stop. Christ as *Agape* imparts His wholeness to us so that inward contradictions begin to melt thus, peace reigns in our life. We become a whole person because Christ made us whole. Wholeness releases the two voices that press to be heard and strive for ascendancy. The one voice is that of the shepherd who said: "My sheep hear My voice and I know them" (John 10:27).

The third problem is *relational alienation*. Too many of us have been through religious politics, church splits, and doctrinal wars. The relational problems in churches, marriages, and families are chronic issues. Hurt, pain, and alienation are everywhere, sometimes more in the family of God than outside of it! God's solution is to *Agape our neighbor*. When we replicate Father's love we love someone *because* God loves him—smelly, drunk, miserable, obnoxious, stubborn, whatever. The person is not required to change for us to love him because we learn to love that which God loves in him. Relational alienation begins to cease and *joy* emerges.

Our love for God causes the unending conflict between people, families, nations, and denominations to become minimal and even to cease. Christ as *Agape* Incarnate takes us to His Father, causing a cessation of unnatural resistance. He teaches us to forgive, release, and love our enemies. He designed this government of righteousness, peace and joy to be enjoyed in the presence of our enemies. What a marvelous gift of God!

Thoughts and Questions

- In what ways have you found yourself resisting God?

- Which of the three internal problems have you struggled with the most?

- How can you see *Agape* as the solution to all three problems?

READING 15

Rich Man, Poor Man

The poor man utters supplications, but the rich
man answers roughly (Proverbs 18:23).

WHEN I WAS STUDYING medicine, one of my patients was a very wealthy Jewish man who had slipped in the bathtub and hit his head, precipitating an internal brain hemorrhage. A few days later he died. He was wrapped in a body bag, and I took him to the morgue. That same day, an African-American man who lived on the dump came in to be treated for a life-threatening infection in his lungs. After we finished draining the fluid from his lungs, all he wanted was to talk about the Lord. I sat by him for several hours before he freely received Christ and then died. He also was wrapped in a body bag, and I took him down to the morgue. While I was standing there, I realized that the rich man and the poor man were in the morgue side by side. One of them knew Jesus and I wasn't sure about the other, but I knew his money wouldn't help him. Death is an inexorable equalizer.

In Bible college, I was a heat-seeking missile for God, certain that in the years ahead I would attain the offices of apostle, prophet, pastor, and teacher, just for starters. In a spiritual sense, I thought I was a rich man. However, over the years, God has reduced my strength, modified my voice, purified the expectations, and now, through many shakings, you can hear the "poor man" talking. God lovingly used vocational suffering on the installment plan to crucify me. It is nothing less than a progressive process for a rich man to become a poor man. When we are in consummate unreality, we are prone to think of ourselves as rich, when in reality, we are poor and naked (see Rev. 3:17).

It is difficult for a rich man to *enter* (contrasted to seeing, believing, studying, and preaching) the Kingdom. The difficulty is that because of power, influence, freedom, and wealth, the rich (not necessarily financial) think they really know everything. It is also easy to be a rich man in theology or in philosophy because we *think* we know all about the issues. A rich man's sense of superiority keeps him from *entering* the Kingdom. Surrender of the control that doctrinal, philosophical, or scientific wealth provides is not easy. For the most part, America has related to other nations of the world as a rich man.

Doctrinal know-it-alls are abundant. Speaking like a rich man is the source of many marital and church fights; if either side would just speak softly, like the poor man, most arguments would quickly end. However, in our self-preservation and smart-alec attitudes, we have to defend ourselves, which only makes things worse. As a rich man, I have said things to my wife, Judith, which I wish I could retract.

Jesus said, *"Blessed are the poor in spirit"* (Matt. 5:3). There is a hurting world out there waiting to be entreated. Whenever someone answers you roughly, he or she is most likely dominated or captured by some system other than the Kingdom of God. On the other hand, a poor man asks, "Would you like to know my Father?" An *Agape* answer has the sound of an entreaty.

Thoughts and Questions

- How would you describe a rich man and a poor man?

- In what ways has your behavior toward others been as a rich man or a poor man?

- Why does a poor man use entreaties rather than answer roughly?

PART II

Becoming Father Pleasers

READING 16

Pleased or Not Pleased

This is My beloved Son, in whom I am well-pleased (Matthew 3:17).

THE KINGDOM OF GOD is His government, and the Kingdom comes when Father is pleased. Jesus knew how to please the Father. He said, *"He who sent Me is with Me; He has not left Me alone, for I always do the things that are pleasing to Him"* (John 8:29). Father, however, was not pleased with Israel:

> For you also endured the same sufferings at the hands of your own countrymen, even as they did from the Jews, who both killed the Lord Jesus and the prophets, and drove us out. They are not pleasing to God, but hostile to all men (1 Thessalonians 2:14-15).

When Father is not pleased, the Kingdom gradually or abruptly withdraws. Do you remember a time when you went to a church service where the presence of God was absent? The service went on, but you could feel that God was not there. Father was sick of Israel's feasts, celebrations, and sacrifices, because in their hearts they were not Father pleasers. Listen to the words and heartfelt plea in the voice of the prophet Isaiah:

> *"Why this frenzy of sacrifices?" God's asking. "Don't you think I've had my fill of burnt sacrifices, rams and plump grain-fed calves? Don't you think I've had my fill of blood from bulls, lambs, and goats? When you come before me, whoever gave you the idea of acting like this, running here and there, doing this and that— all this sheer commotion in the place provided for worship? "Quit your worship charades. I can't stand your*

READING 16

Pleased or Not Pleased

This is My beloved Son, in whom I am well-pleased (Matthew 3:17).

THE KINGDOM OF GOD is His government, and the Kingdom comes when Father is pleased. Jesus knew how to please the Father. He said, *"He who sent Me is with Me; He has not left Me alone, for I always do the things that are pleasing to Him"* (John 8:29). Father, however, was not pleased with Israel:

> For you also endured the same sufferings at the hands of your own countrymen, even as they did from the Jews, who both killed the Lord Jesus and the prophets, and drove us out. They are not pleasing to God, but hostile to all men (1 Thessalonians 2:14-15).

When Father is not pleased, the Kingdom gradually or abruptly withdraws. Do you remember a time when you went to a church service where the presence of God was absent? The service went on, but you could feel that God was not there. Father was sick of Israel's feasts, celebrations, and sacrifices, because in their hearts they were not Father pleasers. Listen to the words and heartfelt plea in the voice of the prophet Isaiah:

> *"Why this frenzy of sacrifices?" God's asking. "Don't you think I've had my fill of burnt sacrifices, rams and plump grain-fed calves? Don't you think I've had my fill of blood from bulls, lambs, and goats? When you come before me, whoever gave you the idea of acting like this, running here and there, doing this and that— all this sheer commotion in the place provided for worship? "Quit your worship charades. I can't stand your*

trivial religious games: Monthly conferences, weekly Sabbaths, special meetings—meetings, meetings, meetings—I can't stand one more! (Isaiah 1:11-13 MSG).

The Greek word *euarestos* and its derivatives, translated "pleased, well-pleasing, or acceptable" (Strong's Nos. 2100-2102), are used more than 40 times in the New Testament; 14 of them refer to pleasing God with morality and behavior. Many Scriptures give evidence that the New Testament is Father's love letter that shows us how to be a Bride to the Bridegroom and a son or daughter to the Father. If something is acceptable to God, there must likewise be things that are unacceptable. There are two references to not pleasing the Father and both have to do with behavior.

1 Corinthians 10:5: *"Nevertheless, with most of them God was not well-pleased."*

1 Thessalonians 2:15: *"…who both killed the Lord Jesus and the prophets, and drove us out. They are not pleasing to God, but hostile to all men."*

As God and Creator, He can be pleased or displeased, and no one can alter that because He's God. If we are displeasing and Christ is pleasing, it is obvious that we need Jesus!

Thoughts and Questions

- Why would the Kingdom gradually or abruptly withdraw if Father is not pleased?

- What do you think God was saying in Isaiah 1:11-13?

- In what ways do you think pleasing the Father has to do with our behavior?

Pleasing Behavior

*Therefore we also have as our ambition, whether at home
or absent, to be pleasing to Him* (2 Corinthians 5:9).

JESUS WAS A FATHER pleaser. He did not come to die; He came to do the will of the Father, which included dying. His death was pleasing to the Father: *"But the Lord was pleased to crush Him, putting Him to grief"* (Isa. 53:10). What pleases or displeases God as a Father is important because it re-establishes a long-neglected truth of biblical purpose in human suffering. When Christ arrived at Gethsemane, there was a clash of wills between Father and Son. Three times Jesus asked the same question: "Father, is there any other way to accomplish this task?" (See Matt. 26:39-44) When we ask for anything three times, we have to admit that we are seriously considering the cost that lies before us. After Father said no for the third time, Jesus yielded and said, *"Not My will, but Yours be done"* (Luke 22:42). Many of us have walked with the Lord Jesus long enough to know that when the personal cost is evident, yielding is not always easy.

Like Jesus, we can learn what pleases and doesn't please Father. Ephesians 5:9–10 says, *"The fruit of the Light consists in all goodness and righteousness and truth, trying to learn what is pleasing to the Lord."* The Message translates it more freely: *"The good, the right, the true—these are the actions appropriate for daylight hours. Figure out what will please Christ, and then do it."*

What if the Christian life really could be concentrated down to this one principle? It seems this would confirm Father's intention to reduce all of the Ten Commandments to one: love God with all your heart, soul, mind, and strength.

Paul saw pleasing the Father as freedom:

For you were called to freedom, brethren; only do not turn your freedom into an opportunity for the flesh, but through love serve one another. For the whole Law is fulfilled in one word, in the statement, "You shall love your neighbor as yourself." But if you bite and devour one another, take care that you are not consumed by one another (Galatians 5:13-15).

Suppose that as brand new believers, we were given a mentor who taught us right from the start how to be sensitive to what is pleasing and not pleasing to the Lord. That is what religion thinks it is doing, but it focuses on sin management, legalities, and works—how to manage your life so you can be acceptable and perfect. However, Father says: "Love Me and I will do the managing. You will know that which pleases Me, and the result will be holiness of mind and purpose and moral maturity!"

Thoughts and Questions

- What are some behaviors in the Scriptures that are pleasing to the Father?

- In what ways do you think pleasing the Father gives us more freedom?

- Does managing our own lives in order to be pleasing work? Why or why not?

Learning What Is Pleasing

And try to learn [in your experience] what is pleasing
to the Lord [let your lives be constant proofs of what is
most acceptable to Him] (Ephesians 5:10 AMP).

ONE OF THINGS THAT pleases God is to care for the poor, hurting, disenfranchised, and widows. One of the things that is not pleasing to Father is talking critically about one of His kids. Sometimes it requires serious discipline for us to learn what is pleasing to God.

I vividly remember a time when I had to learn what was pleasing to the Lord. I was walking downtown and saw a bag lady with a shopping cart full of all her belongings. The Lord suddenly told me to give her $20. In my great wisdom, I knew that she would use the money for wine so I gave her $5 instead. The Lord said, "I didn't tell you to give her $5; I told you to give her $20." I wrestled with it for several minutes as I walked away, and finally I got up the courage to do what I knew was pleasing to Father. I turned around, walked back to the bag lady and gave her the $20. She grabbed my hand and kissed me up the arm and I started to weep.

At that moment, this is what was pleasing to Father. However, it is possible that I could give another bag lady $20, and it would be displeasing to the Father. This would be especially true if I gave the $20 in an attempt to repeat a past performance or to regain a past blessing. We want Him to be pleased with us, so we tend to do the same thing over and over, even though it has no life in it. If we have all the patterns and formulas, we don't need a relationship with God. Everything boils down to one word: *Agape.* *Agape* begins in God, goes out to us, and then comes back to God. Stated as simply as possible: "*We love* [Agape] *because* [for this reason] *He first loved*

[Agaped] *us*" (1 John 4:19). God loved us not based on any merit of our own. Now, He is asking us to return to Him, in as pure a form as we are able, that love (*Agape*) that He gave us in the person of His Son. If we do that, He will be pleased!

After my rather dramatic encounter with the Lord when He stated that He wanted my love, I set myself to eagerly learn the skill of being more sensitive to the prompting of the Holy Spirit by asking, "What is it, Father?" As an 80-year-old, I am equally eager to declare and impart what I believe to be the Kingdom lessons of pleasing God as a Father for the postmodern youth and new believers who are beginning their own journey. In trying to learn what is pleasing to God, we need to learn to make distinctions. *Agape* is not relative; it is an absolute. We can know when we are pleasing and when we are not, when we are givers or when we are takers. Giving is pleasing; taking is displeasing. It is that uncomplicated and amazingly simple. If this idea of pleasing the Father rings your chimes, it will provoke a heart response.

Thoughts and Questions

- Why do you think it is pleasing to the Lord to care for orphans, widows, and the poor?

- Describe an experience where you learned a painful lesson about what was pleasing or not pleasing to the Lord.

- Explain why *Agape* is an absolute.

Love Like That

*Watch what God does, and then you do it, like children who learn
proper behavior from their parents. Mostly what God does is love
you. Keep company with him and learn a life of love. Observe how
Christ loved us. His love was not cautious but extravagant. He
didn't love in order to get something from us but to give everything
of himself to us. Love like that* (Ephesians 5:1-2 MSG).

BECAUSE NOT MANY OF us are able to love (*Agape*) like that, we need
to be born-again. Jesus gives us the new birth, which consists of His
inseminating the Eternal Seed (see 1 Pet. 1:23) into us—and we begin to
cultivate the *Agape* of God. As we continue to embrace the Kingdom reality
of the new birth, our capacity to be pleasing to Him increases. As we learn
to "love like that," we know before the words are out of our mouths that we
are injuring someone. Our response to His heart is the cause and motivation for us to begin to change our behavior so that it will please our Father.
Agape becomes our new standard of behavior (see 2 Cor. 5:14).

What happens when we don't love like that? Although we are born-
again believers, there are times when we do not love like that—maybe even
a minute ago. When I started to teach and embrace *Agape* as the essence of
the Kingdom, I did not want anyone to think that I had it all at home in
my garage. *Agape* has become the most confrontational concept in the entire
Bible. In Ephesians 3:17, Paul said that *"Christ will live in you as you open
the door and invite him in. And I ask him that with both feet planted firmly on
love"* (MSG). When we are not pleasing to our Father, we can let Christ in
us be His pleasure. Christ did it all: *"If you keep my commands, you'll remain*

intimately at home in my love. That's what I've done—kept my Father's commands and made myself at home in his love" (John 15:10 MSG).

Christ kept all of Father's commandments so He could give them to us. We don't have to worry about keeping all of the commandments because He kept them for us. We now only have one command: *Agape.* This is stated clearly in John 13:34-35. He gave us Christ to make up for all the crazies so that He could love us and we could love Him. Christ perfectly loves the Father for us. Most people are taught to fake it until they make it.

We must learn to see ourselves *in Christ*—that is where He covers us with His love while we learn to please Him. During the process, we may feel the pain of failure, but there is no condemnation. He covers us so that we can start the lesson again. Some of us repeat the same lesson over and over until we're sure we've seen that territory before. This reminds me of the guy who had to marry the teacher to get out of fourth grade. The more we grow in *Agape*, the more pleasing we are to the Father.

The Lord's Supper is one of the tools God uses to help us "love like that"—to love God and to love others as He loves them. The bread is His Body, given to us for the unqualified purpose of imparting to us His love; we need it to become Father pleasers. The cup of wine is His blood, given to us for the remission and forgiveness of the multiplied times that we failed to love as He loves. His forgiveness comes without rebuke or condemnation. Seen in this light, the Eucharist takes on family and fatherly overtones that make us want to mature in His love with deep gratitude for His provision.

Thoughts and Questions

- How does our capacity to "love like that" increase?

- What motivates us to change our behavior to be pleasing to Father?

- In what ways has Christ perfectly loved the Father for you?

READING 20

Walking in *Agape*

*Staying right at the center of God's love, keeping your arms open
and outstretched, ready for the mercy of our Master, Jesus Christ.
This is the unending life, the real life!* (Jude 1:21 MSG)

BECOMING A FATHER PLEASER is best discovered in the biblical idea of abiding. Walking in *Agape* requires sensitivity. I saw a refrigerator magnet that said, "Wine is evidence that God loves us and wants us to be happy." Father is pleased when I drink the first glass of wine. He may be pleased when I drink the second one. By the third one He might say, "That's not for you." We really can learn that degree of sensitivity so that we are alerted the moment we cross the line. For some, this needed sensitivity might be in the area of going to the movies, eating out, or shopping. It could be in many other areas, such as finances or proper nutrition.

I was talking to a friend who prayed about investing his inheritance in a new business. He didn't really find that measure of Father's pleasure he was looking for but thought a hefty profit was inevitable, so he sent off a check for $25,000. A few days later, the check was returned with a notification that it was made out improperly. In spite of the inner feeling that he should not do it, he ignored the sense of warning and eagerly wrote and mailed another check. A few weeks later, the whole company went under and took his money with it. He told me that the temptation to gain the promised interest overcame his sense of reluctance from God as a Father. Had my friend taken the time to find out whether or not Father was pleased with the business investment, he could have spared himself a lot of pain and regret. This was a costly lesson of learning to walk in the Spirit and learning what pleases or displeases Father.

Another friend of mine has two sons. He described what it meant to him to be a Father pleaser. He said, "If either one of my boys got up tomorrow morning and said 'Daddy, today what would be pleasing to you?' From the experience of being a father, I would say two things: 'First, I want you to believe that as your dad, I want the very best for you. Second, I want you to love your brother.' If my two sons believed that I would take care of them no matter what, and they were determined to love each other, nothing could make me happier as a father."

Walking in *Agape* is that uncomplicated; it is a dad speaking to His kids, "Trust Me, son, I want you to know My love for you, My intent toward you. Your brother may not be all that easy to love, but build yourself up in the faith and keep yourself in the exact center of My love" (see Jude 21 MSG). In the next verse it says,

> *Go easy on those who hesitate in the faith. Go after those who take the wrong way. Be tender with sinners, but not soft on sin. The sin itself stinks to high heaven* (Jude 1:22-23 MSG).

Sometimes it is difficult to be tender with sinners; it is easier to write them off if they don't follow our rules. But that is not the heart of a Father pleaser.

Learning to please the Father could involve $25,000, or it could be learned over a loaf of bread. A young woman described her experience of learning to please the Father. As she was starting to gather the ingredients to make bread, she heard Father tell her not to bake bread that day because He didn't want her spending her time that way. Instead of listening, she went ahead and prepared the dough. It was a disaster, and she was all upset so she ended up fighting with her husband and yelling at her kids. If we are not sensitive to pleasing the Father, all kinds of other issues take priority.

Jesus taught us what pleases the Father:

> *If you abide in Me, and My words abide in you, ask whatever you wish, and it will be done for you. My Father is glorified by this, that you bear much fruit, and so prove to be My disciples. Just as the Father has loved Me, I have also loved you; abide in My love* (John 15:7-9).

In an abiding relationship, fruit grows on the vine.

When I first wrote *Agape Road*, I thought the idea was to get on the *Agape* road and never get off. The reality is that most of the time we stay on the road for about four minutes. As we mature, we can walk in *Agape* for 12 minutes and then 15. Before long, we find that we really are learning to please our Father. We become easier to relate to and really learn how to care for the hurting. The excitement of gaining the skill of abiding, i.e., staying on the *Agape* road for consecutive periods of time, leads to the joy of becoming increasingly pleasing to Father.

Thoughts and Questions

🐝 In what ways do you think becoming a Father pleaser requires sensitivity?

🐝 Why does Jude 21-23 express the heart of a Father pleaser?

🐝 Explain the connection between being a Father pleaser and bearing fruit.

Reading 21

Steps to Growing Up

Brethren, do not be children [immature] in your thinking;
continue to be babes in [matters of] evil, but in your minds
be mature [men] (1 Corinthians 14:20 AMP).

THERE ARE SEVEN CLEAR steps in the normal spiritual growth of believers. Unless there have been significant or insurmountable interruptions in that growth, the biblical sequence goes like this: infant, child, trained child, Kingdom citizen, priest/king, ambassador, and Father pleaser. In this session we will look at the first four of these growth phases.

⚘ *Infant.* "*For everyone who partakes only of milk is not accustomed to the word of righteousness, for he is an infant*" (Heb. 5:13). An infant is born into the Kingdom—inseminated with the Eternal Seed of the Kingdom, which is Christ in Seed form. We have almost trivialized the new birth by setting it into the solitary context of heaven and hell. The new birth is ultimately designed to give Father His inheritance, which consists of a people of His own (see Eph. 1:18). Like the acorn, which contains the DNA of an entire oak tree, so the new birth has the DNA to conform us to the image of God's Son, which is Jesus Christ our Lord (see Rom. 8:29).

⚘ *Child.* "*As long as the heir is a child, he does not differ at all from a slave although he is owner of everything*" (Gal. 4:1). The institutional church is slow to allow us to enjoy our childhood. Religion, for a variety of reasons, teaches us to perform with the goal, conscious or subconscious, of making us useful to the organization.

In many ways, life itself does not allow us to enjoy our childhood. Religious performance may be the most complex and insidious hindrance to the joy of childhood and learning to please our Father. When we become effective performers, the complexity and challenge to release all of that for Kingdom simplicity is not easy.

❦ *Trained child.* "*But solid food is for the mature, who because of practice have their senses trained to discern good and evil*" (Heb. 5:14). The necessity of growing up when the time for growing up has come is rather self-evident. Being trained in the joy of pleasing the Father and developing the skill of abiding in Christ so that we can love like He loves involves serious life lessons. Father does not expect or demand behavioral perfection. A trained child has learned the simplicity and reality of walking on the *Agape* road. (If you have not read *Agape Road*, I would encourage you to do so; it is foundational for being a Father pleaser.)

❦ *Kingdom citizen.* "*Giving thanks to the Father, who has qualified us to share in the inheritance of the saints in Light. For He rescued us from the domain of darkness, and transferred us to the kingdom of His beloved Son* (Col. 1:12–13). This step involves becoming a functioning and productive citizen in the Kingdom government. Our citizenship is a transfer into another Kingdom by reason of our new birth and water baptism. We are no longer members of the governmental entity of darkness, which keeps us prisoners. We are, by virtue of Jesus' own Kingdom, transferred into His governmental authority of Light. This suggests a behavioral change because we are now citizens of a new governing force.

Thoughts and Questions

❦ Explain the purpose of the new birth in the infant stage.

❦ In what ways have you become a trained child?

❦ What is the result of becoming a Kingdom citizen?

68

Phases of Growth

Until we all attain to the unity of the faith, and of the knowledge of the Son of God, to a mature man, to the measure of the stature which belongs to the fullness of Christ. (Ephesians 4:13).

Continuing from Reading 21, we now look at the remaining 3 steps in the normal spiritual growth of believers.

* *Priests and kings.* "*But you are a chosen race, a royal priesthood, a holy nation, a people for God's own possession*" (1 Pet. 2:9-10). Kingdom citizens grow into priests and kings. As we mature, we become more capable of embracing the intercessory burden and authority Christ gave us to disciple the nations, which Oswald Chambers points out does not mean making more converts. The priesthood of the believer encompasses five aspects: absorb human failure, love without reward, vocational suffering, intercessory behavior, and extender of mercy. If you would stick these on your bathroom mirror and own them every day, they would help you understand what God means when He calls us to be priests in His Kingdom.

* *Ambassadors.* "*Therefore, we are ambassadors for Christ, as though God were making an appeal through us; we beg you on behalf of Christ, be reconciled to God* (2 Cor. 5:20). This is a governmental term used several times in the New Testament. We are governmental representatives of the Kingdom not of the church, denominations, or doctrines. When we adjust our concept of who we are and realize that we are Kingdom representatives, it changes our behavior. When we go to the hospital to minister, we pray

for everyone in need, not just those in our persuasion. An ambassador is out to reach the whole world; he represents a Kingdom government with a King, Jesus Christ, who Himself is a Father pleaser! Paul said, *"I am an ambassador in chains; that in proclaiming it I may speak boldly, as I ought to speak"* (Eph. 6:20).

🌱 *Father pleaser.* "You are My beloved Son, in You I am well-pleased" (Luke 3:22). A Father pleaser is a person whose ultimate desire and purpose is to preserve and maximize the sense of Father's manifest presence and approval. A Father pleaser seeks to walk in His favor at all times and under all circumstances. Our failure is covered in His grace, and that failure is forgiven without condemnation. The reward for which the Father pleaser waits is approbation. Being a Father pleaser is our gift to Him; we are returning to Him the love He gave us in Seed form in the new birth in as mature a form as possible. Father desires this clear growth factor. Father pleasers are charged with and primarily concerned about knowing and bearing Father's manifest presence. A Father pleaser's personal goal is to walk at all times, under all circumstances, and without compromise in the favor and expectations of Father's Kingdom. If we purpose to do that, we soon discover ourselves in trouble with the world systems: its financial system, church system, family system, etc. The reward Father gives affects us emotionally, spiritually, and psychologically. Each of us, deep in our person, needs to hear: "well done." Approbation is more than gratitude. Real approbation contains no flattery; it motivates us. Kingdom Father pleasers will risk their lives to hear Him say "Well done!" (see Acts 15:26; Matt. 25:21).

Thoughts and Questions

🌱 Why would being a priest require us to absorb human failure and love without reward?

- In what ways are you a governmental representative of the Kingdom?

- Why is being a Father pleaser our gift to Him?

READING 23

Kingdom Resurgence

The kingdom of heaven is at hand (Matthew 4:17).

T HE WORD RESURGENCE CARRIES the idea of "that which was once strong and influential having lost its place of influence." Resurgence includes the ideas of renaissance and revival. Resurgence means the Kingdom is becoming increasingly evident; it is taking its place in world history and once again requiring and forcing man, in all his strength and stubbornness, to recognize the place and necessity of His Kingdom. God, as a Father, is now increasing the demands, expectations, and government of that Kingdom. This pressure, as I understand it, will continue and increase until we discover the necessity of functioning as Father pleasers. In my understanding, the Father pleaser will then discover himself or herself caught in Kingdom resurgence between two conflicting personal demands:

1. *Preservation of our reputation and status quo.* Status quo, loosely translated, means the mess we are in. Everyone, regardless of education, religious persuasion, or financial status, knows that change is here to stay. Attempting to preserve our preferences in the turmoil will cause unlimited confusion. The ultimate issue is being conformed to the image of Jesus Christ who was the ultimate Father pleaser.

2. *Preservation of our integrity.* If we have the advantage of knowing these pressures are coming, we also know that such pressures will force us to preserve our personal integrity before the presence of God the Father. Who we are and what we believe will be pressed

until we pass from the ideal to that which is real, workable, and existential. There is simply no place to hide.

This Kingdom dimension will force all of us, globally, into a rather severe and unpleasant reassessment. Unreality and religiosity have had their day. Kingdom reality is upon us in every known way and in every known discipline. Present-day Christianity compromises many things on the assumption that God will forgive us. Compromising our integrity is simply not pleasing to the Father. There is a serious difference between the integrity of Joseph and that of David. Joseph refused to be seduced by Potiphar's wife; David intentionally took Bathsheba to bed. Both were faced with real life situations; one denied His name, the other did not. Somehow, Kingdom reality has been hidden in spheres of doctrine and compromise, but there is a reward for the man or woman who knows how to stand.

Although grace and forgiveness are the centerpiece of the *Agape* paradigm, forgiveness is not the Father's ultimate purpose or pleasure. Father pleasers with more mature personal integrity are simply unable to compromise; they understand Joseph's motive for not yielding to Potiphar's wife. For Father pleasers, our options are limited, and compromising is not one of them. As America and the other Western nations degenerate and fragment into anarchy, hedonism, personal idealism, and entitlement, my sense is that our having learned to be Father pleasers will be expensive, rewarding and, may save our spiritual lives. The implications of what I am saying need to be heard and applied with a full grasp of grace, forgiveness, and freedom. There is no legalism here. If we disobey, compromise, or fail to stand, we are not in danger of losing our salvation. Father forgives us at His own expense. The issue is whether or not we will have pleased Him as a Father.

Thoughts and Questions

- Why would preservation of our reputation and status quo affect the coming of the Kingdom?

- Explain how Christianity compromises behaviors based on the assumption that God will forgive us.

- If forgiveness is not Father's ultimate purpose, what is?

Three Kingdom Spheres

For the [whole] earth is the Lord's and everything
that is in it (1 Corinthians 10:26 AMP).

HERE ARE THREE KINGDOM spheres that function in a simultaneous manner. There are not three successive stages, but three aspects of the Kingdom that occur simultaneously. To fully grasp these three spheres, we need to see them in light of God's providence and sovereignty.

Sphere One—Kingdom of Nature

This has to do with God's sovereignty. It is His rule as preserver of all He created. God's sovereignty in the Kingdom of nature means that God rules everybody and everything, all the time and in all places. There simply is no place we can hide or escape His sovereignty! The whole earth is the Lord's: *"If I ascend to heaven, You are there; If I make my bed in Sheol, behold, You are there"* (Ps. 139:8). The sovereign God is a Father, but His governmental function in this realm severely limits His freedom to function as a Father; He functions as King and Creator. This is what the writer to the Hebrews meant when he wrote, *"It is a terrifying thing to fall into the hands of the living God"* (Heb. 10:31).

Sphere Two—Kingdom of Grace

Grace is like the rubber room of Father's instruction. This can be seen clearly in Titus 2:11–12:

> *For the grace of God has appeared, bringing salvation to all*
> *men, instructing us to deny ungodliness and worldly desires and*
> *to live sensibly, righteously and godly in the present age.*

This covenantal God reveals His Father's heart of providence by using all things in our lives, including sin and failure. Grace gives us the freedom to fail because Father can use that failure in a way that makes all things work together for good (see Rom. 8:28). The Kingdom of God is Father exercising His will in a providential manner; it is an offer, never an imposition. He extends His influence and rule to those who receive Him in the person of Christ (see John 1:12). God's providential rule is the present Kingdom of God. He rules the earth as He has always done, but now in Christ, He has offered us the privilege of coming to know Him, to see and enter a realm called the Kingdom of God. It is a sphere in which we can learn providentially how to please Him. Thus, we are taught to pray, "*Your kingdom come. Your will be done, on earth as it is in heaven*" (Matt. 6:10). He is looking for ambassadors of that Kingdom who will see things providentially.

Sphere Three—Kingdom of Glory

This is the Kingdom in future revelation best understood as not now and not yet. The glory of God is very simple: God Himself will indwell all creation as His living temple, and "*the earth will be filled with the knowledge of the glory of the Lord, as the waters cover the sea*" (Hab. 2:14). Each of the prophets declared that the whole earth would be filled with His glory. We know that "*at the name of Jesus every knee will bow, of those who are in heaven and on earth and under the earth*" (Phil. 2:10). Learning to see the future as Father's glory revealed is a serious Kingdom advantage. When God causes every knee to bow, it will be extremely demanding and turbulent.

Remember, all three of these spheres are going on at the same time: the sovereign Kingdom of nature, the providential Kingdom of grace, and the Kingdom of glory. Paul identifies the believer who has learned to be a Father pleaser as Father's own inheritance. These spheres work together simultaneously for the purpose of Father's own inheritance becoming a reality (see Eph. 1:18).

Thoughts and Questions

- In what ways can you see the sovereign God limiting His freedom to function as a Father?

❦ In what ways has the providential God used sin and failure for good in your life?

❦ Why do you think it will be turbulent when God causes every knee to bow?

Changes in Our Identity

The dominion (kingdom, sovereignty, rule) *of the world has now come into the possession and become the kingdom of our Lord and of His Christ* (the Messiah), *and He shall reign forever and ever* (for the eternities of the eternities)*!* (Revelation 11:15 AMP).

THE KINGDOM'S RESURGENCE WILL precipitate seven changes. We will look at all seven over the next sessions. These changes, by their very nature, will be seen as extraordinarily inflammatory because they will disrupt religious know-it-all dogmatism, God-denying materialism, extensive emotional and religious skepticism, and man's idealism; consequently, Kingdom reality will be established. They are also reformational because God Himself designed them for the intentional reforming of the Church on earth. In my understanding of Father God and His government, all seven of these changes are designed to be transitional in that they involve unmanageable and disorderly organizational transitions that can be seen as His intentional purpose. That purpose is to move us from living under His sovereignty to knowing Him as Father in a providential manner. Providence disrupts self-validation.

These changes are also inexorable in that they are unpreventable and uninvited; they come as a result of the demands and expectations of His governmental Kingdom. As we see these unfold in the next few years, it may look like death is happening, but Father pleasers will see it as the Kingdom birthing. The present global and financial crunch is just the beginning of the resurgence of that Kingdom, which will inexorably produce the birth pangs the apostle Paul refers to in Romans 8:21-22. God, in His sovereignty, retains the right to use all things to conform us to the image of His Son.

🌱 *Restoration of God's Fatherhood.* It is helpful to understand the Kingdom as Father's intrusion or invasion into the sphere of human willfulness and obstinacy—and it could get very turbulent. Discovering the strong motivation of being a Father pleaser will increasingly become an urgent necessity. Our sovereign God, who has been essentially and practically dismissed by His own Creation, will reassert His rights and authority as the Father of all that He has created. *"The kingdoms [plural] of this world have become the Kingdom [singular] of Our God and of His Christ"* (Rev. 11:15 KJV). Salvation is complete when I intentionally receive Christ and allow Him to take me to His Father.

🌱 *Sonship.* This change will demand shifting our identity in titles and offices to the greater, more inclusive identity as God's sons and daughters. Jesus said, *"I and the Father are one"* (John 10:30)—not one person, but one entity, one life, one expression. This is what Charles Spurgeon saw when he said something like "I looked at Him, He looked at me, and we were one forever." Once we really grasp Fatherhood, the idea of titles and offices as our identity will seem to lose its charm and authority. While some titles are useful, we need to sublimate all concepts of titles and offices into our sonship because the office or title is not who we are; it only describes what we do. Who we are is a son or a daughter of the providential Father. Offices such as apostles, prophets, and teachers are all real, but if we take our identity from them, we incline toward superiority, which seems to produce defensive and non-receptive responses. Our reputation should not be defined by our title. Authentic titles are needed, but we should not center on them. We are to act like sons and daughters seeking to please Father.

Thoughts and Questions

🌱 In what ways can you see God reforming the Church?

❦ Why will Father asserting His rights and authority over all He created be turbulent?

❦ Why is it important to shift our identity from titles and offices to being sons and daughters of the Father?

READING 26

Change In Motivation

*In [this] freedom Christ has made us free [and completely
liberated us]; stand fast then, and do not be hampered and
held ensnared and submit again to a yoke of slavery [which
you have once put off]* (Galatians 5:1 AMP).

THE NEXT THREE OF the seven changes are reformational and will be precipitated by the Kingdom's resurgence.

❦ *Father pleasers.* There is coming a necessary change from legal, argumentative, and religious use of the Scriptures to a more human, love-filled, and Christ-centered application of what does or does not please the Father. How would God as a Father, operating in His providential manner, with limitless forgiveness in Christ and unlimited affection, handle a particular failure or disappointment? This pleasure is fully demonstrated in the life and ministry of Jesus Christ. The spirit or attitude and/or voice in which a Bible text is used may be more important than the text itself. It is amazing, but where the most Bible is preached, there seems to be the least amount of love because we use the Scriptures in a way that expects or demands things from each other instead of trying to please the Father. Jesus came to do the will of the Father, so to the woman caught in adultery He said, *"Woman, …did no one condemn you? I do not condemn you, either. Go. From now on sin no more"* (John 8:10-11).

❦ *Transformation of our motives for ministry.* This is a change from taker to giver. The world sees the present-day Church as a taker, because it has increasingly become so. Like the temple of old, Jesus' statement that "You have made my Father's house a robbers' den" (see Matt. 21:13) is becoming increasingly true. God is a giver. His Son is a giver. His children must become givers and not takers. There are three words we need to take hold of: possess, acquire, and control. Do not allow your denomination or church to possess you. The entire spirit or atmosphere that surrounds evangelism has become increasingly acquisitive, wanting to acquire members as contrasted to concern for the person as an individual.

> *Woe to you, scribes and Pharisees, hypocrites, because you travel around on sea and land to make one proselyte; and when he becomes one, you make him twice as much a son of hell as yourselves* (Matthew 23:15).

The mature Father pleaser becomes increasingly responsible to know whether he or she is being acquired, possessed, or controlled. We were called to freedom (see Gal. 5:1), and freedom means we are being changed from takers to givers. We are required to be free people if we are to set our hearts on being Father pleasers.

Change in objective. This change involves the transition from the goal of getting to heaven to living on earth with a Kingdom purpose. Many people have one desire—to make heaven their home. If you are a Christian and you die, you have to go to heaven—there is no place else to go. Heaven is not a goal; it is a destiny. Neither heaven nor hell is the Kingdom's primary issue. Paul states that our Kingdom objective is that *"creation itself also will be set free from its slavery to corruption into the freedom of the glory of the children of God"* (Rom. 8:21). The Kingdom purpose of the redemptive act is to make us sons and daughters. When the redemptive act is understood and applied from the perspective of the Father and the joy of our becoming His inheritance, everything seems to shift in purpose and meaning. It causes the entire New Testament to be read in a more relational and Father-centered manner.

Thoughts and Questions

- How would our providential, affectionate Father handle a failure or disappointment?

- Why is it important to be aware of being acquired, possessed, or controlled?

- What is the Kingdom's primary purpose?

READING 27

Change in Doctrine

*By abolishing in His [own crucified] flesh the enmity [caused by] the
Law with its decrees and ordinances [which He annulled]; that He
from the two might create in Himself one new man [one new quality of
humanity out of the two], so making peace* (Ephesians 2:15 AMP).

T HE LAST TWO CHANGES are really inflammatory and disruptive to
religious dogmatism and religious skepticism but are inevitable for
Kingdom reality to be established.

* *Measurable disruption in doctrine.* Due to the dramatic and unexpected intrusion of the Kingdom of God, there is now and
  will be an increased and measurable disruption in the biblical concepts of doctrine. After years in a Nazi prison, Dietrich
  Bonhoeffer asked for religion-less Christianity. He also stated
  that the world he knew was now coming of age. He could see
  that we were entering a sphere of global inclusion that would
  minimize and perhaps trivialize many of the immature doctrines to which we cling. For example, some believe that if
  you do not belong to this or that group, you cannot possibly be
  saved. In an attempt to keep the Kingdom clean, some churches will not allow visitors to take communion. The Kingdom
  of God asks for and expects us to walk in *Agape* rather than to
  posture ourselves in narrow doctrinal and denominational distinctions. *"You search the Scriptures… and still you are not willing
  to come to Me"* (John 5:39-40 AMP). We are to walk in *Agape*
  and be living epistles that people can read rather than to walk
  in doctrine.

Doctrines shift and change, but the Kingdom cannot be shaken, and the basics of our faith have never altered. English poet Alfred Tennyson in his well-known poem described the disruption in doctrine well:

> *Our little systems have their day;*
> *They have their day and cease to be,*
> *They are broken lights,*
> *And Thou, Oh Lord, are more than they.*

The Kingdom expects inclusivity, not doctrinal exclusivity.

🌱 *Change in unfolding eschatology.* The Greek word *eschatos* (Strong's Greek No. 2078) means "the very end." Biblically, Jesus is the *eschatos*; everything and everyone is consummated in Him. While still in seminary, I pulled a big book on eschatology off the shelf, and the first sentence that I read said that no one has yet been able to accurately predict future events. I put the book back on the shelf. The change in eschatology is centered in the "one new man" (Eph. 2:15). There have been five transitional men in our redemptive history: Adam, Abraham, Moses, Christ, and the one new man. This one new man is the corporate person, *"Christ in you* [plural], *the hope of glory"* (Col. 1:27). God is pinning all of the future on this one new man: Christ and His Body. At this moment there are more than 1.5 billion Jews and Gentiles who make up that one new man. Alister McGrath, in *Christianity's Dangerous Idea* (2006), says that there are 500 million to 600 million believers in the world who are baptized in the Holy Spirit. Imagine how many more there are today. Suppose Father has spent all these years preparing stones in the field, getting them ready to build His building. Whatever your eschatology, don't fail to include and calculate the involvement of this one new man.

Thoughts and Questions

🌱 In what ways can you see a measurable disruption in the biblical concepts of doctrine?

- Rather than focusing on doctrine, what does the Kingdom expect?

- In your own words, explain the change in the focus of eschatology from future events to the one new man.

READING 28

How Jesus Pleased the Father

I saw the Lord constantly before me, for He is at my right hand that I may not be shaken or overthrown or cast down [from my secure and happy state]. Therefore my heart rejoiced and my tongue exulted exceedingly; moreover, my flesh also will dwell in hope [will encamp, pitch its tent, and dwell in hope in anticipation of the resurrection]. (Acts 2:25–26 AMP).

I N THE NEXT TWO sessions we will look at seven things from Acts 2:25-28 that Jesus used to please the Father. You may discover in these the ability to walk in freedom until you are 85 and white-haired! Take a few minutes and read the entire chapter, noticing the words "My" and "Me."

- *Vision therapy* (Acts 2:25). "*I saw the Lord constantly before me.*" Jesus always saw the Father in His presence, so He conducted Himself as if He could see the Father and the Father could see Him. "*Where there is no vision, the people are unrestrained, but happy is he who keeps the law*" (Prov. 29:18). The first step to getting in trouble is to take our eyes off Jesus. Peter walked on the water, took his eyes off the Lord, and sank. The minute we get distracted and look at the mortgage, or the sickness, or the nagging neighbor, we begin a downturn.

- *Spiritual strength* (Acts 2:25). "*For He is at my right hand that I will not be shaken.*" Most of us have walked with the Lord long enough to know that there are things in life that really do shake our bush. To name a few: betrayal, death, financial issues, and mega failures can rock our whole foundation. Jesus saw the Lord at his right hand and drew spiritual strength from Him so that

He would never be shaken. When Judas and Peter betrayed Him, He was unshaken. When the whole Jewish system turned against Him, He was unshaken. The Christian life is not difficult; it is impossible. In the final analysis, Jesus puts steel up our backbone and makes us stand. It's not our will power or great prayer life. If we don't know how to draw spiritual strength from Him, we will fall on our faces…but at least we will be pointing in the right direction!

- *Worship* (Acts 2:26). "*Therefore my heart rejoiced and my tongue exulted.*" Jesus was a worshiper. Worship is a vital part of being a Father pleaser, and the Lord asks for a heart of worship. First Corinthians 14:2 says, "*For one who speaks in a tongue does not speak to men but to God.*" Worshipping in other tongues is more than important; it is the source of learning to please God as a Father.

- *Hope* (Acts 2:26). "*My flesh also will dwell in hope.*" Hope doesn't mean, "I hope it doesn't rain tomorrow." Hope is something we live for. The reason people commit suicide is because they've lost hope. Hope is a duty or a responsibility. It is one of the most powerful factors in being a Father pleaser. When we lose hope, we are in serious trouble. Like a punching bag with sand in the bottom, hope is resilient and keeps popping back up after it is punched. Obtain your hope from Jesus as Lord, and then guard your hope well.

Thoughts and Questions

- In what ways would seeing the Lord constantly before you affect your behavior?

- Describe an experience in which God enabled you to stand in the midst of a difficult circumstance.

- Why is losing hope a serious issue?

READING 29

Becoming a Father Pleaser

For You will not abandon my soul, leaving it helpless in Hades
(the state of departed spirits), *nor let Your Holy One know decay*
or see destruction [of the body after death]. You have made known
to me the ways of life; You will enrapture me [diffusing my soul
with joy] with and in Your presence. (Acts 2:27–28 AMP).

From the last session's Scripture in Acts 2:25-28, we continue to look at the seven things that Jesus used to please the Father.

* *Death and Resurrection* (Acts 2:27). *"For You will not abandon my soul, leaving it helpless in Hades, nor let Your Holy One know decay."* It seems that over the past few decades we have become more determined to feel good. Because of this, we are increasingly experiencing Cross-less Christianity. God doesn't use rubber nails, but if we don't embrace death, we can never enjoy resurrection. Because the Church has refused death, it is running out of fuel. Preaching the Cross in a legalistic manner is not what I am talking about. We must be careful of receiving the message of the Cross from those who only speak death. There are many who are ignorant of the joy of the Cross and the end result of the Resurrection. Death is normal in the Christian life when it is followed by resurrection. Water baptism is a symbol of death and Resurrection. Father pleasers embrace death and Resurrection as a way of life. When some form of death comes knocking at your door, it is the Cross. Father is asking you to embrace it in order to impart and disclose that necessary Kingdom life which comes out of death.

❦ *Leadership* (Acts 2:27). *"You have made known to me the ways of life."* Leadership comes at many levels. If you're out in the bush and your eight-year-old son knows where the jeep is, he's the leader. If you know just one more thing than somebody else, you become the leader. During the Jesus movement, the church elders were the youth who had been saved two weeks before the others! They may not have been the best leaders, but they knew something the rest of the youth didn't, and that's what made them the leaders. Leadership has both joy and responsibility. Whether you realize it or not, there are men and women in your life, perhaps in your neighborhood or at work, school, or church who are following you. It is important to be Father pleasers because they are watching your life and hoping you're real. They want to believe that you know where you're going.

❦ *Satisfaction* (Acts 2:28). *"You will enrapture me [diffusing my soul with joy] with and in Your presence."* Notice that in our first point, we start by being in God's presence, and we also end by being in His presence. Father pleasers are full of joy. We live in a discontented and materialistic society, and advertising makes it even worse. We must acquire a better model, the latest edition, the one with bells and whistles. Rather than valuing spiritual matters, society pressures us to value material things. Jesus wants to satisfy something deep in us, so that we will be full of gladness in His presence. Once we get our vision clear and see the Lord, we will not be shaken but learn to be satisfied.

As ambassadors of Christ's Kingdom we must accept the responsibility of leadership, even at great personal cost. We must learn to disclose the inner workings of our journey, so that in every aspect of our lives we can become Father pleasers.

Thoughts and Questions

❦ Describe an experience in which you embraced the process of death and resurrection in your life.

- Who are the men and women in your life who might be looking to you for leadership?

- In what ways have you experienced deep satisfaction in Father's presence?

PART III

Fatherhood

READING 30

Church as Mother, Kingdom as Father

However, when everything is subjected to Him, then the Son Himself will also subject Himself to [the Father] Who put all things under Him, so that God may be all in all [be everything to everyone, supreme, the indwelling and controlling factor of life. (1 Corinthians 15:28 AMP).

THE CHURCH IS THE Mother and the Kingdom is the Father. Like Mary, the mother of Christ, the Church is designed to embrace newborn believers and take them to the Father by cultivating and nourishing them in His Kingdom purpose. Mother, however, has a tendency to use her intimacy with Father and anointing from Him for her personal advantage. She uses the anointing to prosper financially, build ministries, meet human needs, and gain power rather than doing the will of the Father. This is the essence of humanism.

The most serious issue in the Church today is not evangelism but the manner and content with which people are being discipled. Refusal or failure to introduce a Kingdom agenda leaves us victimized by the cultural vagaries of each individual church group or denomination. Because the climate in the Church is determined by the essence of the diet being offered, when we are nursed on *Eros*, the end result is a church full of crying babies—bless me, help me, visit me, strengthen me, teach me, show me. The adage is: as goes the church, so goes society. We experience one revival after another; meanwhile the people are nursed on an *Eros/Agape* mixture, so spiritual nourishment is very much lacking, resulting in bad fruit or even worse, spiritual injury. The whole idea of *Eros* darkness is almost totally unknown or ignored, though it badly needs to be isolated, identified, and broken.

The Church is certainly mothering, but we don't have much Fathering. Few Mothers explain and enforce the authority of the Father for fear of diminishing their own authority. Without an authority outside of her own, Mother tends to struggle on the same level with the children. When she understands the government and authority of Father, she can appeal to and impart that authority to others. This induces the believer to conform his or her behavior to biblical standards because both the individual believer and the Church are required to respond to the will of the Father. This is not domination and control because the Scriptures state plainly that Father's commandments are not burdensome (see 1 John 5:3); even the Son can do nothing on His own initiative (see John 5:19)—He came to do the will of His Father.

> *I am the Vine; you are the branches. Whoever lives in Me and I in him bears much* (abundant) *fruit. However, apart from Me [cut off from vital union with Me] you can do nothing* (John 15:5 AMP).

If we are to bear fruit, we must be tapped into the Vine. This involves doing Father's will on earth as it is in Heaven —His Kingdom authority being acknowledged on earth. God's authority is central and primary, and both individual believers and the corporate Church should honor Him because God is all in all. The only standard for life, ministry, and godly behavior is Father's will. If Mother could return to this, it would bring about a global reformation.

Thoughts and Questions

- Explain the difference between the Church and the Kingdom.
- What is the result of being nursed on *Eros*?
- Why does Mother need to enforce Father's authority?

Loss of Father's Will

Don't suppose for a minute that I have come to demolish the Scriptures—
either God's Law or the Prophets. I'm not here to demolish but to
complete. I am going to put it all together, pull it all together in a vast
panorama. God's Law is more real and lasting than the stars in the
sky and the ground at your feet. Long after stars burn out and earth
wears out, God's Law will be alive and working. Trivialize even
the smallest item in God's Law and you will only have trivialized
yourself. But take it seriously, show the way for others, and you
will find honor in the kingdom (Matthew 5:17-19 MSG).

IT IS IMPORTANT TO understand how the loss of Father's will occurs within the paradigm of the Kingdom as the Father and the Church as the Mother. Over the centuries, Church leadership has broken, annulled, relaxed, and trivialized the instructions of the Father. A loose translation of the Greek word for *annul* is that of Church leadership using its vested authority to issue permission slips for the purpose of personal advantage, political popularity, or to avoid conflict. An example is the Roman Catholic Church's stand on divorce versus annulment of marriage. While the church does not support divorce, if someone has sufficient money, influence, or political pull, he or she can get a marriage annulled that has lasted for many years and produced several children. The person is then seen as never having been married and is free under religious law to marry again. In many ways, the Church does the same for homosexuality, political and financial schemes, denominational advancement, etc. The motivation behind it all is to avoid the conflict and suffering that Jesus promised we would face.

When the Church annuls or trivializes Father's instructions, it does not abrogate or abolish the validity and power of the Kingdom. It does, however, demonstrate the division between the Father and the Mother in the home. As a wife or mother, she is undermining and abusing the authority of the home, seemingly for her own advantage or agenda. Solomon described this behavior as: "*The wise woman builds her house, but the foolish tears it down with her own hands*" (Prov. 14:1). She undermines the very authority she claims to represent and then wonders what went wrong.

Father's Kingdom always contains greater perspicuity, breadth, and permanence than the Church. It will survive the abuse and misuse of principles given to the Church because Jesus has provided for that. The Kingdom is unshakable because Father's omnipotent will transcends individual will, contrary applications, and overt misuse for personal advantage. Jesus never promised that the Church would be unshakable. What He did promise is that the gates of hell would not prevail against her, which is quite a different matter (see Matt. 16:18).

Thoughts and Questions

- In what ways has the Church broken, annulled, relaxed, and trivialized the instructions of the Father?

- What does this demonstrate?

- Have you experienced your authority being undermined? How did you respond?

READING 32

The Importance of Fathers

But an hour is coming, and now is, when the true worshipers will worship the Father in spirit and truth (John 4:23).

WHEN JESUS TALKED TO the Samaritan woman at the well, it was not about heaven or about the possibility of hell if she did not change her ways. He spoke to her on a deep level about an essential need. He was asking her to open herself to the Father who had come to her through Him. Jesus was giving her *security* in the midst of total insecurity and *belonging* and *identity* in Himself by allowing her to have the authority to be one of His own children. He was redefining her heritage to be part of His family.

Jesus' entire mandate was to take us to the Father. Everything in evangelism should be focused on finding our true Father who was lost to us in the Fall of Man. We are dead and live in darkness, waiting for the Father in whom is Light and no shadow of darkness (see James 1:17). His intention is for us to know security, identity, and belonging. The single purpose of the redemptive act is the replication of Father's *Agape*, DNA, or character in those who believe, so that we would be fully mature as Father is fully mature. Jesus demonstrated maturity by the manner in which He treated His enemies. He is asking that we learn to do the same.

When we fail to follow Jesus to the Father, we cannot conduct ourselves as His children. We have a Father, but are acting as though we are *bastards* or illegitimate sons (see Heb. 12:8). The only way to minister to the bastards is to lead them to their Father. The word *Father* is used more times than *Lord Jesus Christ* in the Gospel of John—it is an important issue to God. Jesus says that no man can come to the Father except by Him (see John 6:44). The road to Father's house is the pathway of intimacy. Jesus is always pointing us to the Father because He is the One from whom every family in heaven and earth derives its name.

When I was twelve years old, my father abandoned our family. As the only male in the family, I felt the need to take responsibility for my mother and five sisters. For the rest of my life, I struggled with this warped idea of fatherhood by feeling the need to take responsibility for everyone. If anyone failed or missed the exit, I was sure it was my fault.

Fatherhood is a fundamental issue both spiritually and naturally. The cry and urgent need for spiritual mothers is equally critical. If we know the Father, we can conduct ourselves as surrogate, spiritual fathers or mothers for the purpose of imparting security, identity, and belonging to those who are hurting, resulting in life.

As Father, He wants to let a hurting world know of His love. He does this by teaching us, like the woman at the well, to worship Him in Spirit and truth and to open ourselves to love our enemies and pray for those who persecute us, so that we can look and act like His very own children. Learning to do this is a process of maturing or becoming perfect (Greek: *telios*)—as our heavenly Father is perfect and mature (see Matt. 5:44-45, 48). God is taking us on a journey to be *like* Him—a loving Father.

Thoughts and Questions

- In what ways have you misinterpreted the nature of God the Father?

- Explain why fatherhood is the essence of evangelism.

- Why does God want us to love our enemies and pray for those who persecute us?

READING 33

Covenant between the Father and the Son

The Father loves [Agapes] the Son extravagantly. He turned everything over to him so he could give it away—a lavish distribution of gifts (John 3:35 MSG).

FOLLOWING ARE THREE FOUNDATIONAL Scriptures that offer a practical understanding of the reciprocal love Father God and His Son have for one another. The essence of *Agape* is essentially Trinitarian and is a sweet society.

First: *"So that the world may know that I love [Agape] the Father, I do exactly as the Father commanded Me. Get up, let us go from here"* (John 14:31). This obedient response of our Lord to His Father should become part of our earthly mission statement because it demonstrates our love for God. To accomplish this, we have to get moving and let the hurting world know that we love the Father. There is a particular joy in becoming a life source of Father's love for others. The glory of God is to let His love and extravagant goodness shine through our earthly life. To do so, we must learn to become spontaneous and risk-takers. Put some $20 bills in your pocket to give away when you see someone hurting. Don't be so insistent to witness to witness to someone, just put a little cash in their hand and say, "Here, the Father loves you!" To many people, a $20 bill can make a big difference.

Second: *"If you keep My commandments, you will abide in My love; just as I have kept My Father's commandments and abide in His love"* (John 15:10). Jesus gave us His two commandments—love God and love one another (see Matt. 22:40). He kept all of His Father's commandments that Moses recorded, doing so in our behalf. The Law of Moses is fulfilled in Christ; all He asks us to do is to keep *His* commandments. The whole world would begin to experience transformation if we would only do the one thing He asked of us—*Agape* one another.

Third, *"For Christ did not enter a holy place made with hands, a mere copy of the true one, but into heaven itself, now to appear in the presence of God for us"* (Heb. 9:24). The covenant is not between *me and God*; the covenant is between the Father and the Son. Jesus keeps the covenant for us, and then invites us into an intimate relationship with Himself and His Father. God accepted the sacrifice of Christ as perfect redemption for every one of us. We have nothing to fear because we have already been at the judgment seat in the person of Christ—Christ is *Agape*, and perfect *Agape casts out fear* (see 1 John 4:18). All we have to do is learn to replicate that *Agape* in daily life.

For years, I kept trying to get God to move in my life, not understanding that He was waiting to take me into His. I was worrying about my own concerns, while Jesus was waiting for me to share His. When I finally saw what was happening, my whole direction changed. When we allow God to take us into His life and purposes, we release our death grip on our own little world, giving Him freedom to do what He intended in our lives. This is part of being seated with Christ in heavenly places. Our position is relational, allowing us to see things from His viewpoint. When the Kingdom comes, it will not be different from what we have now; there will just be more of it. We are living in the real Kingdom, it is called *Agape*—the life of God.

Thoughts and Questions

🌱 Why is it necessary to demonstrate our love for God?

🌱 Explain your place in the covenant between the Father and the Son.

🌱 In what ways are you or are you not comfortable in God's presence?

READING 34

God's Paternity

You loved Me before the foundation of the world (John 17:24).

Each of us has experienced our parents or family members being embarrassed because of the way we represented the family name. I had five sisters who were pretty sophisticated, while I, as the only male, was a raw, sweaty, and an unpredictable Mumford. Occasionally, they did not even want to claim me as their brother because I was an embarrassing, mouthy kid.

If you want to find out whose kid you are, all you need is a piece of hair and a DNA test. The Father is looking for the same evidence—His DNA characteristics evident in our behavior. But, what test can we use to determine our spiritual paternity? John tells us that the DNA evidence is if we have love for one another (see John 13:35). When we were born, God's DNA was planted in us whether we liked it or not. We were created in His

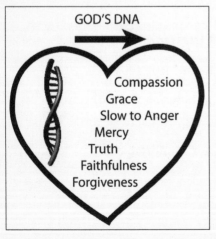

image and born into a fallen world. This is why it is against our nature to tell a lie, but it does not prevent us from doing so. Even when we do not act like it, we are still one of God's kids—His DNA, the mysterious Seed, is just dormant in us. In this diagram, the straight *Agape* arrow is God's paternity—His *Agape* given to us at the new birth. When we are born-again and receive Christ, the mysterious Seed containing the seven attributes of God's

DNA begins to grow in us. It is on this basis that the apostle John builds his epistemology. He was looking for evidence, or the lack thereof, of the DNA of God. Jesus said, *"I know you, that you do not have the love of God in yourselves"* (John 5:42). If we had the love of God in us, we would love and receive Him and His Father. It is exciting to know that our name was written in Christ's DNA *before* the foundation of the world.

When I was backslidden, I had a big Harley-Davidson motorcycle. I used to come home at night with weeds in the wheels and scratches on my face, and I didn't even remember where I'd been. I used to say to my friends, "Ride with me and you're safe." Without knowing it, I was leaning into His plan for me that was established at the foundation of the world! I could feel God's grace on me and I felt like I would never die. When we are young and immature, God puts up with this, but when we become more mature in the Lord, it becomes presumption.

At the beginning of our relationship with the Lord, we only see God as our Redeemer. As we develop a deeper relationship with Him, we begin to understand that He is our Creator as well as our Redeemer. As we continue to mature in our relationship with Him, we get to know Him as our Father. Most of the Church knows God as the Redeemer, and some believe He is the Creator, but a great many have lost their concept of Father. In order for us to know God, we have to know 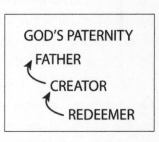 Him in all three roles: as our Father, our Creator, and our Redeemer. It is our Father who plants His DNA in us and meets us in our time of need.

Thoughts and Questions

- 🐝 Describe what it meant for you to carry your family name well when you were young.

- 🐝 What is the DNA evidence God is looking for in your life?

- 🐝 Describe your relationship to God in His three roles: Redeemer, Creator, and Father.

READING 35

God's Paternity Is the Incorruptible Seed

*Your new life is not like your old life. Your old birth came from
mortal sperm; your new birth comes from God's living Word. Just
think: a life conceived by God himself!* (1 Peter 1:23 MSG).

JESUS SAID, "*I AM the way, and the truth, and the life*" (John 14:6). God
incarnated Himself and came from eternity to provide us the Way.
Then, He designated that road as the one that takes us back to Himself.
He birthed Himself in us a Truth and gave us His DNA as Life. God's
paternity is *Agape*, the Incorruptible Seed, and the New Testament is full
of examples of God's paternity. Simeon and Anna may not have seen it
very clearly, but like the disciples, they saw God Almighty as Redeemer,
Creator, and Father. They saw that Jesus was the Son of the living God—
God incarnate. Simeon and Anna were waiting for the Kingdom while the
temple was still standing. Paul, too, understood God's paternity when he
saw the glory of God in the face of Christ.

God inseminated us with the tiniest of Seeds—His DNA—so that
Christ could dwell in our hearts by faith (see Eph. 3:17). In order for the
Seed to grow, it needs water baptism so that our old nature can be buried
and our new nature can be resurrected. This is simply cleaning up all the
crazies in our life so that the Seed can grow. As it increases and grows,
Christ is being formed and perfected in us. God is *Agape*, so He comes as
Agape incarnate and brings us to Himself. We love because He first loved
us; *Agape* meets *Agape*.

AGAPE MEETS AGAPE

God gave me His paternity and His incorruptible Seed began to grow in me when I was 12 years old. Even though I rejected it, the Seed kept on working. As a little kid, I knew something had been planted in me; even though I did not know what it was, I knew I wanted it. I was baptized in water about four times, and if there was prayer for ingrown toenails, I went because I did not want to miss anything. I answered every altar call just in case I didn't do it right the first time. I didn't know it then, but I was trying to give the Lord clean soil for the Seed to grow. Unfortunately, thorns crowded out the Seed, and it was another 12 years before I came back to the Lord.

If you have ever been backslidden for a period of time in your journey, you will have experienced the Seed's ability to survive. Fortunately, the Seed does not depend on you. If you had your choice, you would probably still be backslidden, but the Seed prevailed. In my backslidden state, I'd get about half drunk sitting in a bar. Alcohol works like a truth serum; so when it kicked in, I would start telling everybody in the bar about Jesus because the Seed in me was still at work. I felt deep compassion for those around me, but I did not know what to do with it. Their response was usually, "Well if He's so great, why aren't you walking with Him?" When the incorruptible Seed is in your life, no matter how deep it is buried, you can see a glimpse of God's character. We are cleansed with His blood and fed with His bread at the Lord's Table giving us fertile ground for His *Agape* to grow in us.

Thoughts and Questions

- Explain the significance of water baptism being essential for the Seed to grow.

- Describe how the incorruptible Seed has survived in your own life.

- What role does the Lord's Table play in the Seed planted in you?

READING 36

God Is Father

*If God were your Father, you would love [Agape] Me, for I
proceeded forth and have come from God, for I have not even
come on My own initiative, but He sent Me (John 8:42).*

WHEN JESUS WAS 12 years old, His family was returning home from Jerusalem. After a couple of days into the journey, Jesus' parents could not find Him, so they returned to the city to look for Him and found Him in the temple. His response was,

> *How is it that you had to look for Me? Did you not see and know
> that it is necessary [as a duty] for Me to be in My Father's house
> and [occupied] about My Father's business?* (Luke 2:49 AMP).

Jesus did not come to earth for Himself; He came to reveal the Father and take us to Him. As followers of Jesus, we have one job description: to know the Father and commit our whole life to making Him known.

God's Fatherhood has been grossly misrepresented. Many people suffer deep wounds from things their earthly fathers did or did not do while they were growing up. We need to be cleansed of our distorted perceptions and get to know Him as a person. *Our only redeeming factor is God's DNA.* God's self-revelation in Jesus shows us the intrinsic makeup of His person. When I saw His Son, I started to fall in love with the Father. I thought if the Father has a Son like that, He must be some Papa! A hurting world wants to know that the Father is like you.

His self-revelation allows us to walk away from our long-held fears of coming judgment and our innate fear of facing Him. Jesus actually *wants* us to be with Him: "*Father, I desire that they also, whom You have given Me, be with Me where I am*" (John 17:24). At first I did not believe this, so I kept repeating this Scripture out loud for over a year so that I could know the love He has for me. Because of the deep rejection I experienced as a child, I always felt that I wasn't worthy to be in the group and that I should just go out and wait in the car. Many of us would be more comfortable waiting in the car, but Jesus wants us to be seated with Him in heavenly places. His chair is big enough for all His children to fit in. He knows we are a little weird, but His DNA is planted in us and He really wants us to be with Him! We can know the love God has for each of us because of the evidence of His Son. The Crucifixion proves this.

Many people believe lies about God the Father's nature. He is never cruel or capricious. These accusations come from the accuser. He does care about us and He will not abandon us. But, we must know *whom* we love before we can really release our affections and place our confidence in Him.

Thoughts and Questions

- As followers of Jesus, what is our job description?

- Are you comfortable being seated with Christ in God's presence? Why or why not?

- Do you feel there is enough of God for you personally as well as for all His other kids? Why or why not?

READING 37

Playing Father to God's Kids

*If I want him to remain until I come, what is that
to you? You follow Me!* (John 21:22).

THERE IS OFTEN COMPETITION and jealousy among God's kids. We don't have any trouble with our neighbor buying a Mercedes-Benz 450, but when our Christian brother buys one, all kinds of reactions surface. We complain, "Lord, this person is mishandling Your money!" What we are doing is using borrowed authority and attempting to play God or act parental toward His other children. We are being sheriffs rather than gardeners. We would do well to pay attention to our own walks with God and release others to the care of their own Father. Each of us was uniquely created, and Father, amazingly enough, responds differently to each of His own. Oswald Chambers said, "Let God be as original with other people as He is with you."[1]

When Judith and I were raising our four children, I travelled a great deal. I would bring presents home on many of the trips, but when I started to see envy and competition among the kids, I began bringing a gift home for only one of them. It put the other three through their changes, but they learned that life is not equal or just. They also looked forward to the time it would be their turn.

Because I suffered such rejection in my early life, I did not think there was enough of Father to go around, so I didn't want others to love my Father; I wanted Him for myself. God's name is I AM, meaning, "I will be what I need to be to meet the needs of My people." We must get free from our possessiveness of Father God and set Him free to be the God to us and to others that He wants and needs to be. God's Fatherhood in each believer's life is something we can learn to depend on. We have security, identity, and belonging in Him; therefore, we can love everyone whom God loves, and we can do so without envy or competition. It takes a degree of maturity to weep with those who weep and rejoice with those who rejoice. We *can* grow up enough so that there is a cessation of envy or competition in the family because we all have the same Father. We must set the Father free to be I AM to each of us.

If trying to possess, acquire, and control God as Father is an issue in your life, try this prayer: "I do not seek to possess You, Father. I choose to not be jealous of Your other children. I do not want to acquire You or use You as my servant; I want to be Your servant. I am Yours to command. I consciously give You back Your freedom, Father. I do not seek to control You or make You do what I think You ought to do. Be my Father and help me to follow You."

Thoughts and Questions

- Describe a situation where God's borrowed authority was used on someone.

- To what degree are you able to allow God to be Father to His other kids?

- In what ways do you need to set God free to be I AM to His other kids?

NOTES

1. Oswald Chambers, *My Utmost for His Highest: Selections for the Year,* "June 13," electronic ed. (Westwood: Barbour, 1996), c1993 Logos Library Systems.

Idolatry as Misplaced Affection

Yet I will leave 7,000 in Israel, all the knees that have not bowed to
Baal and every mouth that has not kissed him (1 Kings 19:18).

WHEN WE READ THIS, we should weep. It does not take much effort to feel the heart of God as a husband or Father watching Israel, His Bride, struggling with *misplaced affection*. The issue is not just morality or doing what is right; it has to do with idolatry in the form of misplaced affection. God is looking for preferential love. He wants to be loved and preferred over other things, including money and work—they, too, can become idols.

Love for God as Father involves removing our misplaced affection from everything in the world and firmly and intentionally placing it upon God. This is what it means to love Him with all our heart, soul, mind, and strength. Father's response goes something like: "Ah, I've been waiting a long time for that!" God wants us to collect all of our stray affection and place it upon Him.

The Christian wedding ceremony is symbolic of preferential choice. The bride walks down the aisle to meet her bridegroom, who is waiting for her. They are both saying to the world, "I prefer this man's/woman's love to any other; I will be faithful and will give him/her my life." Not everyone is able to stay faithful to that vow; but when it is broken, it is serious, because a commitment or *vow of preference* was made before God and man.

When man detaches from Father God and from His glory, he attaches or reattaches to the things that are on the earth and begins to worship animals and creeping things (see Rom. 1:21-23). The results are tragic. *"What then? Are we better than they? Not at all; for we...are all under sin"*

(Rom. 3:9-10). We know that the law cannot justify us in our relationship to God. Fortunately, *"what the law could not do, weak as it was through the flesh, God did"* (Rom. 8:3). The flesh (*Eros* as ungoverned desire) is everything in us that is rebellious, idolatrous, and causes us to have a harlot spirit or to love everything but God. "God did" is good news! God cured our wound. God was in Christ reconciling Himself to the world. The entire redemptive process is a love affair.

Many people picture God as terribly angry and Jesus standing between them and God like a shield to keep them from being consumed in judgment. That is a gross misrepresentation of who God is; He is a Father full of love and compassion. God saw the depth of the wound in the human condition and did something indescribable and incomprehensible about it. His *Agape* love was so intense that He turned His own wrath and weapons upon Himself. God, Who knew no sin, made Himself to be sin that we might become the righteousness of God (see 2 Cor. 5:21). To love God with all of our heart, soul, mind, and strength means to prefer Him over everything.

Thoughts and Questions

- Describe how you think God must feel about misplaced affection.

- What does preferential love involve?

- In what ways is the statement "God did" good news in your life?

Difference Between Anointing and Intimacy

He who does not love [Agape] has not become acquainted with God [does not and never did know Him], for God is love (1 John 4:8 AMP).

BECAUSE ANOINTING IS A gift of grace, experience tells us that many people can have a strong anointing apart from a deep relationship with God. In more than 50 years in ministry, I have seen men and women with powerful anointing for evangelism, including manifestations of the supernatural and the prophetic. I have been involved in much of it myself. However, when I began to see a clear distinction between anointing from God and intimacy with Him, I said to the Lord, "I'm interested in more than anointing. I don't care what it costs; I want to know You!"

It is important that we understand the difference between anointing and intimacy because God as Father is looking for intimacy. Anointing is for the purpose of *doing* something. It involves the presence of the Holy Spirit for accomplishing a task such as evangelism. Intimacy—in-to-me-He-sees—is something that God shares with us because of *who we are*; it is the state of being closely related. It is a conscious search to know God and understand His Nature.

> *But if one loves God truly [with affectionate reverence, prompt obedience, and grateful recognition of His blessing], he is known by God [recognized as worthy of His intimacy and love, and he is owned by Him]* (1 Corinthians 8:3 AMP).

Intimacy includes being comfortable with Father implementing "all things" in order to grow His Seed in us. This involves cultivation and continual development of a vital relationship, which Jesus described by saying,

> *The person who has My commands and keeps them is the one who [really] loves Me; and whoever [really] loves Me will be loved by My Father, and I [too] will love him and will show (reveal, manifest) Myself to him. [I will let Myself be clearly seen by him and make Myself real to him]* (John 14:21 AMP).

God actualizes this intimacy by giving us a consciousness of His presence. Intimacy is very delicate. When it is neglected, injured, or broken, the sense or awareness of His presence is withdrawn.

Intimacy is tied to *Agape* and is the route to the supernatural. When intimacy is present, evangelism, prophetic anointing, words of knowledge, miracles, and healing take on new meaning because God's *character* is being revealed. The supernatural is an inevitable result of increased intimacy because *Agape* is His nature. Because of grace, God can heal people through us when we're sick ourselves because healing has nothing to do with us. I've been sick with the flu and hardly hanging onto the pulpit when someone would come up and say, "Bob, would you pray for me?" When I prayed, the Lord would heal them. You may say, "If it's really God, you would have been healed, too." No, God does what He wants to do—He flows through the vessel and heals people irrespective of what is going on in the person who is being used by Him. This is the difference between intimacy and anointing. This kind of grace can also be applied to failure, sin, and weakness.

Some of the worse times for a pastor are what I refer to as the Sunday morning spirit. Everything goes wrong—the children rebel, the coffee boils over, and the car won't start! Judith and I have had some of the worst fights on our way to church. When we walk through the front door and say, "Good morning, church," the grace of God takes over, and His anointing goes through us. Then we get back in the car and finish the argument. God enjoys using weak vessels.

Thoughts and Questions

❦ Describe a situation in which you saw God's anointing in someone.

❦ What is one of the characteristics of anointing?

❦ In what ways can you see intimacy as a route to the supernatural?

PART IV

Priesthood

Reading 40

Kingdom of Priests

*You yourselves have seen what I did to the Egyptians, and how I bore you
on eagles' wings, and brought you to Myself. Now then, if you will indeed
obey My voice and keep My covenant, then you shall be My own possession
[special treasure] among all the peoples, for all the earth is Mine; and you
shall be to Me a kingdom of priests and a holy nation* (Exodus 19:4-6).

THERE ARE SEVERAL ROLES or identities described in the Scriptures that
believers have inherited: sons and daughters, heirs, disciples, friends,
servants, witnesses, priests, etc. One identity that most Christians are not
well-practiced in is being priests. We would rather have someone accomplish priesthood functions on our behalf. However, all of us have been
called to be priests in God's Kingdom. Unfortunately, time, pressure, and
culture have disallowed that concept to be cultivated and made workable in
our lives.

Since the creation of Adam, God has maintained one unchanging desire:
that we become a kingdom of priests and a holy nation. Notice the phrases
in this session's Scripture that denotes sole ownership: "to Myself," "My
own possession," "to Me." These phrases suggest intimacy and relationship.
God continues to emphasize our role as priests in the New Testament:

> *But you are a chosen race, a royal priesthood, a holy nation,
> a people for God's own possession, that you may proclaim the
> excellencies of Him who called you out of darkness into His
> marvelous light* (1 Peter 2:9).

Even in Revelation, God is calling us to be priests:

To Him who loves us and released us from our sins by His blood and He has made us to be a kingdom, priests to His God and Father—to Him be the glory and the dominion forever and ever (Revelation 1:5–6).

We were "purchased" (Strong's Greek No. 59— *agorazo*: "to buy in the marketplace") by Christ with His own blood *not for ourselves*, but for the privilege and responsibility of ministering as priests and reigning upon the earth (see Rev. 5:9-10). The basis of our authority or "reign" on the earth is directly linked to the fulfillment of our calling as priests to God individually and corporately. If the members of the Body of Christ would awaken to their individual and corporate identity in Christ, the reformation of the Church, which is so urgently needed, would happen. Over the next few sessions, we'll look at the specific duties that God wants from us in our role as His priests.

Thoughts and Questions

- What other Scriptures can you find about the significance of our priesthood?

- Why has God continued to emphasize the priesthood from Genesis to Revelation?

- In what ways can you see the Kingdom on earth affected by our functioning as priests?

READING 41

The Priesthood of the Believer

*For every high priest is appointed to offer up gifts and
sacrifices; so it is essential for this [High Priest] to have
some offering to make also* (Hebrews 8:3 AMP).

SEVERAL YEARS AGO, I met a salty, 77-year-old cowboy, one who wore
authentic Levis and pointy boots and seemed as tough as nails. He told
me that seven years earlier he had died in a hospital room. While he was
lying there, clinically dead, God said to him, "You didn't do what I called you
to do. Do you want to go back and do it?" I don't know many people who got
this kind of deal! The cowboy said, "Yes, Lord, I want to go back and do it."
He had been clinically dead for about six minutes, and when he woke up, his
wife screamed. A few days later, he asked the Lord what He wanted him to
do. The Lord said, "Go to the Shell station every morning at 5 A.M." So every
day at 5 A.M. he got a cup of coffee and sat there. Before long the prostitutes
and winos, lonely cowboys, and those who were hurting all started coming
for him to love on them and minister the life of the Lord. People came from
everywhere to *the priest of the Shell station*. For many years, he was faithful to
his call, except for the week that he had his quadruple bypass.

We mature, respond to His call, and preferentially choose our way into
a priestly role; we do not automatically become priests. What does a mature
believer look like? When *Agape* is perfected in us, it causes us to respond in
a similar way that Christ responded—*we begin carrying the burden of the Lord
and start to feel and experience priestly things*. Jesus taught us how to be His
priests and minister to others. He entered into every detail of human life.

*Then, when he came before God as high priest to get rid of
the people's sins, he would have already experienced it all*

himself—all the pain, all the testing—and would be able to help where help was needed (Heb. 2:17-18 MSG).

Another translation says that He would "be able to run to the cry." What a beautiful picture!

In order to run to the cry, we must be authentic people made up of body (physical), soul (personality), and spirit (spiritual) all in healthy balance. We are one person but everything that happens in our lives—physically, naturally, or spiritually—flows into every other area of our lives. In order to respond to the cry, we must learn how to listen to our whole person on both a conscious and unconscious level. The Lord is in process of releasing an army of lovers who will carry His burden. I would like to grow up enough to at least be a private in that army.

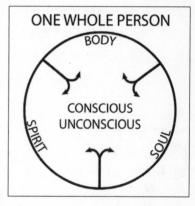

The priesthood of the believer encompasses five aspects of the burden of the Lord: absorb human failure, love without reward, vocational suffering, intercessory behavior, and extender of mercy. We will look at each of these in the next sessions. If you would stick these on your bathroom mirror and own them every day, they would help you understand what God means when He calls us to be priests in His Kingdom.

We are called to respond in a priestly manner. Father waits for each one of us to see and enter that sphere of His love.

Thoughts and Questions

- Explain what it means for priests to carry the burden of the Lord.

- In what ways have others acted as priests on your behalf and run to your cry?

- Why do the three aspects of our person make us healthy individuals?

Absorb Human Failure

*Let us then fearlessly and confidently and boldly draw near to
the throne of grace* (the throne of God's unmerited favor to us
sinners), *that we may receive mercy [for our failures] and find grace
to help in good time for every need [appropriate help and well-timed
help, coming just when we need it]* (Hebrews 4:16 AMP).

GRACE IS GOD'S LOVE given to *absorb* the failures, self-determination, and rebellion of all people. When we are functioning in New Testament priesthood, we are required to cease being critical and religiously judgmental of the failures of others; our response as New Testament priests is to model Christ. We seek to absorb and identify with failure. Of course, you will feel your own frailties, quickly discovering that this treasure is in earthen vessels, maybe even in a Styrofoam cup! God knows our frame and is mindful that we are but dust (see Ps. 103:14). He absorbs our failures, then asks that we do the same for others.

If we are unprepared or unwilling to absorb human failures, our inflexibility will prevent us from ministering to others. God absorbs all three tons of our failures and refuses to rebuke us for it! You may find that you are the person in the office who people come to to dump their issues; at times, you may feel like a human garbage can. Sometimes people are not really looking for answers; they just need someone to listen to them with a sense of confidence and absorption. It is wise to refrain from quoting Bible verses when they are trying to get their story out—often that is very dishonoring. We have not been called to *correct* everyone we meet. We are asked to *absorb* other people's weirdness, failures, idiosyncrasies, and strange behavior as part of our call to priesthood. God is big enough and smart enough to sort out all the issues with His own children; He does not really need our help.

A minister came to me seeking a place to dump his pain. The details were most nauseating. As he was speaking, he was breaking and crying. In the middle of it I thought, "Lord, I can't stand this! I wish I didn't know what he's telling me!" The Lord responded, "You *can* stand this; I've called you to the priesthood." We can only absorb human failure when we have our own security, identity, and belonging in Father God. We can, however, get to the point of super saturation if we are not careful. Priesthood requires us to keep ourselves close to the Source; only He can enable us to absorb others' failures and remain healthy ourselves. We can only be effective priests when our intimate relationship with God is intact. To be a son/daughter of our Father, we must mature spiritually so that we are able to help others shoulder their burdens. Absorbing human failure will involve acting as loving priests even to our enemies, so that we can function as sons and daughters of our Father.

Thoughts and Questions

- In what ways has God absorbed your failures?

- Why is it important to absorb other people's weirdness, failures, idiosyncrasies, and strange behavior as part of our call to priesthood?

- Explain the significance of intimacy with God in our role as priests.

READING 43

Love Without Reward

For if you love those who love you, what reward
can you have? (Matthew 5:46 AMP).

Mother Teresa is often the first person we think of as loving without reward. A priest cannot have hooks, a hidden agenda, a hard heart, or remain inflexible. Our motivation for priestly behavior is God's glory and the extension of His Kingdom. Jesus said, *"As the Father has sent Me, I also send you"* (John 20:21). This is the straight *Agape* arrow that functions without immediate reward.

Loving without reward can be as simple as active listening. A man was talking to an old friend for about 15 minutes and all he talked about was himself. Then he said, "Enough about me, let's talk about you. How did you like my new book?" By listening to someone without thought of gaining anything, we have increased insight into the *Eros* phenomenon and the depth of all that is self-referential, allowing us to begin functioning as Kingdom priests on Father's behalf.

Luke 6:35 (AMP) shows us what it means to absorb the failures of our enemies. It requires a full dose of *Agape* to love and do good to our enemies:

> *But love your enemies and be kind and do good [doing favors so*
> *that someone derives benefit from them] and lend, expecting and*
> *hoping for nothing in return but considering nothing as lost and*
> *despairing of no one; and then your recompense* (your reward)
> *will be great* (rich, strong, intense, and abundant), *and you*
> *will be sons of the Most High, for He is kind and charitable and*
> *good to the ungrateful and the selfish and wicked.*

I mentioned earlier that the Lord told me to keep some $20 bills in my pocket and give them away when He instructed. I call this my *Agape* money. When the Lord told me to give the bag lady a $20 bill, the sheriff in me quickly arose. "I can't do that. She might use it for wine and I'm a steward of this money." I could *feel* His negative response. After finally surrendering, I handed it to her and told her that God really did love her. She grabbed my arm and kissed my hand repeatedly, then began to kiss up my sleeve, moving me to tears. The Father was providing a lesson in priesthood, teaching me to spontaneously love her without reward. I encourage you to not put all your finances in the system; keep some out just to give away to those who can't reward you. As Jesus said, be careful not to let your left hand know what your right hand is doing:

> *When you help someone out, don't think about how it looks. Just do it—quietly and unobtrusively. That is the way your God, who conceived you in love, working behind the scenes, helps you out* (Matthew 6:3-4 MSG).

Who would think it could be so simple? *Agape* allows us to minister to hurting people and to do it without reward, not even for a tax deduction. Invite someone to dinner who cannot invite you back. Love without reward because *you* need to, not because others do.

Thoughts and Questions

🦌 Describe an experience where someone has loved you without reward.

🦌 From Luke 6:35, explain what it means to love without reward.

🦌 What are some ways you can love without reward as a Kingdom priest?

READING 44

Vocational Suffering

*Through many tribulations we must enter
the kingdom of God* (Acts 14:22).

S OME SUFFERING IS NOT due to sin or personal failure. There is a kind
of suffering which comes simply because we belong to God and desire
to enter the sphere of His government. Christians endure a certain kind of
suffering that no one else endures. Vocational suffering is allowed or cir-
cumscribed by the will of the Father. Please do not think that I am talking
about having cancer for Jesus. We are called to resist evil and do all that
is possible to receive physical healing. Vocational suffering comes because
of *who we are*, not what we did. It is allowing the floodwaters that come
through our lives to conform us to Christ. Only in Christ can human suffering transform us into His image.

Even though Jesus was God's Son, He entered into every detail of
human life and learned obedience through suffering (see Heb. 5:8). His
suffering had nothing to do with sin or failure; Jesus was teaching us vocational suffering so that we could be His priests and be given the capacity
needed for imparting life to others.

> *Then, when he came before God as high priest to get rid of the*
> *people's sins, he would have already experienced it all himself—*
> *all the pain, all the testing—and would be able to help where*
> *help was needed* (Heb. 2:17-18 MSG).

He showed us how "to run to the cry." He comforts us in our afflictions
so that we can comfort others. We must allow the Lord to put tears in our

voices through vocational suffering. When we embrace suffering, we allow God to work His character, His own DNA within us.

A story is told about six powerful horses that were trained to run to the fire when the alarm went off. In their eagerness and immaturity, they dashed to the scene of the fire but forgot the fire engine. They were first to the fire, but had no *equipment* to put it out. Too many Bible colleges, seminaries, and churches get us to the fire, but have neglected or failed to give us the equipment to deal with the real issues.

My sister, Peg, walked through a painful experience when her husband was dying of cancer. She prayed and stood by him to the end, grieving deeply during the process. Soon after, she went out to breakfast by herself, and in the booth next to her was an elderly woman who had lost all her hair due to chemo treatments. The Lord quietly said, "Go sit with her." As soon as Peg slid into the booth and said "Hi!" the woman started to cry. A priestly encounter followed. The Lord allows certain experiences to flow through our world in order to equip us to run to the cry and arrive at the fire with the equipment to help when we get there. Part of that equipment is what we learn through vocational suffering.

Thoughts and Questions

- Explain your understanding of vocational suffering.

- Why did Jesus have to learn obedience through suffering?

- In what ways have you experienced and learned from suffering that benefitted another?

Intercessory Behavior

I admonish and urge that petitions, prayers, intercessions,
and thanksgivings be offered on behalf of all men
(1 Timothy 2:1 AMP).

INTERCESSION IS THE ACT of praying or asking God for something on behalf of another in contrast to asking for ourselves. It is an extension of Christ's priestly office and is a living sacrifice because Jesus *lives* to make intercession for us (see Heb. 7:25). He is our advocate, pleading with God on our behalf for our continual transformation, moving us from being takers to givers. We are called to intercede for our family, friends, neighbors, city, and nation. When Simon's mother-in-law was sick, those in the house interceded for her and asked Jesus to heal her of a severe fever. Intercession tends to bring healing to the whole person.

Intercession is also the function of a peacemaker. Peacemakers are called *"sons of God"* (Matt. 5:9). As intercessors, we are called to mediate for the transgressors or the rebellious (see Isa. 53:12). We intercede for our own children when they are rebellious and wayward. As God's priests, we can intercede for others' sins.

Intercession brings God's blessings on others. While pastoring, I paid a visit to one of my elders. When I got to the doorstep, I heard loud voices and anger inside. Like a good pastor, I listened for a few minutes before knocking on the door. The husband and wife were hostile toward each other because of their inability to have children. As we talked, an intercessory burden came over me, and I laid hands on them and said, "It is not the will of God for you to be childless. God is going to give you children. In Jesus' Name I release the conception!" Then I went out to my car and said,

"Father, if You ever backed up anyone's word, please back up this one!" Ten months later, they had their first baby.

Paul says, *"Be unceasing in prayer"* (1 Thess. 5:17 AMP). There are many forms of intercession, and some are not verbal; we can intercede by just being there. As sons and daughters of God, our simple presence, which bears His presence, can be a form of intercession. The power of the listening ear is also a form of intercession. We do not have to talk or quote Scripture; just listen with compassion and honest care. We can also pray in the Spirit as a form of intercession for others because the Spirit *"comes to our aid and bears us up in our* [own] *weakness"* (Rom. 8:26 AMP).

Each of us in the Body of Christ is called to intercede; but if the spiritual gift of intercession is one of your primary gifts, guard it with great care because it is an aspect of *Agape*. Do not allow that precious, rare, and needed function to become *Eros*-driven. Many are the traps awaiting the intercessor. Guard yourself in the sphere of *Eros* payoffs. Refuse, if possible, to make it known that you are interceding for some particular person or circumstance; sometimes it is better to keep quiet and let the fruit reveal itself.

Thoughts and Questions

🦟 Describe what intercessory behavior means to you.

🦟 What does intercession do for others?

🦟 Why does our priestly role of intercession have to be guarded?

READING 46

Extender of Mercy

Go figure out what this Scripture means: "I'm after mercy, not religion.
I'm here to invite outsiders, not coddle insiders." (Matthew 9:13 MSG).

IT IS A PRIESTLY act for those who have received mercy to extend it to others in need. Like receiving forgiveness and failing to give it, failure or refusal to give mercy to others becomes a serious issue with Father God. James tells us that we are to *speak* and *act* as people

> who are to be judged under the law of liberty [the moral instruc-
> tion given by Christ, especially about love]. For to him who has
> shown no mercy the judgment [will be] merciless, but mercy [full
> of glad confidence] exults victoriously over judgment (James
> 2:12-13 AMP).

Showing mercy to others gains us mercy with the Father. He greatly prefers to show mercy to us than to condemn us. Mercy is a strong preventative measure to keep us from acting like sheriffs.

Extending mercy involves helping someone with a flat tire, listening to a hurting heart, or helping someone with a crying baby. I was heading home after one ministry trip, and a young man and his infant were on the long and crowded flight. The baby would not stop crying, and everybody on the flight had the same thought: "Get that baby hushed!" Finally, while everyone was becoming increasingly irritated (including me), a lady got up, picked up the infant, and cradled and loved on him until he quieted down and went to sleep. Would you have responded in a manner similar to the older woman? A little later in the flight, we discovered that the man's young wife had died while giving birth to this child. He was completely inexperienced as a father with an infant and was in urgent need of mercy. Could we have read the circumstance with more maturity? Can we see the necessity of Father teaching us mercy?

Jesus' ministry to the woman caught in adultery is a good example of extending mercy in a priestly manner. While most people would have rejected her, Jesus, in mercy, refused to condemn her. Jesus doesn't attempt to clean His fish until after they are caught. It is after we are received and loved that we can give someone permission to correct or adjust us. That is the nature of a priest.

Our oldest son came home late one night. He had been drinking and was slightly happier than usual. As he was standing in the doorway weaving to and fro, all kinds of things were going through my mind: "After everything I taught... what are people going to think...?" While I was deciding whether or not to communicate my displeasure, I heard the Lord say, "Give him mercy." In response, I said to him, "It's all right, go on to bed." The next morning he got up, quite physically distressed, genuinely sorry and, to my knowledge, never abused alcohol again. Mercy has a way of bringing a form of correction all its own. *"Mercy triumphs over judgment"* (see James 2:13).

Extending mercy may involve or require the dimensions of healing, demand the use of the prophetic and, very often, the ministry of deliverance. Each of us should have an intentional *Agape* agenda; our priestly call is to extend the mercy of Christ to a hurting world.

Thoughts and Questions

🐝 What are some motivations for extending mercy?

🐝 In what practical ways has mercy been shown to you?

🐝 How can you have an *Agape* agenda of mercy?

Seven Steps to Becoming a Priest

For what the Law could not do, weak as it was through the flesh,
God did: sending His own Son in the likeness of sinful flesh and as
an offering for sin, He condemned sin in the flesh (Romans 8:3).

WHAT MAN COULD NOT do, *God did*. Let me explain what God did. When we find ourselves Kingdom-centered, we begin to see God's ultimate purpose, which is the creation and release of His own kings and priests within the framework of His governmental structure. This call was originally given to Israel, but their failure to represent Father and His purpose correctly led to the loss of their Kingdom inheritance, and it was given to a people who would produce the fruits of it (see Matt. 21:43). The creation and release of His own kings and priests is the focus of the entire New Testament (see 1 Pet. 2:9-10). What God did is to provide an incremental way for us to fulfill our call as kings and priests. The progression to become kings and priests goes like this:

1. *The new birth.* We are inseminated with the *Agape* of God at our new birth. As *Agape* grows, our internal capacity for obedience from within increases and the laws become written on our heart causing us to become Father pleasers.

2. *Infancy.* Infancy is not time-related; it has to do with maturity. As newborns, we desire the sincere milk of the Word. Paul uses the word *infancy* when he says, *"Do not be children [immature] in your thinking"* (1 Cor. 14:20 AMP). In the Book of Hebrews, he uses it as a rebuke:

For everyone who continues to feed on milk is obviously inexperienced and unskilled in the doctrine of righteousness (of conformity to the divine will in purpose, thought, and action), *for he is a mere infant [not able to talk yet]!* (Hebrews 5:13 AMP).

3. *In training.* In the original Greek language, we translate this as *pedagogy* or being trained or discipled in the things of the Kingdom and the Holy Spirit. This is the rubber room.

4. *Citizenship.* When we come of age in the faith, we progressively receive the governing factors of the New Jerusalem in our hearts and minds. Functioning as a real citizen within the government of God is an exciting goal.

5. *Mature sons/daughters.* A basic Kingdom principle is that every citizen should come to a maturity that would allow his or her involvement in the extension of God's purpose in the earth. Note that both God's sons and sons of the evil one mature (see Matt. 13:38).

6. *Kings and priests.* Father's ultimate goal is that we function as kings and priests in all five areas: absorbing human failure, loving without reward, vocational suffering, intercessory behavior, and extending mercy. Functioning priests are vital in our hurting world.

7. *Ambassadors.* Making ourselves available for the extension and presentation of the Kingdom government to the other nations and governments of the world is more than exciting.

It is embracing these seven incremental steps that causes the Kingdom to take on the excitement and conflict that is described in the New Testament.

Thoughts and Questions

In your own words, explain what God did.

🌱 Can you see these incremental steps in your own journey? Explain

🌱 Why do you think these steps would cause excitement and conflict in your life?

Redefining Spiritual Maturity

This is how My Father shows who He is (John 15:8 MSG).

S PIRITUAL MATURITY IS NOTHING less than the replication of God's own love (*Agape*) within the hearts of His people (see Matt. 5:43-48; 1 Pet. 1:22-23). Replicating God's *Agape* means replicating His glory—the manifestation of His nature and DNA. When we function as priests, we replicate God's *Agape*. A helpful motivation here is the not-so-obvious fact that human knowledge *cannot* be brought to maturity because knowledge puffs up; it is *Agape* that must be brought to maturity.

Becoming priests requires that we mature and build our lives on Kingdom reality because as the pressures of life come, it involves the shaking of that which is unreality. He will shake created things so that the uncreated can remain (see Heb. 12:27). In this process He displaces *Eros* and fills us with *Agape* which never fails or breaks down; it is the real thing. God is *Agape*.

This process of *Agape* displacing *Eros* through shaking poses some hard questions: Are we willing to be used by God in a priestly manner? Are we willing to absorb human failure? Are we willing and ready to be treated wrongly or sinned against without *reacting*—for the purpose of revealing God's glory? This can be frightening, but mature *Agape* drives out fear! To be priestly, we must be prepared to be the garbage can because people will dump their issues and problems on us, and as priests, we must be mature enough to properly respond to them. God's glory can shine through us when we refuse to react when mistreated. This is not about human strength or the White Knuckle Club; it is about allowing God to reveal Himself through us as priests.

In French novelist Victor Hugo's *Les Misérables,* a thief breaks out of prison and is found on the street and invited into the home of a priest. During the night, the thief steals the silverware from his host and runs away. The police catch him with the silverware in the bag and bring him back to the priest, expecting the priest to testify against him. The priest graciously admits that it was his silverware, but says it was *given* to the man, not stolen. The priest then hands two silver candlesticks to the thief and says, "Here, I forgot to give these to you." When the police leave, the priest tells the thief to use his redemption well. This act of *Agape* is the pivotal point in the complete transformation of the life of the thief. Progressively, he begins to help others by creating a factory and hiring the hopeless in the town. The story is *Agape* in action.

Paul says that it would be better to be cheated, defrauded, and robbed than to take a brother to court because that would be a dishonor to God's glory (see 1 Cor. 6:6-7). The basis of Paul's appeal is *Agape*. Take the loss. Surrender. Refuse to demand to be right and have it your way. Jesus will make it up a thousand times. Spiritual maturity involves replicating God's glory in every aspect of our lives. As priests, this is our calling and vocation.

Thoughts and Questions

🦌 Are you willing to be used by God in a priestly manner?

🦌 What are some of the real-life implications of being used as God's priest?

🦌 Describe your understanding of spiritual maturity.

Love for Truth

They did not welcome the Truth but refused to love it that
they might be saved (2 Thessalonians 2:10 AMP).

A HUNTING DOG SAW THE rabbit. As he had been trained, he started pursuing it. All the other dogs picked up the scent and started to follow. They ran and ran, but one by one the dogs started to drop off—except the one dog that first saw the rabbit. In 1954, I *saw* the Kingdom. It was not a complete or full picture, but I did see the rabbit and I am still running.

The Scriptures tell us that not everyone who starts this race finishes it. My heart's desire is to see each of us keep on keeping on. I would like to meet you ten years from now and know that you are still running. The lessons about being one who "loves truth" will keep you running and could possibly save your spiritual life.

Because we were infected and affected by the original Fall, we have an internal twist in our thinking that causes us to love (*Agape*) darkness rather than light (see John 3:19). I have often said that *truth is almost always negative in its first appearance*. We do not really *want* to know the truth because when that truth first comes to our attention, it seems negative and often disagrees with what we would want it to say. As the adage goes, "My mind is made up; do not confuse me with the facts!" Judith and I still laugh over my reaction to her wanting me to get on the bathroom scale. The truth was, I was enjoying the darkness and did not want to know how much I weighed.

Sometimes we are *inconveniently enlightened* when truth (the person and character of Christ) comes and tells us something we don't particularly want to hear, or disruptively disagrees with what we were sure were the facts. We are then forced to choose between loving darkness and loving truth. When truth disagrees with our beliefs, loving it is the essence of learning to follow the person of Christ no matter how inconvenient it may be. Choosing truth over beliefs involves a preferential choice.

When the 12 disciples began to follow Jesus, they were sure that they understood the whole program. Fully confident that they knew what they were doing and where they were going, they asked "Master, where do You dwell?" They were indicating a personal desire for Him to be their rabbi and to teach them what He knew. Little did they suspect that He was the Son of God, the Messiah and the one who would run into conflict with the powers that were in place. Over time, they began to assume that He would quickly overthrow the Roman government, set up the earthly Kingdom, and make Judah head of the nations. When He began to say "My Kingdom is not an earthly Kingdom...My purpose is to die and be resurrected..." their response was "Not so, Lord!" (See Matt. 16:21-23.) Even in the first chapter of Acts they were still waiting for a natural Kingdom. Truth was about to break upon them:

> *It is not for you to become acquainted with and know what time brings...you shall be My witnesses in Jerusalem and all Judea and Samaria and to the ends...of the earth"* (Acts 1:7–8 AMP).

Jesus never took His eye off the Kingdom. We may not fully know all that Father intends for us and our future, but we can ask Him to give us a love for truth so that we can keep our eye on the Kingdom, know His voice, and follow Him, irrespective of the cost or disruption.

Thoughts and Questions

🐾 Have you seen the rabbit? In what ways are you still chasing it?

🐾 Why is truth almost always negative in its first appearance?

🐾 In what ways have you been inconveniently enlightened?

PART V

Seers and Sayers

READING 50

Seeing the Eternal Seed

Who do people say that the Son of Man is? (Matthew 16:13).

T HE 430 YEARS BETWEEN the Old Testament and the New Testament was a time of absolute silence. Not a sound of any kind came from heaven. Yet Simeon and Anna served in the temple night and day waiting expectantly for the Kingdom of God to come. After a lifetime of waiting, God directed Mary and Joseph to bring baby Jesus into that temple for both Simeon and Anna to see. What they saw was the fulfillment of the prophetic vision given to them many years before. They saw the glory of God in the face of the Christ child. Bypassing all that was in place, they saw into the future and the unfolding purposes of the God of Israel. Something totally new had begun.

Simeon saw that finally, the mysterious, Eternal Seed had been birthed, and the secret aims of many hearts would be revealed. He became not only a *seer*, he also became a *sayer:* he blessed God for the coming of the child, and he blessed Mary and Joseph for the rejection they were going to face because of Him. Simeon also saw that Jesus was sent as the stone that would cause men to stumble, and which was the foundation of God's building. Finally, Simeon saw that Jesus was the sign of God's salvation and that God's sign would be rejected (see Luke 2:29-35).

Anna was a prophetess who immediately recognized that with the Christ child redemption or divine deliverance had come. She became more than a *seer*; she also was a *sayer* who praised God for His grace. Anna continued to talk *"of [Jesus] to all who were looking for the redemption (deliverance) of Jerusalem"* (Luke 2:38 AMP).

When Jesus said, "Who do people say I am?" He was waiting for the 12 disciples to see that *God*, the I AM of Exodus, had now come to them as He had promised. This living Christ said, *"He who has seen Me has seen the Father"* (John 14:9). When Peter finally became a *seer*, he also became a *sayer*, declaring: *"You are the Christ, the Son of the living God!"* (Matt. 16:16). Peter saw that the foundation stone had been laid, and on that understanding, Christ could build on him. Simeon, Anna, and the disciples saw God's glory and DNA reflected in Christ. This is the coming of the Kingdom.

We do not become authentic believers until we have actually and spiritually *received something from heaven.*

> *To open their eyes that they may turn from darkness to light and from the power of Satan to God, so that they may thus receive forgiveness and release from their sins and a place and portion among those who are consecrated and purified by faith in Me* (Acts 26:18 AMP).

When we become seers, we receive that which Father has provided for us in the person of Christ: forgiveness given to us by faith. Salvation is more than an intellectual assent to given truth; it is an encounter with the Holy Spirit who comes to reveal Christ and make His Kingdom known. When we become *seers,* it is relatively easy to become *sayers,* for our assignment is to be witnesses to what we have seen as His Kingdom enters our time-space world.

Thoughts and Questions

- What were Simeon and Anna waiting for?
- What did Simeon and Anna say when they saw the Kingdom?
- What did Peter see? How did it affect his life?

Paul Became a Seer

Who are you, Master? I am Jesus, the One you're
hunting down (Acts 9:5 MSG).

T HE APOSTLE PAUL WAS a conservative, zealous, and blameless Pharisee who lived according to the law, but he also fervently persecuted the Body of Christ. He knew that Jesus ate with immoral and unclean people like tax-gatherers who betrayed their nation, prostitutes who broke all the moral laws, and fishermen who ate without the ritual washing. He knew Jesus accepted them into the Kingdom reserved for the pious Jew. Then he saw a crucified Messiah hung upon a tree as a curse. How could God act like this? He thought the actions of Jesus would destroy everything the Jews held sacred, confuse the issues, and eventually dethrone God's own people.

Paul's first glimpse of God's glory was in Jesus' own disciple Stephen. Paul was watching as Stephen was stoned, and he heard him pray, "*Master Jesus, take my life*" (Acts 7:59 MSG). Later, when Paul was knocked off his donkey in his encounter with the resurrected Messiah, he actually *saw* the glory of God in the face of Jesus Christ (see 2 Cor. 4:6). His encounter with the disciples who knew Jesus and effectively reflected God's DNA helped Paul see the Kingdom with his own eyes. He knew that God had come and that *Agape* fulfilled the whole law including the sacrificial and priestly system. Paul saw that Jesus came to change our definition of holiness from keeping the law to increasing in love for all men, so that our hearts could be without blame (see 1 Thess. 3:11-13). When Paul saw the knowledge of the glory of God in the face of Jesus Christ, it changed him. From that moment on, he did everything for the glory of God (see 1 Cor. 10:31). It is on this basis that Paul could re-enter the synagogue, irrespective of the beatings and persecution.

Every act, business deal, and relationship we enter into must contain the seven hidden attributes of God's own nature. Our generation is waiting for God to come, but the minds of the unbelieving are blinded to *the light of the gospel of the glory of Christ, who is the image of God*" (2 Cor. 4:4). This ability to see is also hidden from much of institutional Christianity. When we see the glory of God in the face of Christ, religion falls aside. Like Paul, once we have seen God's nature, we are seers and we then become sayers who give witness to His nature in us. When this understanding of who Christ is becomes ours, we have touched the treasure and the pearl.

Thoughts and Questions

- Describe what Paul saw or understood after he was knocked off his donkey.

- In what ways did this change Paul?

- If you have not seen the glory of God in the face of Christ, ask God to open your eyes.

Seeing Through or Looking At

But at present we do not yet see all things subjected to him [man].
But we are able to see Jesus (Hebrews 2:8-9 AMP).

A VITAL PRINCIPLE THAT ENABLES us to effectively walk in the Kingdom is learning to *see through* rather than *look at*. Remember that truth is almost always negative in its first appearance. If we want to know the truth, we must be willing to develop the skill of *seeing through* what appears to be something negative or what we ordinarily would not want to see. When we see something as it really is, it is not usually like we first thought or imagined. This is true of our church or the politician for whom we voted. Remember, once we see through, people and situations may appear worse, not better. When we begin to see through, the wonderful business deal that was too good to be true suddenly becomes full of false promises and sales hype, saving us much pain.

Seeing through involves working through disillusionment. One cannot be disillusioned without first having an illusion. When I was young, my desire was to be a surgeon; I was fascinated with the whole medical world. In my immaturity, doctors simply could do no wrong; I was illusioned. Then I began studying medicine in preparation for the mission field. During training I became disillusioned when I was able to see through the image and weaknesses of the medical profession.

Seeing through is a function of the living Word of God.

> *His powerful Word is sharp as a surgeon's scalpel, cutting through everything, whether doubt or defense, laying us open to listen and obey* (Hebrews 4:12 MSG).

I have been forced to see things, people, and situations as they really are, not just in the image or manner I desired. Only God knows the end from the beginning.

We all know that life can change in about a minute. We think we have our future plans all mapped out, when suddenly, we get one phone call, and our whole life is upside down. If you are struggling with life's circumstances, find yourself broken-hearted, confused, or disillusioned over how events have unfolded, or have lost confidence in your prayers being answered, the concept of *looking at or seeing through* could be a lifesaver. Hindsight is almost always 20/20. Once we have walked through a difficult situation, our vision is much clearer as we have seen how God was orchestrating events. It is not so easy to perceive God working in the midst of a situation, and we can often feel trapped by the circumstances. However, with some training, we can learn to see through. In the midst of the difficulty, we need to ask ourselves whether we are looking at the difficulty and complexity of circumstances or seeing through them. Seeing Jesus rather than man or circumstances gives us the ability to see through spiritually. Jesus is moving all things in our lives toward the fulfillment of His Father's Kingdom, but we must have spiritual illumination to be able to perceive it.

Thoughts and Questions

- If we want to know the truth, what must we do?

- In what circumstances have you been looking at rather than seeing through?

- Why is spiritual illumination and seeing through important?

READING 53

Walking in Truth

For the time is coming when [people] will not tolerate (endure) *sound and wholesome instruction, but, having ears itching [for something pleasing and gratifying], they will gather to themselves one teacher after another to a considerable number, chosen to satisfy their own liking and to foster the errors they hold, and will turn aside from hearing the truth and wander off into myths and man-made fictions* (2 Timothy 4:3-4 AMP).

In order to walk in truth, we must address a certain kind of sin. These are internal mental strongholds and attitudes that no one but Jesus can touch or adjust.

> *What comes out of the mouth gets its start in the heart. It's from the heart that we vomit up evil arguments, murders, adulteries, fornications, thefts, lies, and cussing* (Matthew 15:18-19 MSG).

Eventually, these internal strongholds can and do lead to other actions that are outward. Rather than look at internal attitudes with outward judgment and a critical mind-set, we need to *see through* to the heart issues so we can deal with root causes.

God's glory is the quintessence of the Kingdom of God. Without exception, attitudinal sin puts us all in the category of *"falling short of the honor and glory which God bestows and receives"* (Rom. 3:23 AMP). Jesus seeks transformation of the heart and mouth, which comes as we seek to *see through* rather than *look at*. Religion, on the other hand, creates all kinds of compensating devices for human failure. All of them are based on the inexorable fact that we love darkness more than light and *insist that others tell us what we want to hear.* This is a fatal form of self-deception. We can look at Israel's failure in the people's response to God as Father, or we could begin to see through the deeper issues and discover that the real problem was the deceitfulness of sin. Israel's complexities began as internal mental and attitudinal rebellions that progressed to spiritual failure, resulting in loss of the Kingdom as their inheritance.

As the result of Christ's love, we have been given the eyes to see an entirely new realm called the Kingdom of God. *The Kingdom is in the Holy Spirit.* The primary reason that the Kingdom comes without observation (see Luke 17:20-21) is because it is in the Holy Spirit. We are not able to see that Kingdom without or apart from the new birth. If we do not start seeing things spiritually, we will not understand how the Kingdom works. As we develop a spiritual capacity or ability to see, those things that are unseen become visible to us. We can then say, "Ah, I know what's going on here!" In the days ahead, the need for discernment will become increasingly urgent. Physical things like jobs, houses, and cars are not going to endure because they are temporal. From a Kingdom perspective, such things are not real. The real, permanent, and everlasting things are unseen, and no one can take them from us once they become our own possession. Like the dog that caught sight of the rabbit, we must never stop pursuing the Kingdom because it is eternal and uncreated.

Thoughts and Questions

- ❦ Why do we have to address internal strongholds and attitudes in order to walk in truth?

- ❦ Describe a time when you insisted that others tell you want you want to hear. Why is this a form of self-deception?

- ❦ Why does the Kingdom require that we see things spiritually?

The Lesson of the Yeast

*On their way to the other side of the lake, the disciples discovered they
had forgotten to bring along bread. In the meantime, Jesus said to them,
"Keep a sharp eye out for Pharisee-Sadducee yeast." Thinking he was
scolding them for forgetting bread, they discussed in whispers what to
do. Jesus knew what they were doing and said, "Why all these worried
whispers about forgetting the bread? Runt believers! Haven't you caught
on yet? Don't you remember the five loaves of bread and the five thousand
people, and how many baskets of fragments you picked up? Or the seven
loaves that fed four thousand, and how many baskets of leftovers you
collected? Haven't you realized yet that bread isn't the problem? The
problem is yeast, Pharisee-Sadducee yeast"* (Matthew 16:5-11 MSG).

SEEING THROUGH IN THIS instance is most valuable. These simple and
uncomplicated disciples were not credulous or overly concerned that the
Lord would do a miracle. They were embarrassed that they had forgotten
to bring lunch and had the thought of food on their minds while listening
to Jesus talk about the yeast of the Pharisees. "Runt believers" elsewhere is
translated "you men of little faith." Jesus was referring to the absurdity of
their interpretation, rather than rebuking them. Twice the disciples wit-
nessed Jesus' ability to meet human need by feeding thousands of people
with a few pieces of bread and fish. They *knew* He could take care of their
needs, so they should not have been so distracted with something as insig-
nificant as forgetting the food. He rebuked them because they were *looking
at* the bread not *seeing through* to what Jesus was really talking about.

Yeast itself can be a good influence—Jesus said that the *"kingdom is
like yeast that a woman works into the dough…and waits while the dough rises"*

(Matt. 13:33 MSG). However, it is also used in a negative way throughout the Scriptures. When leaving Egypt, the Israelites were told to get rid of all yeast and to eat only unleavened bread. "In verse 5 the disciples were, "on their way to the other side of the lake." Crossing the lake could be compared to leaving Egypt. Jesus took the occasion to warn the disciples about the danger of Pharisaical influence, which was hypocrisy and Jewish legalism, as well as Sadducee influence, which was secular and heathen.

Only when error is perceived and removed does the truth of the Kingdom have freedom to gain entrance. Legalism and hypocrisy are not side issues. Paul said they would *spread like gangrene*" (2 Tim. 2:17). Both are infectious and dangerous. Learning to perceive the magnitude of the issue is a major part of the action needed to correct it.

Jesus was warning that hypocrisy and legalism have the effect of yeast— they influence everything in which they come into contact. Pharisaical yeast causes us to lose our Kingdom focus through religious activity and it can happen in about 30 minutes. Like light and salt, the Kingdom is pure *Agape* yeast given to influence, preserve, and heal.

Thoughts and Questions

- Explain what Jesus was trying to get the disciples to understand when He was talking about the yeast.

- What happens when we lose our Kingdom focus?

- Do you know others who have been snared in the leaven of the Pharisees?

Seeing the Word Made Flesh

What are people saying about who the Son of
Man is? (Matthew 16:13 MSG).

FROM JESUS' FIRST SIGN of turning the water into wine, the disciples were shown glimpses of God's glory, causing them to believe in Him. Just after Jesus gave the lesson of the bread and the danger of the yeast of the Pharisees and Sadducees, He went into the region of Caesarea Philippi and asked His disciples a question:

> *Who do people say that the Son of Man is? And they answered,*
> *Some say John the Baptist; others say Elijah; and others Jere-*
> *miah or one of the prophets. He said to them, But who do*
> *you [yourselves] say that I am? Simon Peter replied, You are*
> *the Christ, the Son of the living God. Then Jesus answered*
> *him, Blessed* (happy, fortunate, and to be envied) *are you,*
> *Simon Bar-Jonah. For flesh and blood [men] have not revealed*
> *this to you, but My Father Who is in heaven* (Matthew
> 16:13-17 AMP).

Many people in Jesus' hometown were scandalized by Him. They simply saw the son of Joseph, not the Word made flesh. Hadn't they known Him since He was a boy? They simply could not or would not see through. The opinions and rumors about Jesus' identity were everywhere. Peter, however, was able to see through and he said, "I know Who You are! You are the Christ, the Son of the Living God. You're the coming One!" (see Matt. 16:16). Jesus said, "Ah, Peter, My Father showed you that!" Peter *saw through* to who Jesus was physically and perceived His real nature. I AM had come.

For Peter, who was a Hebrew, this was a major step. It was a supernatural illumination. Jesus then said,

> *And now I'm going to tell you who you are, really are. You are Peter, a rock. This is the rock on which I will put together My church, a church so expansive with energy that not even the gates of hell will be able to keep it out* (Matthew 16:18 MSG).

Jesus was looking for something in the disciples that is just as urgent for us: *Can we see the glory of God in the face of Jesus Christ?* (see 2 Cor. 4:6). When we are able to see through instead of look at, we are someone on whom God can build His unshakable Kingdom.

Paul, a Pharisee of the Pharisees, took pride in his Jewish pedigree. It was so persuasive that Father clearly chose him to extract the Kingdom of God from the roots and fruits of Judaism. Jesus, born of the line of David, also had a pure Hebrew lineage. Jesus was baptized as a Jewish Messiah but was brought up out of the water as the universal Son of the living God—thus showing us that death must come to the old creation so that our new lineage could be resurrected. His Kingdom is not out of this world system. When asked about His natural heritage, He said, "Those who do the will of My Father are My family, My sisters and My brothers" (see Mark 3:35). Being born into the Kingdom of God is a result of the Resurrection of Jesus Christ, not Hebrew lineage (see Matt. 12:50; John 1:13). The outworking of our being a new creation in Christ Jesus is eating His flesh and drinking His blood. Jesus is a cosmic Christ moving toward a universal Kingdom that is far beyond any human limitation, including our Jewish heritage.

Thoughts and Questions

❦ Why did Jesus ask the disciples who the Son of Man was?

❦ Describe how you see Jesus.

❦ Why is God able to build on people who can see through?

READING 56

Seeing the Kingdom in Glory

From that time forth Jesus began [clearly] to show His disciples
that He must go to Jerusalem and suffer many things at the hands
of the elders and the high priests and scribes, and be killed, and on
the third day be raised from death (Matthew 16:21 AMP).

SIMON PETER HAD JUST seen through Jesus' humanity to know that
He was "the Messiah, the Son of the living God" (see Matt. 16:16).
However, because of his own personal interests, he could not see all the
way through to God's full intentions for the Messiah. Peter was not looking
for Christ's spiritual Kingdom; he wanted a real, earthly realm without the
Romans and with him and Jesus running the show from Jerusalem. When
Jesus said He was going to Jerusalem not to conquer but to suffer, Peter's
gears were stripped—*"This must never happen to You!"* Jesus' response was

> *Get behind Me, Satan! You are in My way [an offense and*
> *a hindrance and a snare to Me]; for you are minding what*
> *partakes not of the nature and quality of God, but of men*
> (Matthew 16:22-23 AMP).

Jesus was not saying that Peter was literally possessed by Satan but that
Satan was using him as an accuser or opposer of God's eternal purposes.
Peter's personal interests and ambitions kept him from accepting the ulti-
mate intentions of the Father.

I, too, have opposed God's sovereign purposes because I could not see
through my immediate circumstances into God's ultimate plan. Presently,
Jesus is unfolding His eternal Kingdom on the earth in the hearts of men.
This Kingdom will not ultimately be discovered in the earthly Jerusalem

in Israel but in the heavenly Jerusalem of Hebrews 12:22 and Revelation 21:2, descending out of Heaven. The New Jerusalem is the Kingdom of God—the Father's will being done on the earth as it is in Heaven. It is precisely what the Church has prayed for for more than two thousand years! Though God's ultimate intention in our lives may bring present blessing, His eternal purpose for us is to help us become mature sons and daughters—and through that relationship, to extend His spiritual Kingdom and glory to the hearts of people everywhere.

God is a Spirit and He operates primarily in the spiritual sphere. Transitioning from an earthly to a heavenly mind-set is most important if we are going to see through present circumstances into God's eternal purposes. "Seeing through" is both a developed skill and a gift that we are encouraged to ask for in faith (see 1 Cor. 2:9-10).

After correcting Peter, Jesus says to His disciples,

> *If anyone desires to be My disciple, let him deny himself [disregard, lose sight of, and forget himself and his own interests] and take up his Cross and follow Me [cleave steadfastly to Me, conform wholly to My example in living and, if need be, in dying, also]* (Matthew 16:24 AMP).

If our self-denial is not rooted in a revelation of the Father's ultimate intentions, it can degenerate into an exercise of religious asceticism, which only develops our toxic self-righteousness. When we are unable to see through to God's ultimate purposes in present circumstances, we can become a stumbling block or a hindrance to ourselves and to others. May God give us grace to deny the temptation of personal ease for the high prize of walking as sons and daughters of the Kingdom.

Thoughts and Questions

- In what ways has your inability to see through cost you?

- What circumstances have you opposed in your life because you could not see the Kingdom?

- Why is seeing through essential in order to deny yourself?

READING 57

Seeing the Kingdom Revealed

*Recently he spoke to us directly through his Son. By his Son,
God created the world in the beginning, and it will all
belong to the Son at the end* (Hebrews 1:2 MSG).

THE EMPHASIS ON NATURAL Israel is, in my opinion, a serious application of *looking at* rather than *seeing through* because the Old Testament contains the shadows and types of all that Christ came to fulfill. Paul opens this spiritual dimension in several of his writings and shows us how deep and pervasive it is:

> *For in Him the whole fullness of Deity* (the Godhead) *continues to dwell in bodily form [giving complete expression of the divine nature]. ... Such [things] are only the shadow of things that are to come, and they have only a symbolic value. But the reality* (the substance, the solid fact of what is foreshadowed, the body of it) *belongs to Christ....For [even the whole] creation* (all nature) *waits expectantly and longs earnestly for God's sons to be made known [waits for the revealing, the disclosing of their sonship]. For the creation* (nature) *was subjected to frailty* (to futility, condemned to frustration), *not because of some intentional fault on its part, but by the will of Him Who so subjected it—[yet] with the hope that nature* (creation) *itself will be set free from its bondage to decay and corruption [and gain an entrance] into the glorious freedom of God's children* (Colossians 2:9,17; Romans 8:19-21 AMP).

Christ is more than Mary's Son of the line of David and the tribe of Judah. Those were the physical instruments God chose to reveal the eternal Word—God made flesh. Jesus is *God's final speech*, meaning everything Father previously said was a type and shadow for the Word to be made flesh and that speech cannot be changed or added to in any manner. This can be inconvenient enlightenment to many who have been caught up in the natural and find themselves unable to *see through* the feasts and holy days. With all love and sincerity, perhaps we should stop and ask Father if we are looking at natural Israel or seeing through to the emergence of the Kingdom. No matter what it costs, we need to see what the greater spiritual issues are and allow God to penetrate our soulish understanding. It is essential that we see through to the glory of God in the face of Jesus Christ in the same manner that precipitated Paul's conversion to Christ.

There is only one born without *Eros*—the incarnate Son of God. The entire creation waits for this cosmic Christ to be reproduced in others so that we can *be free from corruption* for all eternity. John saw that this freedom is God's glory having been so worked into our spiritual and physical person and nature, that the entire world will be able to see Christ as the way to the Father (see John 17:21-26). May we never trade *seeing through* to the Kingdom for *looking at* a restored temple in Jerusalem for this is the fulfillment of all that the cosmic Christ purchased in His Crucifixion.

Thoughts and Questions

- In what ways is the focus on natural Israel a result of the lack of seeing through?

- Describe your understanding of God's universal Kingdom as the whole Creation.

- If you are willing, ask God to show you the more significant spiritual issues of the Kingdom.

Seeing Clearly

*His appearance changed from the inside out, right before
their eyes. Sunlight poured from his face. His clothes
were filled with light.* (Matthew 17:2 MSG).

JESUS TOOK PETER, JAMES, and John with Him up the mountain but
left the other nine disciples behind. That does not seem very fair, but
it is possible that Jesus took Peter, James, and John because they could *see
through* more clearly than the others. I have a saying that if you pout when
you're left out, you'll puff up if you're let in. There will be times when you
will be left out; it is important that you learn to handle it well. See through
the circumstances; do not get all bent out of shape. Learn how to properly
respond to life and see God as sovereign no matter how the circumstances
may appear.

On the mountain, the disciples saw Christ's physical person and
clothing undergo a change. The Transfiguration was not a symbol of the
Resurrection but of the coming of the Kingdom. As Jesus stated: *"There are
some of those who are standing here who will not taste death until they see the
Son of Man coming in His kingdom"* (Matt. 16:28). This was the Kingdom
being revealed, and His face and garments shone with the glory of God.
Peter, true to his nature, said, "Oh, this is great! I'm going to make three
tabernacles—one for You, one for Moses, and one for Elijah." Peter typi-
cally did not wait to see through what was happening. On that mountain, a
major *kairos* event was occurring. In the unfolding of the eternal Kingdom,
it was time for Moses (representing the Law) and Elijah (representing the
prophets) *to surrender their teaching offices to the person of Christ*. We know
that *Agape* is the fulfillment of the Ten Commands and of the Law, the

prophets, and the psalms, resulting in freedom of the entire, created universe. (The Amplified Bible gives us 69 instances of the Law and the prophets being abrogated).

While Peter was still speaking, a cloud composed of light, who was the Father Himself, overshadowed them, and a voice from the cloud said, *"This is My beloved Son, with whom I am well-pleased; listen to Him!"* (Matt. 17:5). Jesus was God's final speech.

There isn't anything else to say or add after Christ. Peter, James, and John were still reaching into the past, but when the cloud lifted, *all they could see was Jesus* because He is God's final speech. For our Kingdom foundation, we must always begin with Christ, teach Christ, and end with Christ.

Christ as God's Son is the source of our new birth and He opens our entrance into the Kingdom of God. Like the disciples, we receive His Words and believe, which enables us to see something of the glory of God in the face of Jesus Christ. The new birth is the introduction into the skill of seeing through. You cannot even see the Kingdom until and unless you have been born from above! We *know* we have been forgiven, loved, and that He has moved on our behalf because we *know* He is *Agape* incarnate. Healing, answered prayer, and provision all become authentic and available due to the discovery of God in Christ revealing His redemptive love and nature to our hurting person and to our hurting world. He loved us to the uttermost. The Crucifixion and Resurrection were His crowning glory so that we could *see* God's nature—His *Agape*. Though His humanness He allows us to see clearly, so we can know who God is and what He is like, and, as a result, know eternal life.

Thoughts and Questions

- Why is it important to see God as sovereign no matter how the circumstances appear?

- Explain why Jesus on the Mount of Transfiguration was the coming of the Kingdom.

- In what ways have you seen the glory of God in the face of Christ?

READING 59

Exam Time

*But take heed; behold, I have told you everything
in advance* (Mark 13:23).

M Y BASIC DRIVE IS that of a teacher. I have a great appreciation for the classroom—one with several blackboards and media connections is very satisfying to me. One of the more complex aspects of loving truth and seeing through is the not-so-obvious Kingdom principle that *once the exam starts, the teacher does not speak*. It is quite contrary to the ordinary idea of how Jesus responds to us during a crisis. It seems to work like this: Jesus carefully teaches, gives illustrations, asks questions, applies principles, and often allows input from other sources. After all of these aspects are in place, then comes exam day, the one for which He has prepared us. It is only out of the testing process that we can know existential reality. Often, I have desperately wanted to give my students an exam, but the Lord has repeatedly said, "No, you give the teaching; *I will give the exam*." After the exam is over and the papers are in, the Teacher becomes very free with His input and advice, assessment, and evaluation. He then patiently reaffirms, corrects, and, without rebuke, adjusts our understanding.

Most people have the false assumption that during an exam all they have to do is ask the Teacher for help. Not so. He always gives open book exams with the freedom of using our Bible or notes, or referring to other sources of reference. This is one reason why it is increasingly important to keep a journal of what God is saying and teaching us. However, during the exam the Teacher will seldom break the silence or attempt to add to the guidance because it is not the time to reinterpret what has been taught. This is what Scripture means by *"take care how you listen"* (Luke 8:18). It has to do with *how* as compared to *what* you hear. Ask the Father to allow you to see through. Ask Him to teach you how to love that which is not agreeable. Ask for a love for truth that is more than your love for darkness. You will begin to see not only what is happening in the natural circumstances but also to see right through to the spiritual events.

Exams are successful when we consistently abide with strong confidence in the nature of God the Father. Take them in a manner similar to taking the elements of His Body and His Blood at the Lord's Table. We are not to count the exam as something strange but rather as a constituent part of the growth process. It is only when we have passed the exam that we can say we have bought the Truth, which we will not sell.

As we mature and give mental assent and then admission or perhaps *permission* to the exam and its spiritual and practical lessons, Kingdom fruitfulness is guaranteed. The Eternal Seed will bring forth the fruit after its kind.

Thoughts and Questions

🖋 What is the point of an exam in our lives?

🖋 What is one of the benefits of keeping a journal?

🖋 In what ways has the Lord been saying, "Take care how you hear" to you lately?

Spiritual Discernment

*Buy truth, and do not sell it, get wisdom and instruction
and understanding* (Proverbs 23:23).

SPIRITUAL DISCERNMENT—SEEING THROUGH AS compared to looking at—involves four specific ingredients: spiritual warfare, departure from our comfort level, entering the spiritual realm, and permeability of the human spirit. Let's look at each of these:

Spiritual warfare. Warfare usually begins when we are faced with truth that may appear negative. We may think that these particular circumstances could not be God, and like Eve, question: "Has God really said?" Discernment is a skill that requires intentional cultivation to see past the bread to the yeast as Pharisaical influence, or past our immediate reward to see the spiritual Kingdom. Discernment involves both positive and negative insight. We discern what God is doing; we also discern forces in the created universe that do not originate in God. When we start to see through spiritual issues, we open ourselves to spiritual warfare. This may be some of the logic behind the adage, "Ignorance is bliss"! Discernment is required when all outward appearances seem to be in place but something causes our whole person to withdraw. The wise woman said: There ain't nothin' wrong, but somethin' ain't right! Looking through is not the gift of suspicion but a manifestation of the Spirit of truth, which causes us to be aware of that which we could not possibly know apart from His love and provision. Truth is valuable but expensive—it will cost us.

Departure from our comfort levels. When we begin to see through, we have to leave our comfort level behind because it requires that we be persistent and diligent in chasing the rabbit. Other people can drop off and quit but not us. Our own comfort level is not as important as a Kingdom understanding of the real issues.

Entering the spiritual realm. When we cease looking at that which is natural and begin to see the eternal and the spiritual, we should be issued another passport because in reality we have entered another country. The spiritual realm has a different language, value system, and way of measuring things. When we take the time and make the effort to repeatedly turn to the Father and ask, "What is this all about?" we will begin to see through, which will cause us to emigrate from one realm or country to the Kingdom of God.

Developing a permeable spirit. When we begin to see through, our spirit and person become permeable or porous, and we are able to receive and absorb the things God shares with us. Rather than taking a risk and remaining childlike and vulnerable, many people harden and lose permeability to prevent injury.

Loving truth means we are determined to allow God as our Father to show us reality irrespective of the discomfort. We are unafraid that this journey will take us away from orthodox truth—for Christ is the Spirit of truth who has come to make the things of God real for us. We want to know God's final speech in the person of Christ, irrespective of its personal discomfort or cost. Each of us should be increasingly intentional in our lives to begin with Christ, to teach Christ, and to end our journey in Christ. Christ is the reflection of Father's glory. We should be increasingly unafraid to press into God for His Kingdom reality.

Thoughts and Questions

- What does spiritual discernment involve?

- In what ways is your comfort level unimportant compared to Kingdom issues?

- Describe why a permeable spirit is needed for God to share things with you.

PART VI

God's Final Speech

READING 61

Seeing the Invisible Father

In many separate revelations [each of which set forth a portion of the Truth] and in different ways God spoke of old to [our] forefathers in and by the prophets, [But] in the last of these days He has spoken to us in [the person of a] Son, Whom He appointed Heir and lawful Owner of all things, also by and through Whom He created the worlds and the reaches of space and the ages of time [He made, produced, built, operated, and arranged them in order] (Hebrews 1:1-2 AMP).

EACH "SEPARATE REVELATION" (SOME translations say "many frag-ments") sets out a portion of the truth in type and symbol of what was to come, but it is not the whole picture. The revelations that formed the Old Testament were many: Abraham; Joseph; Moses' Law and the exodus journey across the wilderness; the cloud and fire; the ark, tabernacle, and temple; the system of animal sacrifices, the priesthood and its garments; Elijah and the prophets; and the Sabbath. Each of these speaks to us in some manner of the coming of Christ. For instance, in the Old Testament, redemption from sin was accomplished by the priest laying his hands on the head of a lamb or goat and then sending it out into the wilderness to carry away all the sins of the people (see Lev. 16:10). This picture was a fragment of what was to come in Christ.

These fragments or separate revelations continued in the New Testament. Then John the Baptist came and said, "This is He! This is the One we've been looking for." He was a forerunner to prepare the road for the Lord and make His highways straight (see Matt. 3:3). Simeon and Anna, who waited many years for the Christ, also were given a glimpse of what was to come.

But all this was shadow, not substance. *"The reality (the substance, the solid fact of what is foreshadowed, the body of it) belongs to Christ"* (Col. 2:17 AMP).

In the Old Testament, Christ was concealed; in the New Testament, Christ is revealed as the final speech of God. God gathered up all of the Old Testament fragments and put them into the person of Christ. He spoke to us in a final voice that could not be added to or changed. Christ was preexistent and, as the Triune God, created the whole world. God appointed Christ heir and lawful owner of all things.

Jesus showed us God's essential nature:

> *No man has ever seen God at any time; the only unique Son, or the only begotten God, Who is in the bosom [in the intimate presence] of the Father, He has declared Him [He has revealed Him and brought Him out where He can be seen; He has interpreted Him and He has made Him known]* (John 1:18 AMP).

When you look at someone you can see what they look like, but you can't see their nature until you get to know them. I really want to know God the Father. To see and know someone, we must know the essence of his or her person. Jesus revealed the Father and brought Him out where He could be seen, interpreted, and made known. The Son as the final speech actually showed us what the nature of the invisible Father was like.

Thoughts and Questions

- In what ways have you seen only a fragment of a circumstance rather than the whole picture? What was the result?

- What could Simeon and Anna only see a portion of?

- Explain how all the fragments were gathered up and put into the person of Christ.

How God Reveals His Glory

*Whom we have heard, Whom we have seen with our [own]
eyes, Whom we have gazed upon [for ourselves] and have
touched with our [own] hands* (1 John 1:1 AMP).

GOD CAN NOW BE seen, heard, touched, and understood because God poured everything He was into the person of Christ. He was the full embodiment and the mirror of God's glory. This is God in disguise! God didn't send a committee; He came Himself. God was in Christ reconciling the world to Himself (see 2 Cor. 5:19).

Because God is a Spirit, He chose to reveal Himself by the use of the incarnation—"the word made flesh" (see John 1:14). You shall call His name Immanuel—God with us. Jesus was God's final speech, so that we could understand how God speaks. The opening words in the Gospel of John present the concept of the incarnation as the self-revelation of God put into fleshly form so that we could know, understand, and love God, who is a Spirit. The thrust, meaning, and purpose of the incarnation is Jesus' state-ment: *"Anyone who has seen Me has seen the Father"* (John 14:9 AMP).

Matthew is one of the few writers who explains God the Father as incarnational. He wrote the beautiful phrase, *"No one fully knows and accu-rately understands the Son except the Father"* (Matt. 11:27 AMP). In a moment of deep, personal spiritual insight, he saw the Father and the Son as one person, each revealing the other—the Father loves the Son and the Son loves the Father. They relate to each other by means of the *Agape* paradigm.

How does the world see God's glory? Through you and me. Of course we are not Jesus, but because Christ is being formed in us, we begin to look like Him. We are the light of the world. Our goal is to live our lives so that people can see the Father. If they could see that we have been with Christ, they would see compassion, grace, mercy, slow to anger, truth, faithfulness, and forgiveness written on our countenance and hear it in our voice. God's glory is going to be revealed in the earth and it has to be through us.

Paul stated that,

> *You yourselves are our letter of recommendation* (our credentials), *written in your hearts, to be known* (perceived, recognized) *and read by everybody* (2 Corinthians 3:2 AMP).

Letters of recommendation or living epistles are an incarnational revelation of God intended to replicate and demonstrate His DNA in everyday life. People cannot see God who is a Spirit, but they can see you and me in whom the *Agape* of God, the Eternal Seed, has been brought to manifestation and fruition by the new birth.

Thoughts and Questions

❦ Describe your understanding of Jesus being God in disguise.

❦ How does Jesus, as God's final speech, help us understand how God speaks?

❦ As letters of recommendation or credentials, in what ways are we to replicate and demonstrate God's DNA in everyday life?

King of the Kingdom

But as to the Son, He says to Him, Your throne, O God, is
forever and ever (to the ages of the ages), *and the scepter of*
Your kingdom is a scepter of absolute righteousness (of justice
and straightforwardness) (Hebrews 1:8 AMP).

THE KINGDOM IS THE Kingdom of God the Father—it is His government. God's government didn't do too well in all the fragments and the pieces, so He brought forth a different aspect: He gave the Kingdom to the Son by issuing the person of Christ the scepter of righteousness: "*Your throne, O God, is forever and ever.*" This scepter is the authority and commission to bring God's people into conformity with the image of God's Son, and it has to do with the perpetuity of His Kingdom. When the Son picks up the Kingdom, He fulfills Father's commands, keeps the law of God, and does everything the Kingdom requires, including praying for the sick and casting out devils.

He will exercise His governmental authority in a present and practical manner in life as it is in this time/space world. If the predicament is as torturous as Isaiah and Luke described when they talked about valleys, mountains, and crooked and rough places (see Isa. 40:4; Luke 3:5), we are in desperate need of effective and permanent relief from each of these.

The issuance of a scepter has indeed happened, but it is almost entirely lost and/or ignored by the western church. Only this scepter is absolute; it has the inherent ability to measure and evaluate all things in a manner that produces justice and equity. Father's governing force, represented by that scepter, functions in an absolute, straightforward, and just manner by reason of the *Agape* incarnate in the person of Jesus Christ. When God the

Father assigns His government to His Son, the final outcome is destined to victory.

Thus, God's final speech in the person of His Son becomes operable by the executive administration of the Holy Spirit. Because the Kingdom is, in reality, *in the Holy Spirit,* that Kingdom comes without observation by the human eye. It is not an organization, but a living Body whose internal cohesion is the *Agape* of God Himself. Consequently, the new birth gives us eyes to see that Kingdom, which is an entirely spiritual dimension. Being filled with the Holy Spirit and intentionally refusing to ignore, injure, or grieve Him becomes increasingly critical for all of us who are seeking to enter that Kingdom sphere and embrace the Kingdom scepter as our very own.

Thoughts and Questions

- Explain the purpose of the Kingdom scepter.

- What will the scepter do in your life if you embrace it?

- Why has Christ's Kingship been lost or ignored by the western church?

READING 64

Promise of the Father

And all of these, though they won divine approval by [means of] their faith, did not receive the fulfillment of what was promised, because God had us in mind and had something better and greater in view for us, so that they [these heroes and heroines of faith] should not come to perfection apart from us [before we could join them] (Hebrews 11:39-40 AMP).

THROUGHOUT THE SCRIPTURES, WE can see the redemptive acts of the Almighty God as they unfold, bringing the promise of the Father to pass. The promise is referred to in Genesis 28:14 AMP:

> *And your offspring shall be as [countless as] the dust or sand of the ground, and you shall spread abroad to the west and the east and the north and the south; and by you and your offspring shall all the families of the earth be blessed and bless themselves.*

Although Enoch, Noah, Abraham, and Isaac were all heroes of the faith, they did not receive fulfillment of the promise.

In the New Testament, Jesus gave us the promise and reiterated it:

> *I will send forth upon you what My Father has promised; but remain in the city [Jerusalem] until you are clothed with power from on high* (Luke 24:49 AMP).

> *He commanded them not to leave Jerusalem but to wait for what the Father had promised, of which [He said] you have heard Me speak* (Acts 1:4 AMP).

The *promise of the Father* is the coming of the Holy Spirit. The Old Testament is more than history; it is what theologians call "acts of God." It is a recording of the promise of the Father from Abraham all the way to its fulfillment when God gives the Kingdom to the Son and the Son gives the Kingdom to the Holy Spirit. It is a progressive moving toward the promise to Abraham that *all the families of the earth* will be blessed, and it includes the whole creation. The manner in which God encountered Isaac and Jacob was to fulfill the promise in the New Testament.

In order for us to experience the promise of the Father, the ravines, mountains, and crooked and rough places must be dealt with so that we can find a smooth road. The coming of the Holy Spirit is the means by which these find their correction. Christ's scepter of righteousness corrects these problems so that we can be blessed and bless ourselves. When we bow to and embrace the scepter, we give Him permission to work us through our own ravines, mountains, crooked and rough places, slaying the Seven Giants—look good, feel good, be right, stay in control, hidden agenda, personal advantage, and remain undisturbed—that precipitate the problems.

Father gave us the promise because He wanted to come to us. He wanted all the families of the earth to be blessed and to be able to bless themselves. The Father orchestrated everything so He could be our Papa and teach us how to say "Abba, Father." The Holy Spirit comes because of the promise of the Father. He will show us the things of Christ, and, if we will allow Him, He will take us to the Father and show us what the Father is really like. The result is the intimacy with God, which we so desperately seek. It is the cultivation of the Eternal Seed, which is the hope of the entire created universe.

Thoughts and Questions

- In what ways does God want all the families of the earth to be blessed to bless themselves?

- How have you been blessed by the coming of the promise of the Holy Spirit?

- Why must *Eros* be broken in order to be blessed?

READING 65

When God Changed His Address

And Moses certainly was faithful in the administration of all God's
house [but it was only] as a ministering servant. [In his entire
ministry he was but] a testimony to the things which were to be spoken
[the revelations to be given afterward in Christ]. But Christ (the
Messiah) was faithful over His [own Father's] house as a Son [and
Master of it]. And it is we who are [now members] of this house, if we
hold fast and firm to the end our joyful and exultant confidence and
sense of triumph in our hope [in Christ] (Hebrews 3:5-6 AMP).

T HE WRITER OF HEBREWS was addressing a group of Christians, probably in Alexandria, Egypt, who left Judaism and embraced Christ.
These believers faced exceedingly severe opposition due to some having
seen the reality of Christ and His Kingdom while most people diligently
remained true to Moses. Little did they know that God the Father had
moved into a new house and *changed His address!* The Old Testament is
Moses' house and the New Testament is Jesus' house. The fullness of God's
deity moved from Moses' Old Testament temple to abide in the living
temple, who is God's Son. In spite of the political, cultural, and family
pressures that were trying to force the Alexandrian Christians back into
Judaism, the writer of the Book of Hebrews knew that God did not live
there anymore. Consequently, he was encouraging them to stand firm as
believers in the person of Jesus Christ.

If we can see through to who this Jesus really is, we will be able to see
through the pressures and understand the larger issues in our daily lives. In
this Epistle, Moses' Old Covenant is compared with Jesus' New Covenant
13 times, and each time he says the New Covenant is the better, the greater,

and the more complete covenant because it reveals God's essential nature—what the Father is really like. Moses was certainly faithful in the administration of God's house, but his entire ministry was but a testimony to the things that were to be spoken in the final speech—the revelation given in the person of Christ. Paul preached Christ, but he never ran down Moses because Moses made an incomparable contribution to our Christian journey.

A house or household is an important concept in the Scriptures: "*He will speak words to you by which you will be saved, you and all your household*" (Acts 11:14). The inclusive word *house* designates family and also corresponds to God's present address—where Father has chosen to place His Shekinah presence. Christ was faithful over His own Father's house, and we are now members of His house. Father's house is the family of God, not the physical structure. If we return to the Judaistic mold and attempt to reconstruct a physical temple, we are denying Father's house. As members of this house we hold fast and firm to our joyful and exultant confidence in Christ Jesus, who is Father's final speech.

Thoughts and Questions

❦ When and why did God change His address?

❦ What was Moses' valuable contribution to God's house?

❦ Why is house and family important to God?

Reading 66

Entering Father's Family

But to as many as did receive and welcome Him, He gave the
authority (power, privilege, right) *to become the children*
of God, that is, to those who believe in (adhere to, trust
in, and rely on) *His name* (John 1:12 AMP).

How did we get to be part of this family? My goal in answering this is to help you plant your sneakers firmly so you can say, "Here I stand!" rather than get pushed and pulled into all sorts of opinions. As John states, we enter Father's family by simply *believing* (see John 1:12). We were carefully and meticulously born into this family through believing in Christ. While all of our roots may be in Moses' family, the fragments or pieces of the prophets and temple are all shadows that lead up to the time when Christ came and God spoke His final speech. Believing in the final speech is how we become part of His family.

> *Whether Paul or Apollos or Cephas* (Peter) *or the universe or*
> *life or death, or the immediate and threatening present or the*
> *[subsequent and uncertain] future—all are yours, and you are*
> *Christ's, and Christ is God's* (1 Corinthians 3:22-23 AMP).

Everything is ours—the universe, life or death, the present, and the future. Why? Because we belong to Christ and Christ belongs to God, and God owns it all. As part of Father's family, the whole universe is ours, including the Baptist and Presbyterian churches down the street. Because it is our Father's house, we should take care of it wherever we find it, including other churches and denominations. When we look across this world and see the condition of our Father's house, we see strange, illegal, and unbiblical conduct. We can isolate ourselves, become self-righteous, and attempt to become doctrinally pure like the Pharisees, or we can simply follow Jesus where He is leading us. If we will follow Him, He will take us to some of the most unusual and exciting situations we could ever imagine.

When I was pastoring I would go to the hospital and would pray for anyone who was sick and would let me. It didn't matter if they were Methodist, Catholic, or atheist. God is concerned about every sick person, whatever their label. We must learn to transcend labels and ignore our little doctrinal franchises, strengthening ourselves to be able to embrace God's people, even the unusual ones. We don't need to fight or criticize others—they are part of Father's family just like we are. I know that God has some really unusual kids, but they actually do belong to Him. When we can see through the idiosyncrasies, it won't confuse us; we can love and enjoy them. Father knows how to be their Father.

> *How is it that you had to look for Me? Did you not see and know that it is necessary [as a duty] for Me to be in My Father's house and [occupied] about My Father's business?* (Luke 2:49 AMP).

We are not called to be occupied with denominational business or our own personal business; it is our Father's business with which we are to be concerned. When we are occupied with advancing the Kingdom and seeing God's grace reach out and touch people, Father's glory can be revealed wherever we are. Glory is Father's business. This is what it means to seek first the Kingdom of God.

Thoughts and Questions

- How do we enter Father's family?

- Why is it important to see through the idiosyncrasies of Father's kids?

- In what ways are you occupied with Father's business?

READING 67

Back Over the Line

For I say to you that from now on I shall not drink of the fruit of the vine at all until the kingdom of God comes (Luke 22:18 AMP).

UNDERSTANDING THE NATURE OF transition is half the battle to successfully navigate through it. This diagram is especially important, as it explains the transition from the Old Covenant to the New Covenant.

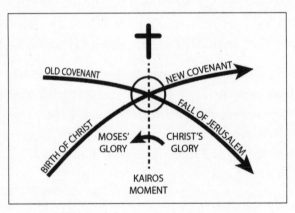

There are two Greek words for time—*chronos* and *kairos*. *Chronos* refers to chronological or sequential time, as in minutes, hours, and days. *Kairos* means the right or opportune moment and signifies a time in between or an undetermined moment of time in which something special happens that determine God's purposes. It is a transitional moment when something stops and something new begins. While *chronos* is quantitative, *kairos* has a qualitative nature. When two planets cross, it is a *kairos* moment. The circle in the middle of this diagram represents an exact *kairos* moment—the moment Christ died, just as all of the events of His life were exactly scheduled for the Passover moment. If you start to see through rather than to look at, you'll begin to perceive exact *kairos* moments when something happened or changed in your own life. Perhaps you unexpectedly met someone, and your life was different from then on, or a circumstance dramatically changed the course of events.

A simple reading of Luke 22:15-20 reveals the exact *kairos* moment at the table of the Lord when four thousand years of Passover history and the Old Covenant ended, and the New Covenant began. The Book of Hebrews states that the Old Covenant, i.e. Moses' Law, is spoken of as having been done away with six times (see Heb. 8:6-10, 13; 9:1, 15-20; 10:16; 12:24). As God's final speech, Jesus came to earth to do Father's business, and at that *kairos* moment He chose to change His address!

On the right of the diagram is Christ's glory and on the left is Moses' glory. Both had glory in their houses, but Christ's glory was so much brighter than Moses' glory that it is hardly a comparison. As the Old Covenant was ending and the New Covenant was being birthed, there was tremendous pressure to return to the things that were temporal: the tabernacle, special garments, shawls, and dietary laws. Because we like to *see* things, all the special clothes and outward symbols make a nice demonstration. When we focus on the Old Covenant, we go back across that line and find ourselves in confusion because we are trying to make the Old Covenant yield what only the New Testament can give us. Paul actually calls going back over the line a transgression:

> *For if I [or any others who have taught that the observance of the Law of Moses is not essential to being justified by God should now by word or practice teach or intimate that it is essential to] build up again what I tore down, I prove myself a transgressor* (Galatians 2:18 AMP).

In biblical simplicity, we could say: God has sovereignly chosen not to live there any longer. In order to live in Father's house and not go back over the line to the Old Covenant, we must learn to rest in what God has provided for us (see Heb. 4:11).

Thoughts and Questions

🌱 Describe a *kairos* moment in your own life.

🌱 Explain the pressure as the Old Covenant came to an end and the New Covenant began.

🌱 Why does Paul consider going back over the line a transgression?

Moving Toward Spiritual Maturity

For even though by this time you ought to be teaching others, you actually need someone to teach you over again the very first principles of God's Word. You have come to need milk, not solid food (Hebrews 5:12 AMP).

ALTHOUGH I HAVE BEEN on my Christian journey for more than five decades, I still feel like a Sunday school student. We need someone to teach us the very first principles. This is the primary purpose of discipleship. As the Book of Hebrews explains, time does not guarantee maturity because true maturity is not just physical growth; it involves the spiritual, emotional, and mental aspects of our personality:

> *Therefore let us go on and get past the elementary stage in the teachings and doctrine of Christ* (the Messiah), *advancing steadily toward the completeness and perfection that belong to spiritual maturity. Let us not again be laying the foundation of repentance and abandonment of dead works* (dead formalism) *and of the faith [by which you turned] to God, with teachings about purifying, the laying on of hands, the resurrection from the dead, and eternal judgment and punishment. [These are all matters of which you should have been fully aware long, long ago]* (Hebrews 6:1-2 AMP).

I'm sure you know a full-grown adult who has the emotional maturity of a nine-year-old. Time, however, can contribute to our maturity if we engage the process. When we are functioning as part of God's family in a state of rest, we begin to move toward maturity.

A mature believer must know how to rest in the righteousness of Christ rather than go back over the line to Moses' law.

> *For being ignorant of the righteousness that God ascribes [which makes one acceptable to Him in word, thought, and deed] and seeking to establish a righteousness* (a means of salvation) *of their own, they did not obey or submit themselves to God's righteousness* (Romans 10:3 AMP).

If we don't embrace God's righteousness, we have to establish a righteousness of our own. That is a lot of work and is the opposite of rest. Becoming spiritually mature involves learning from our failures while resting in God's righteousness. The words *let us go on* in Greek mean "allowing Christ to influence us and carry us along to the more mature things" that He wants to open to us.

As we know, time itself is unable to bring us to spiritual maturity. We need a building permit: *"If indeed God permits, we will [now] proceed [to advanced teaching]"* (Heb. 6:3 AMP). One cannot continue building on a shaky foundation. As we respond to Father drawing us, we mature, and then He opens up new levels of Himself to us. Building permits are issued to those who, with a rather reckless abandon, begin to make the Kingdom their central priority.

If you are dissatisfied with your own spiritual maturity, allow the Father to clearly lead you to the place where He has chosen to dwell. He dwells in His fullness in the person of Christ. It is vital to understand that Christ is not an end in Himself; His promise is to take us the Father.

Thoughts and Questions

- What does Hebrews Chapter 5 define as spiritual maturity?
- Why does becoming spiritually mature involve learning from failure?
- What role does rest play in spiritual maturity?

Being an Enlightened Kingdom Receiver

For it is impossible [to restore and bring again to repentance] those
who have been once for all enlightened, who have consciously
tasted the heavenly gift and have become sharers of the Holy
Spirit, and have felt how good the Word of God is and the mighty
powers of the age and world to come (Hebrews 6:4-5 AMP).

THERE ARE THE FIVE components of a *Kingdom receiver*. These five pieces of equipment give us the ability to see through rather than look at a situation:

1. You are once and for all enlightened. 2. You have consciously tasted of the heavenly gift—salvation in the person of Christ (see 1 Pet. 2:3). 3. You have become sharers of the Holy Spirit. Christian leaders interpret this Scripture differently, but for me this suggests baptism in the Holy Spirit as the normal Christian life. 4. You have felt how good the Word of God is. It is existential reality, meaning you have had the Word illumined and come alive to you. If you have ever had a Scripture open to you like Fourth of July fireworks, you can identify with this. Illumination of the Word of God is more than revelation. 5. You have tasted of the powers of the age to come. This has to do with understanding the supernatural forces that have brought the future Kingdom into present reality. Three of these points are fairly evident; I want to deal with the first and last: you are once and for all enlightened, and in the next session, you have tasted of the powers of the age to come.

Being enlightened has little to do with knowledge because it is impossible to *know* only once—we progressively know. So, enlightenment has to be experiential rather than an increase in knowledge. To be once enlightened is a reference to what occurs when we are water baptized. As Paul points out, it involves a transfer:

> *Giving thanks to the Father, who has qualified and made us fit to share the portion which is the inheritance of the saints (God's holy people) in the Light. [The Father] has delivered and drawn us to Himself out of the control and the dominion of darkness and has transferred us into the kingdom of the Son of His love* (Colossians 1:12-13 AMP).

Water baptism has to do with being transferred from darkness to light.

> *But if your eye is unsound, your whole body will be full of darkness. If then the very light in you [your conscience] is darkened, how dense is that darkness!* (Matthew 6:23 AMP).

Water baptism is part of being enlightened because He delivered us out of the control or dominion of darkness and transferred us into the Kingdom of His Son.

On his fourth birthday I asked my son, Eric, what he wanted for his gift. I thought he was going to say a bicycle or a red wagon, but he looked at me and he said, "I want to be baptized in water with all my church there." So we invited our little home group over, and I baptized him in water. He came up out of the water praying in the language of the Holy Spirit. He experienced *enlightenment*.

We are walking toward light because Christ is the Light and is the inheritance of God's people. He who denies himself and enters into water baptism is flooded with Light. As we walk, God increases the Light and that is part of our maturity process.

Thoughts and Questions

- Why does being enlightened have little to do with knowledge?

- In what ways does being enlightened involve a transfer?

- Describe how spiritual maturity involves being enlightened.

READING 70

Powers of the Age to Come

*[Having] tasted the good word of God and the
powers of the age to come* (Hebrews 6:5).

T HE POWERS OF THE age to come require seeing through rather than
looking at. Most of us who read this believe that the supernatural and
the gifts of the Spirit are for us today. We believe that it is God's desire to
heal the sick, break the power of the demonic, and give us the gifts of ministry and prophecy—these are all the unfolding of the powers of the age
to come.

Jesus was born in both *chronos* and *kairos* time. He came to us in the
incarnation, bringing the age to come into this very age in which we live.
He was fully aware of what the future held. So the powers of the age to
come are now present by virtue of the fact that He *is* the Kingdom. The
Kingdom in the future won't be different than what we have right now,
there will just be more of it. What we have right now is the real thing.
However, right now we only see in part, but the unfolding purposes of
God's Kingdom are eternal and will last into the ages to come.

During one visit to Australia, a small child with Down syndrome and
a harelip ran up, grabbed me by the legs, and held on to me. Her 25-year-
old mother walked up and said, "Mr. Mumford, the Lord told me to ask
you whether or not God would heal my baby." I was never in a more difficult predicament in all my life. If I said, "Yes, God will heal her," and
God didn't do it, there would be despair. But what if I said "no" and God
wanted to heal her? So I said, "Father, what do You want to do?" He said,
"Tell her, yes! I will heal her child." I spoke with spiritual strength as if I
believed it myself and said, "Yes! God will heal your child." As soon as the

words left my mouth the powers of the age to come nearly overwhelmed me, the mother, and the child. Out of the confidence in the manifest presence of God I reached into the powers of the age to come and immediately prayed for them. When I returned a year later, this same child ran up to me in the hotel lobby and grabbed me by the legs. She was a year older, but as I looked at her I recognized that most of the physical effects of Down syndrome had disappeared from her face, the harelip was healing, and I was told that she was attending a normal school. This is the power of the age to come that came to us in the person of Christ.

Thoughts and Questions

🐝 In what ways are the powers of the age to come present now?

🐝 Why won't the future Kingdom be different than what we have right now?

🐝 How do we access the powers of the age to come?

Reading 71

Damaged Receptor

If they then deviate from the faith and turn away from their allegiance—[it is impossible] to bring them back to repentance, for (because, while, as long as) *they nail upon the cross the Son of God afresh [as far as they are concerned] and are holding [Him] up to contempt and shame and public disgrace.* (Hebrews 6:6 AMP).

THE ENEMY WORKS THE day and night shift using this verse on us all, and as the Church, we have abused it by using it on each other. Have you ever laid your head down on the pillow at night only to hear a voice say, "You are really a loser! Other people can make it, but you will never make it. You have committed the unpardonable sin and God is finished with you. Why don't you just quit and save God the trouble?" I am glad that no one but God has the Lamb's Book of Life because every time we fail, someone would erase our name.

Notice the three statements in the following verse:

How much worse (sterner and heavier) *punishment do you suppose he will be judged to deserve who has spurned and [thus] trampled underfoot the Son of God, and who has considered the covenant blood by which he was consecrated common and unhallowed, thus profaning it and insulting and outraging the [Holy] Spirit [Who imparts] grace* (the unmerited favor and blessing of God)? (Hebrews 10:29 AMP).

This person spurned the Son of God, refused to believe that the blood did what Father said it would do, and thus insulted and outraged the Holy Spirit. These three actions create serious injuries to our receptors. They turn our light into darkness, deviate us from the faith, and cause us to go back over the line.

Two people in the New Testament are recorded as having turned away from their allegiance to Christ. One was Peter, who cursed and denied Jesus, yet Jesus went looking for him and restored him. The other was Judas, who sold his inheritance and was not restored. This distinction is critical. Judas, we know, was willful and intentional in his hidden agenda, while Peter was guilty of using an escape mechanism by seeking to save his own hide.

I have a laptop that hooks into a docking station at my desk. The docking station has all kinds of connection ports on it and the computer has ports to receive all those connections. When I put the computer into the docking station, all my equipment comes alive. If I took a hammer and beat on the docking station, the receptors would not be able to receive the information. Our docking stations were injured when we became dead in trespasses and sins. The new birth restores our capacity to receive—see and enter the Kingdom as Father's spiritual dimension.

The room you are sitting in is full of all kinds of radio waves but if we do not have a radio to pick up the waves, we cannot hear the broadcast. God must give us the receptor or the capacity to hear. When we injure our receivers, God is still there, but we cannot perceive Him. The new birth gives us a new capacity to hear and see because it gives us a new mind (thinking) and a new heart (feeling). This is what was damaged when we injured our spiritual capacity to receive. Peter damaged his receptor by denying the Lord, but he was restored. Judas bashed his receiver with a hammer. When our receiver is injured, we can't see through; we can only look at. There is beauty, but no eyes to see it, and music, but no ears to hear it.

Thoughts and Questions

- What are three actions that cause damage to our receptors?
- What is the end result of a damaged receptor?
- What restores our capacity to receive?

Five Components of a Kingdom Receiver

*For He [God] Himself has said, I will not in any way fail you nor
give you up nor leave you without support. [I will] not, [I will] not, [I
will] not in any degree leave you helpless nor forsake nor let [you] down
(relax My hold on you)! [Assuredly not!]* (Hebrews 13:5 AMP).

THIS SCRIPTURES SAY THAT God will *never* reject, forsake, or leave
helpless one who comes to Him. The Father will not in any way fail
you. The problem is that many people do not look to Jesus for the answer.
Cults, philosophical exploration, and sexual deviance all become very real
options to people who are looking for answers in the wrong places. If the
Cross is God's final speech, and we put the Cross behind us and look for
answers elsewhere, we are saying by our actions that the Cross is powerless; consequently, spiritual renewal becomes most difficult, if not impossible. We find ourselves in confusion because there is nowhere else to go
but the Cross. There are no answers for us if we are unable to see them
in Christ.

For some almost embarrassing reason, Jesus chose to come to us like a
helpless beggar. I don't understand it, but He gives Himself to us in such a
gentle manner, avoiding all encroachment or imposition, and gives us the
power to turn Him away or excuse Him from our lives. When we feel that
little nudge to pray or speak to someone and then think, "I'll pray later,"
we are dismissing the King of the universe. God is not at our disposal,
yet He stands at the door and knocks, waiting for us to open to Him. We
should say, "Lord, please don't knock, just tear the door off the hinges!"
We expose Him to Crucifixion all over again by the way we live our lives;
and sometimes it doesn't even appear that we have grasped or understood

the Crucifixion. When we insist on going our own way, we have forgotten, injured, or stepped past the Cross and all that was given to us in the Cross.

There are five components of a Kingdom receiver. When God is *received* in the person of Christ, He *restores our capacity to see, hear, and feel,* which renews our receivers, making us alive again. He *satisfies our sense of touch deprivation* by coming to us with an awareness of His presence. There is a difference between our being near God and God being near us. When our receptors are damaged, God can be there, but we are unable to perceive Him. This is what happens when we are in a meeting where everyone is experiencing God and we are standing there like a stick. *He holds us and surrounds us with His presence,* creating a safe place. Then, when all of this is comfortable, *He goes on to claim us as His own*—"I am my beloved's and He is mine" (see Song of Sol. 6:3)—and the romance increases. We feel like we really are a Bride of the Bridegroom. Finally, *He dwells in us, which results in intimacy and rest.*

Our personality can begin to progressively and intimately know God's personality because Christ came to reveal God's essential nature. When the five components of becoming a Kingdom receiver are fully functioning (enlightened, tasted of the heavenly gift, sharers of the Holy Spirit, felt how good the Word of God is, and tasted of the powers of the age to come), we can plug in by faith and receive all He intends.

Thoughts and Questions

* What is the end result of putting the Cross behind us?

* Which of the five components of a Kingdom receiver are you in need of most?

* Why are these components so important?

PART VII

A Clear Conscience

READING 73

Remember the Bull

For since the Law has merely a rude outline (foreshadowing) *of the good things to come—instead of fully expressing those things—it can never by offering the same sacrifices continually year after year make perfect those who approach [its altars]. For if it were otherwise, would [these sacrifices] not have stopped being offered? Since the worshipers had once for all been cleansed, they would no longer have any guilt or consciousness of sin. But [as it is] these sacrifices annually bring a fresh remembrance of sins [to be atoned for]* (Hebrews 10:1-3 AMP).

MOST OF US WRESTLE with a troubled conscience. I struggled with a seared conscience for years. After having met the Lord at age 12, I was severely harassed for being a Christian. Somehow I knew that the harassment would cease if God turned away from me, and that offending the Holy Spirit was the fastest way to do that, so I stood in the middle of the road and said blasphemous words. I knew I was doing something wrong, and from that day on I struggled deeply with a conscience gone astray.

In the Old Testament, a person would come to Jerusalem once a year with his bull to present the animal to the priest. The priest would transfer all the man's sins to the animal by laying hands on it, and then the bull would be slain and offered to God for atonement. After the sacrifice, the person could enjoy a clear conscience for an entire year. If he had any problems with his conscience, all he would have to say is, "Remember the bull!"

Even though today the blood of bulls is powerless to take away sins (see Heb. 10:4), we are missing something about Jesus' sacrifice being enough to ease our conscience. Today, most believers ask forgiveness for their sins, but don't have a free conscience from the pew to the parking lot. When we struggle with our conscience, we feel we should read, fast, pray, or witness more. The result is a self-determined effort to be holy, which is not Christianity but religion that capitalizes on injured consciences.

God neither desired nor took delight in animal sacrifices. He never wanted the death of all those animals; they were a shadow of the sacrifice of Christ. Jesus didn't come to simply cover up our sin, but to save us from sin. He said, *"Behold, I have come (in the scroll of the book it is written of Me) to do Your will, O God"* (Heb. 10:7). "I have/am come" is present tense; it transcends time and has an eternal purpose, yet is expressed in events of time. The scroll of the book expresses all that the law and prophets teach about obedience. This obedience is unrolled in the history of the Kingdom and was historically complete when the divine voice could say, *"This is my beloved Son in whom I am well-pleased"* (Matt. 3:17). This is why we can be without condemnation.

The word *perfect* in Greek is *telios*, meaning "to bring to an end, complete, accomplish or finish." The law makes nothing *perfect* and is powerless to transform anyone because transformation begins on the inside, while the law affects externals. Outward obedience to the law only makes us performers. Most of us learned how to perform while still sitting on our little painted chairs in Sunday school. We learned how to say and do the right thing for approval, but because the laws were only written on our minds, not our hearts, we didn't experience an inner transformation. Because the law made nothing *perfect*, God had to change His address and move inside of us to write the laws on our hearts.

Thoughts and Questions

🦌 Explain the Old Testament freedom of remembering the bull.

🦌 Why were sacrifices a shadow of things to come?

🦌 Why is the law powerless to transform anyone?

READING 74

The Sacrificial System Continues

For by a single offering He has forever completely cleansed and perfected
those who are consecrated and made holy. And also the Holy Spirit adds
His testimony to us [in confirmation of this]. For having said, This is
the agreement (testament, covenant) *that I will set up and conclude*
with them after those days, says the Lord: I will imprint My laws upon
their hearts, and I will inscribe them on their minds (on their inmost*
thoughts and understanding), *He then goes on to say, and their sins and*
their lawbreaking I will remember no more (Hebrews 10:14-17 AMP).

T HE SINGLE OFFERING OF the bull in the Old Testament allowed the
offerer a clear conscience for one whole year. The single offering today
is Jesus, who forever completely cleansed and *perfected* us. Jesus' single offering was so complete that it allows God to forever forget our sins and vio-
lations of His law. God wants to imprint His laws of *Agape* on our hearts
inwardly so that we can enjoy Him and be comfortable in His presence.
Unfortunately, the church is so sin-conscious that it can hardly be God-
conscious. Our conscience is so jammed with all the religious crazies that it
is almost impossible for us to stand freely in God's presence and enjoy Him
because the accuser works both the day and night shift.

When Jesus came to do the Father's will, He did away with the first
order of animal sacrifices that expiated sin (the Old Covenant) so that he
might inaugurate the second order—the New Covenant. The moment
Christ died, the new order began. Moses' external law came to an end,
and Christ's internal law began. When we attempt to go back to the Old
Covenant, we are essentially rejecting or treating as superficial all that
Christ did for us.

Jesus came to do the Father's will; He changed the Old Testament law of animal sacrifice by dying on our behalf. That one sacrifice was enough to *perfect* our conscience forever. When our conscience is condemning us, we can now say, "Remember the Lamb!" With Jesus' sacrifice, He instituted a whole New Covenant and asks that we follow Him. Paul shows us in the Book of Romans that the sacrificial system continues, but now it is a new kind that requires us to

> make a decisive dedication of your bodies [presenting all your members and faculties] as a living sacrifice, holy (devoted, consecrated) and well pleasing to God, which is your reasonable (rational, intelligent) service and spiritual worship (Romans 12:1 AMP).

Our living sacrifice involves our whole being—physical, intellectual, and spiritual. It is a New Covenant or Kingdom issue. The new birth awakens in us the ability to see the Kingdom and to begin to embrace the known will of God.

Thoughts and Questions

 When Jesus did away with the first order of animal sacrifice, what did He inaugurate?

 At what point did this transition occur?

 When our conscience condemns us, what can we now say?

Freedom of Conscience

*Therefore, brethren, since we have full freedom and confidence to enter
into the [Holy of] Holies [by the power and virtue] in the blood of Jesus,
By this fresh (new) and living way which He initiated and dedicated
and opened for us through the separating curtain (veil of the Holy
of Holies), that is, through His flesh (Hebrews 10:19-20 AMP).*

T HE WORD *CONFIDENCE* IN Greek is *parrhesia* (Strong's No. 3954),
meaning "freedom or unreservedness in speaking; open, frank or
without concealment, ambiguity or circumlocution; free and fearless confidence, cheerful courage, boldness, assurance." Confidence allows us to act
boldly and press into a situation rather than to shy away from it. The word
confidence is used many times in the New Testament, and it encompasses
everything from our attitudes to our speech:

> *And now, Lord, observe their threats and grant to Your bond
> servants [full freedom] to declare Your message fearlessly"* (Acts
> 4:29 AMP).

> *"And when they had prayed, the place in which they were assem-
> bled was shaken; and they were all filled with the Holy Spirit,
> and they continued to speak the Word of God with freedom and
> boldness and courage"* (Acts 4:31 AMP).

> *"Since we have such [glorious] hope* (such joyful and confident
> expectation), *we speak very freely and openly and fearlessly"* (2
> Corinthians 3:12 AMP).

"I have great boldness and free and fearless confidence and cheerful courage toward you; my pride in you is great..." (2 Corinthians 7:4 AMP).

"In Whom, because of our faith in Him, we dare to have the boldness (courage and confidence) *of free access* (an unreserved approach to God with freedom and without fear)" (Ephesians 3:12 AMP).

God gave us the freedom to enter His very presence through the power and virtue in the blood of Jesus. The veil separating us from the holy of holies was a linen curtain about 18-to-20 inches thick and woven with gold. It was torn from top to bottom when Jesus was crucified (see Mark 15:38). God was violently changing His address! It wasn't so we could get into the holy of holies; but so He could get out because He was going to go to the ends of the earth—to every tribe, tongue, people, and nation. Jesus' physical body was torn so that the veil could be torn and God could get out because He wants to be our Father, to walk in an intimate relationship of love with His sons and daughters. This simply can't happen when He is hidden behind a curtain. God provided a way for us to have a clear conscience and walk with Him in confidence, so that we can live in God's presence and enjoy Him and let Him enjoy us. We have full freedom, a clean conscience, and open confidence to enter God's presence.

Thoughts and Questions

- In what ways are you living in boldness and confidence?

- What do other Scriptures on confidence convey?

- Why did God tear the temple veil?

READING 76

Unqualified Assurance

Let us all come forward and draw near with true (honest and sincere)
hearts in unqualified assurance and absolute conviction engendered by
faith (by that leaning of the entire human personality on God in
absolute trust and confidence in His power, wisdom, and goodness),
having our hearts sprinkled and purified from a guilty (evil) *conscience*
and our bodies cleansed with pure water (Hebrews 10:22 AMP).

UNQUALIFIED ASSURANCE AND ABSOLUTE conviction engendered by
faith do not depend on what we did or did not do. I was getting
ready to pray for a person one time and this strong voice said, "You cannot
pray for her because you have not fasted, and this thing only comes out by
fasting." I stood there paralyzed and thought, "What do I do now?" And
the Lord said, "You didn't fast, but I did, so pray for her on the basis of
My fast." Confidence out of a clear conscience started to rise in me because
it didn't depend on me. When I prayed on the basis of what Jesus did, the
stronghold over the person immediately broke. We have an effective high
priest who knows every bit of our failings and knows how to meet us in a
crisis. He tore open the holy of holies because He wanted to get out saying,
"Let's go take the earth!" He purified us from a guilty (evil) conscience so
that we would be free.

There are five significant implications in this Scripture that we
cannot miss:

1. *Total reliance on Christ's righteousness.* We will never be righteous
    apart from Christ. Learning to draw on that and live there is the
    primary way of dealing with an evil conscience.

2. *Less repentance and more faith.* We need to quit going around apologizing and repenting and simply start believing. We tend to focus on the sin and beat ourselves in an effort to repent and get right with God. By focusing on the Father, asking His forgiveness and believing that He cleanses us from all unrighteousness, we can clear our guilty consciences and begin functioning as Kingdom citizens. Try saying, "Father, You are my righteousness. I believe and stand solely in Your righteousness. You did it for me, on my behalf, and I believe it!" Your conscience will begin to be washed, and you will start seeing things with more clarity. You will also get healed from a guilty conscience more quickly so that you can be free to enjoy walking with Jesus.

3. *Christ is our cleansed conscience.* When you hear the accuser's knock at the door, send Jesus to answer it. Christ is our new conscience. He is our redemption. He lives in your house and mine. He came to give us a free conscience before God.

4. *Resist guilt and condemnation.* The first step in resisting guilt and condemnation is: if you did something wrong, make it right. Ask forgiveness from the Father, make amends with whoever you offended, and then walk in a clear conscience. The Father does not bury us with condemnation; we do that ourselves with the help of the accuser. The moment the accuser starts in, remember that in the Old Testament one bull gave a man a clear conscience for an entire year; Jesus did much more than that for us. Jesus is our righteousness, and we stand in His love.

5. *Be comfortable in God's presence.* God provided a way to make us *perfect* in His sight so that we could be a living sacrifice to Him. He wants us to enjoy His company and He wants to enjoy us, but we have to learn how to be comfortable with Him.

Thoughts and Questions

🦌 Explain why our confidence is based on what Jesus did for us.

❧ What is the primary way to deal with a guilty conscience?

❧ Why do we need to believe more and repent less?

READING 77

Discarding Our Confidence

Do not, therefore, fling away your fearless confidence, for it carries a great and glorious compensation of reward (Hebrews 10:35 AMP).

FLINGING AWAY CONFIDENCE IS what it means to backslide. It is the end result of sin, which,

> *seizing the opportunity and getting a hold on me [by taking its incentive] from the commandment, beguiled and entrapped and cheated me, and using it [as a weapon], killed me* (Romans 7:11 AMP).

When Christ came, we were buried with Him, and raised with Him to new life, and He set us free. Confidence is something we already have been given; we merely hold on to it. We fail four times in a row, then think, "Well this doesn't work. I tried being a Christian. I'm not going to do this anymore." And we throw our confidence out the window. Then we have to wander around until God is able to restore our confidence in the person of Christ again.

I wandered for 12 years. I was still backslidden in the Navy and would go with the guys to the bar. Alcohol is a kind of truth serum, so as soon as I'd start to drink I'd say to everyone in the bar, "You shouldn't be in this bar drinking; you need to be walking with God!" When I would start witnessing, they would all start crying. I didn't know how to lead them to the Lord, but I knew how to get them under conviction!

> *Now faith is the assurance* (the confirmation, the title deed) *of the things [we] hope for, being the proof of things [we] do not*

*see and the conviction of their reality [faith perceiving as real
fact what is not revealed to the senses]* (Hebrews 11:1 AMP).

"Faith is the assurance of things hoped for" is not a definition of faith but
a description of how it works in the life of the believer. It has to do with
the confidence that what we are seeing and experiencing is real, not imaginary; it is substance, not shadow. The word *assurance* is used three other
times in the Book of Hebrews (see Heb. 3:14; 6:11; 10:22), and each time
it has to do with diligence and holding fast or *believing*. This is assurance
by faith, meaning the Christian's faith and divine fact is identical. Faith is
not only certainty that something exists, but is also the present possession
of the object.

If we throw away our confidence, it takes a while to build it back up
again. When you deal with someone who made a mistake, don't go through
all kinds of repentance with the person. Simply walk them through forgiveness and talk to them about restoring their confidence in the completed
work of Christ. All we are doing is taking them back to the Lamb for
the restoration of a clear conscience and a strong confidence. Remember
the Lamb!

Thoughts and Questions

- What is the end result of sin?

- In what ways does assurance or believing line us up with
  divine facts?

- What do you do when you have made a mistake?

PART VIII

Lifting Weights in Father's Gym

Reading 78

A Little More Weight

*For [our earthly fathers] disciplined us for only a short period of
time and chastised us as seemed proper and good to them; but He
disciplines us for our certain good, that we may become sharers in
His own holiness. For the time being no discipline brings joy, but
seems grievous and painful; but afterwards it yields a peaceable
fruit of righteousness to those who have been trained by it [a harvest
of fruit which consists in righteousness—in conformity to God's
will in purpose, thought, and action, resulting in right living
and right standing with God]* (Hebrews 12:10-11 AMP).

THE COMPLETE HISTORY OF the redemptive act of salvation from Adam
and Eve forward can be seen in two phrases: *"Become sharers in His…
holiness"*; and *"those who have been trained"* in Father's gym will yield a
harvest of fruit.

There are seven Kingdom principles that are clearly stated in Hebrews
(see Heb. 12:1, 6, 5, 11, 28).

1. *Jesus*: Author/originator and the finisher/consummation of
   all things

2. *Agape*: Father's nature and purpose

3. *Maturity*: Father's intent for all of His children

4. *Heart*: Revelation of heart-reluctance or heart-responsiveness

5. *Exercise*: Proper response in Father's gym

6. *Fruit*: Evidence of the supernatural Kingdom

7. *Kingdom*: Embrace governing principles that are eternal/ uncreated

The word translated "exercise" in English comes from the Greek word *gumnazo* (Strong's No. 1128). It is the root of our word *gymnasium*, and means "to exercise the body in a school of athletics." The gym is where we workout to gain strength and greater endurance so we can bear fruit, i.e., a better body, better health, lack of disease, a longer life, etc. The gym is a picture of our marriage, work, finances, or other circumstances in which we find ourselves. God, in His sovereign and providential manner, enables life's predicaments to serve as our gymnasium so that He can

> *strengthen* (complete, perfect) *and make us what we ought to be and equip us with everything good that we may carry out His will; [while He Himself] works in us and accomplish that which is pleasing in His sight, through Jesus Christ* (Hebrews 13:21 AMP).

When we embrace the process of His gymnasium, Christ's righteousness is brought to full maturity in us.

Father's promise is to lift us out of our valley of despair; to deliver us from our mountain of pride; to straighten the crooked places, however convoluted or twisted; to redeem the rough places, and to bring us to Himself. This is the Good News of the Kingdom of God! This is the promise of the Father that all of the families of the earth shall be blessed. If we could take hold of this mentally, emotionally, and spiritually, it would motivate us to faithfulness when called upon to lift weights in Father's gym.

Thoughts and Questions

- How can the whole Bible be summarized by Hebrews 12:10-11?

- Describe a situation in your marriage, work, or finances where God asked you to lift a little more weight.

- In what other ways have life's predicaments served as a gym to equip you?

READING 79

Paul's View of Father's Gym

But now put away and rid yourselves [completely] of all these things: anger, rage, bad feeling toward others, curses and slander, and foulmouthed abuse and shameful utterances from your lips! Do not lie to one another, for you have stripped off the old (unregenerate) *self with its evil practices, And have clothed yourselves with the new [spiritual self], which is [ever in the process of being] renewed and remolded into [fuller and more perfect knowledge upon] knowledge after the image* (the likeness) *of Him Who created it* (Colossians 3:8-10 AMP).

BOTH PAUL AND PETER had the same understanding of Father's gym. If we were to interpret these verses to refer to the basic gift of salvation, they simply would not make sense. Paul is approaching this idea from the point of view of our needed maturity and the required exercise of our spiritual person. He proceeds neither from condemnation or guilt, nor from threat or coercion. Right from the start Paul, like his Master, moves in appeal, instruction, and loving care. In Paul's view, there are eight specific weights that need to be lifted in our spiritual workout so that we can nourish the Seed and allow it to grow:

- Anger
- Rage
- Bad feelings toward others
- Curses
- Slander

- Foulmouthed abuse
- Shameful utterances
- Not lying to one another

We can observe several things about Father's gymnasium from Paul's writing. The gym always begins in faith and ends in *Agape* being made perfect or mature. It is not concerned with works or some kind of religious merit system, for it was started or originated by Christ and will be finished by Him. It is the good works or the fruit for which Father, as the good farmer, is waiting. A gym is always progressive and incremental; we do not begin by lifting 300 pounds. I remember first going to the gym and watching people workout, and saying to myself, "I'll never be able to run like that or lift that much weight!" Several months later, I discovered how much I had changed—I was running farther and lifting more.

The increments of maturing in Father's gym look like this:

1. *Put on Christ*—open our hearts to the lessons and embrace the new nature that He has given us.

2. *Eliminate all religious/social distinctions* and outward superficialities.

3. Put on the communicable nature of God the Father that was given to us in Christ as His DNA.

4. *Respond to the requirement to forgive* as we have been forgiven.

5. Finally, *allow everything to be consummated in Agape*, which is the bond of unity. *Agape* is fruit, not a gift. Fruit is produced by cultivation and effort. Therefore, Jesus says, "*You will fully recognize them by their fruits*" (Matt. 7:16 AMP). This must be *cultivated* in Father's gym.

Thoughts and Questions

- Explain why working out in Father's gym does not have to do with our eternal salvation.

🌱 In what ways have you experienced lifting more weight in the eight specific areas mentioned in this chapter?

🌱 How has Father allowed you to grow incrementally?

Peter's View of Father's Gym

For His divine power has bestowed upon us all things that
[are requisite and suited] to life and godliness, through the
[full, personal] knowledge of Him Who called us by and to His
own glory and excellence (virtue) (2 Peter 1:3 AMP).

MANY COMMENTATORS SAY THAT Peter was the lead apostle for the simple reason that he was forgiven in greater depth than the other eleven. He knew by experience what it meant to stumble and fall when he was pressed by circumstances to deny his Lord. Peter understood that failure to work out in the gym could cause serious problems and pain. Like Paul, who states that the goal is that we may share in Christ's holiness, Peter begins with faith and ends with *Agape* but he states it more clearly in terms of our becoming sharers of the divine nature (see 2 Pet. 1:3-4). This one statement takes us to the very essence of the Kingdom of God. We are working from the promises that Christ gave us in Seed form. His nature needs to be cultivated, nourished, and brought to fruitfulness. This is a clear restatement of Matthew 13 and the parable of the sower. The lessons of the gym that Peter gives are clear (see 2 Pet. 1:5-8):

1. *"Add to your faith"* cannot mean religious works or some kind of self-effort to be holy. We add muscle strength in the workout by faith.

2. There are eight new muscles that are being cultivated, flexed, and strengthened for the daily routine of living this Kingdom existence in a world that is not all that friendly. They are diligence,

virtue, knowledge, self-control, steadfastness, godliness, brotherly affection, and Christian love.

3. It is interesting that, like Paul, Peter comes to *Agape* as the final ingredient above which there is nothing more. Note that brotherly love is the focus of attention.

4. Peter ends with *Agape*—that aspect of God Himself that is now being replicated as Jesus is being formed in His Body. Christ's own character is being cultivated and made manifest in us.

Being fruitless and barren (lifeless, without signs of life) is what caused Israel to lose the Kingdom (see Matt. 21:43). Father's gym is the cure for being blind, shortsighted, and forgetful. It is clear that the Kingdom is that priority for which Christ asked:

> *But seek* (aim at and strive after) *first of all His kingdom and His righteousness* (His way of doing and being right), *and then all these things taken together will be given you besides"* (Matthew 6:33 AMP).

Father's gym provides an abundant entrance into the Kingdom. This does not have to do with going to Heaven, but Heaven coming to us as the New Jerusalem. When Christ came to us in Seed form, He came asking, teaching, and expecting us to enter the gymnasium with eagerness, so that we could learn the lessons and grow up.

Thoughts and Questions

🌱 Why do you think becoming sharers of the divine nature begins with faith and ends with *Agape*?

🌱 In what ways does adding to our faith increase our muscle strength?

🌱 How has Father's gym been the cure for you being blind, shortsighted, or forgetful?

A Pickle in My Crème Brûlée

Strive to live in peace with everybody and pursue that consecration
and holiness without which no one will [ever] see the Lord. Exercise
foresight and be on the watch to look [after one another], to see
that no one falls back from and fails to secure God's grace (His
unmerited favor and spiritual blessing), *in order that no root of*
resentment (rancor, bitterness, or hatred) *shoots forth and causes*
trouble and bitter torment, and the many become contaminated
and defiled by it—That no one may become guilty of sexual vice, or
become a profane (godless and sacrilegious) *person as Esau did,*
who sold his own birthright for a single meal. For you understand
that later on, when he wanted [to regain title to] his inheritance
of the blessing, he was rejected (disqualified and set aside), *for*
he could find no opportunity to repair by repentance [what he had
done, no chance to recall the choice he had made], although he sought
for it carefully with [bitter] tears (Hebrews 12:14-17 AMP).

THIS PASSAGE OF HEBREWS asks for something that we very much need in our generation: peace and purity. These are not gifts; they are fruit, which appear out of our gardening efforts or as a result of effective workouts in Father's gymnasium.

In verse 15 the writer of Hebrews uses a strange but most effective use of the Greek when he says, *"See to it that no one comes short of the grace of God...."* Many of us miss the deeper intent and purpose of what he was saying. Like Paul, the writer of Hebrews was saying that the issue is to fall away from grace or to make grace of no effect. He saw this as very serious and quite injurious and identified it as a root of bitterness.

The Greek word *bitter* in English can also mean "pickle"—sour, bitter, and acrid. Many of us know people we could describe as "pickles"—they spread their bitterness with the use of Bible verses and political expertise. Cliques, splits, and disharmony follow these people wherever they go. Ultra-religious, Bible-quoting pickles with roots of bitterness result from failure to cultivate *Agape* in Father's gym. There are more than enough of them, and they defile many!

The popular error of believing that Jesus did it all so we are not responsible to workout in the gym is a result of thinking new and acting old. In order to grow and become stronger, we need to stretch and exercise. This mind-set says, "Christ knows that I am right, so He will vindicate me." When all is said and done, more is said than done. Bitterness does rule and dictate the behavior of a person with this mind-set. In Paul's view of Father's gym, the result is that Christ *"will be of no profit (advantage, avail) to you [for if you distrust Him, you can gain nothing from Him]"* (Gal. 5:2 AMP). Again, this is not referring to the loss of salvation but to coming short of God's glory in the process of maturity in our lives.

Our lifestyle can be an embarrassment to our Father when we fail to share in His holiness or His divine nature. This happens simply because we have never been taught how to workout in the gymnasium.

Thoughts and Questions

- Explain why peace and purity are fruit rather than gifts.

- Why does making grace of no effect result in a root of bitterness?

- If Jesus did everything for us, why do we need to workout in the gym?

Fruit Afterwards

For the time being no discipline brings joy, but seems grievous and painful;
but afterwards it yields a peaceable fruit of righteousness to those who have
been trained by it [a harvest of fruit which consists in righteousness—in
conformity to God's will in purpose, thought, and action, resulting in
right living and right standing with God] (Hebrews 12:11 AMP).

ONLY IN FATHER'S GYMNASIUM can we begin to understand the differ-ence between good and evil because in the gym we learn the lessons, not just the theory. It is vital to understand that God does give exams as part of our instruction—they come in the form of life circumstances. When we are faced with something hard in life, we have to know how to respond when the pressure is on. If we can *see through* the circumstances rather than *look at* them, we are on the way to yielding fruit in our lives.

Before we can have a harvest of fruit, we have to endure the discipline that seems grievous and painful. We enter God's gymnasium on one side, bounce all over the place while we are being taught, and finally exit out the other side. God washes our eyes with tears so that we might see things dif-ferently on the other side. His rubber room is the grace of the Lord Jesus Christ that protects us from ourselves.

During the time of our growing up, we gather all kinds of ideas from our environment in order to create a personality. Young boys are a little bit cowboy and a little bit Superman. We enter the rubber room in our self-created personality: we see ourselves as a lover, a fighter, or deeply spiritual. There is nothing like God's gymnasium to show us just how spiritual we really are. Before long, the humanly created aspects of our spirituality begin to surface, and we realize that most of it is material we have placed upon ourselves. It is in God's gym that we find out what's real and what's not, and it can be shocking.

When God shows us to us, we need to know about grace and Christ's righteousness that has been given to us. When we come out the other side, we find the uncreated person—the person we really are, not the one we thought we were. The grace of God is not a commodity; grace is a person. Jesus, the grace of God, appears bringing deliverance from sin and training us how to reject and renounce the wrong things and how to embrace and love the real things. The end result is fruit. Although it seems a contradiction, if we will allow God to control our life with His *Agape*, it will lead to our perfect freedom. We have been called to freedom not another form of religious bondage. God's gym sets us free and gives us a well-spent and fruitful life.

Thoughts and Questions

- In what ways have you had to endure discipline to produce fruit?

- What have you learned about yourself while in Father's gymnasium?

- Describe an experience where grace has taught you to reject wrong things and love real things.

Failure in the Gym

Exercise foresight and be on the watch to look [after one another], to see that no one falls back from and fails to secure God's grace (His unmerited favor and spiritual blessing)...*That no one may become guilty of sexual vice, or become a profane* (godless and sacrilegious) *person as Esau did, who sold his own birthright for a single meal* (Hebrews 12:15-16 AMP).

OUR PORTION OR SHARE in the ministry is the sphere, limit, and measure God wants us to function in. We have to learn what our portion is. Are you pastoral, or a teacher, or prophetic? Are there evangelistic gifts stirring in you? This is what your portion means.

Esau failed to secure God's grace because he sold it. Judas was counted among the twelve disciples and received his share in the ministry, but he consciously sold his Kingdom inheritance for 30 pieces of silver. Peter failed to do what God wanted him to do but believed in the grace of God and was restored. The Scripture says of Judas, *"Let another man take his office"* (Acts 1:20). The word *office* in the Greek is *bishophood*. It was the calling and anointing that Judas was given. When Judas died, it passed to Matthias. If we fail, God's purpose does not stop; He just calls someone else and puts him or her in the place where we should have been to fulfill His purpose. Don't let anyone take your office; guard it with all your heart. There is a difference between pure failure and the more serious, less-known phenomenon of trading our inheritance. God actually makes allowances for failure as part of our journey, but intentional trading of our inheritance for that which we would personally prefer takes on a totally different dimension.

During my first year of Bible college I had a friend who decided to leave seminary, quit the ministry, and get a job. About six months later he came back to campus for a visit. He was driving a brand new, pink and grey, 1956 Ford Fairlane—the long one with the straight pipes, big tail lights, and leather inside. I was poor as a church mouse, and my GI bill barely allowed me to stay in school. When I came out to greet him, he was sitting in this brand new car that smelled like new leather. After he left, feelings of grief, failure, and envy swept over me. Was all of this worth it? Why not get out of school, make some money, and do something with my life that really mattered? Fortunately, the rubber room protected me until I quit bouncing.

Quite a few years later I realized that my friend had actually traded his inheritance in the Kingdom for a Ford V-8. My failures, however numerous, served to enhance my humility and break the false image of who I was and what I was called to do. In contrast, my friend traded what he had for what he wanted, and *God gave him the desires of his heart.* God also gave me the desires of my heart—more than 50 years of ministry in the Kingdom. But I had seriously considered trading my inheritance for a new Ford that smelled like leather. I sometimes wonder if some of the portion that God gave me wasn't a share that had belonged to my friend who traded his call.

In no way am I saying that full-time ministry is God's highest call and secular employment is not. Never! If you are called to be a schoolteacher, don't shrivel up to become a millionaire. If you are called to the marketplace but are determined to go into full-time ministry, it is equally problematic. Trading your own call for something that you would prefer is the issue. It is the discontent and refusal of Father's preference that determines the issue.

Thoughts and Questions

- If you fail, what happens to God's purposes? Why?

- What is the difference between failure and trading your inheritance?

- Why is trading your own call an act of discontent and refusal of Father's preference?

Visible and Shaken

He has given a promise: Yet once more I will shake and make tremble
not only the earth but also the [starry] heavens. Now this expression,
Yet once more, indicates the final removal and transformation of all
[that can be] shaken—that is, of that which has been created—in order
that what cannot be shaken may remain and continue. Let us therefore,
receiving a kingdom that is firm and stable and cannot be shaken,
offer to God pleasing service and acceptable worship, with modesty
and pious care and godly fear and awe (Hebrews 12:26-28 AMP).

LIKE MY FRIEND'S FORD Fairlane, we are often forced to choose between what is visible and what is invisible. The visible will be shaken. The only thing that can't be shaken is the Kingdom because it is *uncreated*. Churches can be shaken. If you have ever been through a church split, you have experienced this. Elders fighting elders, people fighting with each other, and doctrinal disagreements are all part of the shaking. Hebrews identifies eight invisible, eternal, and uncreated elements that are unshakable (see Heb. 12:22-24):

1. Mt. Zion, God's people in Kingdom order

2. New Jerusalem, city of the living God in heaven

3. Countless multitudes of angels

4. General assembly and church of the Firstborn

5. God, the Judge of all

6. Spirits of righteous men made perfect

7. Jesus, the mediator of the New Covenant

8. Sprinkled blood

None of these are created; they are all uncreated. The Scriptures make a very clear distinction between the two categories: visible/temporal or invisible/eternal:

> *Since we consider and look not to the things that are seen but to the things that are unseen; for the things that are visible are temporal* (brief and fleeting), *but the things that are invisible are deathless and everlasting* (2 Corinthians 4:18 AMP).

Remember these eight unshakable entities when you are tempted to trade your God-given inheritance for something temporal but visible and more appealing. When we can preferentially choose to *see through* the invisible rather than *look at* the visible, we can become unshakable.

All ministries will be shaken; the only thing that is unshakable is the Kingdom. In order to be unshakable as individuals, we must be able to *see through* the shaking to God's Kingdom purposes.

Thoughts and Questions

❦ Explain why the Kingdom cannot be shaken.

❦ Why is it necessary to see through the visible elements in order not to be shaken?

❦ In what ways are God's Kingdom purposes waiting for you to become unshakable?

READING 85

Three-Dimensional Reality

For then would He often have had to suffer [over and over again] since the foundation of the world. But as it now is, He has once for all at the consummation and close of the ages appeared to put away and abolish sin by His sacrifice [of Himself].... Jesus Christ (the Messiah) is [always] the same, yesterday, today, [yes] and forever (to the ages) (Hebrews 9:26; 13:8).

PHILOSOPHICALLY AND THEOLOGICALLY, THESE are very important verses. They confirm and amplify the central point in history: it is Christ alone who brings the Spirit and Life.

Many years ago when I was taking philosophy at the University of Delaware, the professor put an orange plastic chair in front of the classroom. We spent two weeks discussing whether the chair was actually orange or if we just *perceived* the orangeness. After a while, I commented on how unwise these discussions seemed, so the professor invited me to tell the class my philosophy of life. When I stood up, I was shaking like a leaf and could hardly get the words out. I said, "Well, I am a follower of Jesus. I know where I came from, I know where I am, and I know where I am going." The entire class seemed to go berserk: How could anyone know where they came from, where they were, and where they were going? Well, I did because I believed Jesus when He said, *"I am the Light of the world; he who follows Me will not walk in the darkness, but will have the Light of life"* (John 8:12).

The first dimension is our *past*: before the foundation of the world, we were in Christ. The second dimension is the *present* or spiritual reality: perhaps we are in Father's gymnasium or actually functioning in our gifts and callings. The third dimension is the *future*: we are confident in the process of who we will become, knowing that we are as safe on our journey into Christ as we will be when we get there. Now that is a philosophy of life! This is called existential reality. Jesus Christ really is the same yesterday, today, and forever and He lives in us.

Hindsight in Greek means "yesterday"—*as I have been* or *He who was*. It is perception gained by looking backward or seeing *afterward* what happened and understanding what ought to have been different. Hindsight is always twenty-twenty. We gain hindsight when God washes our eyes with tears.

Insight in Greek means "He who is or so I remain." Insight is *seeing through*. It is internal sight, mental vision or perception, discernment, understanding, intelligence, and wisdom.

Foresight in Greek means "He who is yet to come." It is looking into the future or perception gained by looking forward.

Muzungu, an African word for white man, means "aimless wanderer" or "he who goes around in circles." Every one of us has experienced what it means to go in circles. Understanding three-dimensional reality—where we came from, where we are, and where we are going—will keep us from aimlessly wandering. If we allow Jesus to control our life with *Agape*, the result will be freedom. That is the Good News restated in postmodern terminology.

Thoughts and Questions

- In your own words, explain the first, second, and third dimensions.

- Describe a time when you had twenty-twenty vision after a circumstance was over.

- Why do you think hindsight, insight, and foresight are so important?

Exercises in Father's Gym—Functions for the Body

All discipline for the moment seems not to be
joyful, but sorrowful (Hebrews 12:11).

H EBREWS CHAPTER 13 DISCUSSES 15 weights that we must learn to lift in order to cultivate the muscles we need in all four areas of our life— *body, soul, mind,* and *spirit.* We will look at these over the next few sessions. None of them are shakable, created realities; they are all spiritual realities. These are not theories but actual exercises to be practiced in the gymnasium of life each and every day. These exercises in Father's gym involve some degree of suffering and cannot be avoided. There is, however, a purpose in trials and other unexpected difficulties: after training, we reap the peaceful fruit of righteousness (see Heb. 12:11). Inner transformation does not come from success and victory but from complexity and sorrow.

🌱 *Love of the brothers.*

> *"Let love [phileo] for your fellow believers continue and be a fixed practice with you [never let it fail]"* (Heb. 13:1 AMP).

This restates the first commandment: *"Love one another"* (John 13:34 AMP). Jesus said, *"I have called you My friends"* (John 15:15 AMP). We know that the Father loves (*phileo*) the Son (see John 5:20). It is not some religious activity but real and measureable friendship. Friendships become more and more important as we see into the nature of the Kingdom.

🌱 *Show hospitality.*

> *Do not forget or neglect or refuse to extend hospitality to strangers [in the brotherhood—being friendly, cordial, and gracious, sharing the comforts of your home and doing your part generously], for through it some have entertained angels without knowing it* (Hebrews 13:2 AMP).

In Bible times showing hospitality was a vital part of being a godly Christian, especially in the time of opposition and persecution. Benjamin Franklin said "fish and guests in three days are stale." Showing hospitality can be a stretching experience at times.

🌱 *Care for prisoners.*

> *"Remember those who are in prison as if you were their fellow prisoner, and those who are ill-treated, since you also are liable to bodily sufferings"* (Heb. 13:3 AMP).

Wherever you go and whatever you do, make ministry to those in prison part of your life. There are prisoners all over the world. From my own experience teaching in prisons, more than half of prisoners in the United States knew God at some point and turned away from Him. Ask God to give you a love, active compassion, and practical ways to act toward those who missed the road.

🌱 *Doing good and sharing.*

> *"And do not neglect doing good and sharing, for with such sacrifices God is pleased"* (Heb. 13:16).

Take time to stop and help people; don't be like the Levite who had to hurry to get to the prayer meeting (see Luke 10:32). Keep those $20 bills in your wallet to give away when the Holy Spirit directs.

It is evident that in order to grow in these areas, we have to practice in the gymnasium of life each and every day.

Thoughts and Questions

- What is the purpose of trials and other unexpected difficulties?

- Which of these weights have you struggled with the most? Why? What has been the result?

- Why would friendship and hospitality be considered a weight in Father's gym?

READING 87

Exercises in Father's Gym—Functions for the Soul

Take My yoke upon you and learn of Me, for I am gentle (meek) and humble (lowly) in heart, and you will find rest (relief and ease and refreshment and recreation and blessed quiet) for your souls (Matthew 11:29 AMP).

As we continue our study of the 15 weights in Hebrews 13, we can see the importance of cultivating our muscles in all four areas of our lives—*body, soul, mind* and *spirit*. The following exercises do involve some degree of suffering in order for us to grow up.

❧ *Preservation of marriage.*

   "Marriage is to be held in honor among all" (Heb. 13:4).

We should be concerned about the preservation of marriage because it is a type of Christ and His Bride. In the history of the world, the institution of marriage as a type of Christ and His Bride has never been as threatened as it is right now.

❧ *Cultivation of character.*

   Let your character or moral disposition be free from love of money [including greed, avarice, lust, and craving for earthly possessions] and be satisfied with your present [circumstances and with what you have] (Hebrews 13:5 AMP).

LIFTING WEIGHTS IN FATHER'S GYM

God deals with greed, lust, and materialism in His gymnasium. He takes us in, allows us to bounce around, and brings us out on the other side with hindsight so that we see things differently. After our gym workout, we learn to recognize greed and materialism in ourselves and live a contented life within our means. We can rest in the present circumstances, knowing that God will never forsake us.

> *Confidence.*

> *So we take comfort and are encouraged and confidently and boldly say, the Lord is my Helper; I will not be seized with alarm [I will not fear or dread or be terrified]. What can man do to me?* (Hebrews 13:6 AMP).

An over-active need for acceptance and approval leads to the fear of man. It is a snare in the life of many men and women and results in servitude rather than freedom. The fear of God that supersedes the fear of man is the only known antidote. If you have a deep concern about what people think, you may need to try lifting a little more weight by simply believing that Christ is your helper.

These three weights enable us to be unshakable. Remember, inner transformation does not come from success and victory but from complexity and sorrow.

Thoughts and Questions

> Which of these three weights has been the hardest to lift?

> In what ways has materialism been an exercise in cultivation of character in your life?

> Describe a situation where you experienced the fear of man. What was the result?

READING 88

Exercises in Father's Gym—Functions for the Mind

Walk uprightly and live a noble life, acting honorably and in complete honesty in all things (Hebrews 13:18 AMP).

L IKE OUR PREVIOUS SECTION, these final five exercises from Hebrews 13 have to do with inner transformation that comes from success and victory that are a result of complexity and sorrow. As we embrace each of these, we nourish God's Eternal Seed in us. The area of growth here is in the mind—the ultimate battleground.

❦ *Preserve a good conscience.*

> *Keep praying for us, for we are convinced that we have a good* (clear) *conscience, that we want to walk uprightly and live a noble life, acting honorably and in complete honesty in all things* (Hebrews 13:18 AMP).

When our conscience is clean, we can be comfortable both in God's presence as well as warm and open in social and family contexts. We do not have anything to prove or sell. We simply are because He is.

❦ *Various and strange teachings.*

> *Do not be carried about by different and varied and alien teachings; for it is good for the heart to be established and ennobled and strengthened by means of grace* (God's favor and spiritual blessing) *and not [to be devoted to] foods*

[rules of diet and ritualistic meals], which bring no [spiritual] benefit or profit to those who observe them (Hebrews 13:9 AMP).

There have never been so many alien teachings as there are now. While waiting to speak at a large church, I picked up a tract in the lobby entitled "Why Christians are not Healed." I thought, "This ought to be good." To my surprise, it said that Christians are not healed because they eat pork. As Kingdom people, we are not to spend our energies on food and rules and diets because there is no spiritual benefit. We are to take care of our bodies, of course, but not spend our lives focusing on the external, when internal spiritual issues take priority.

❦ *Going outside of the city gate.*

Therefore Jesus also suffered and died outside the [city's] gate in order that He might purify and consecrate the people through [the shedding of] His own blood and set them apart as holy [for God] (Hebrews 13:12 AMP).

We must follow Jesus, not doctrine, denominations, or trends because institutions and systems can capture us.

❦ *Leadership.*

Remember your leaders and superiors in authority [for it was they] who brought to you the Word of God. Observe attentively and consider their manner of living (the outcome of their well-spent lives) *and imitate their faith* (Hebrews 13:7 AMP).

Leaders are called by God to serve, not to capture or control people. They are first of all servants, and as such, we are to pay attention to and imitate how they live their lives.

🌱 *Proper response to leadership.*

> *Obey your spiritual leaders and submit to them [continually recognizing their authority over you], for they are constantly keeping watch over your souls and guarding your spiritual welfare, as men who will have to render an account [of their trust]. [Do your part to] let them do this with gladness and not with sighing and groaning, for that would not be profitable to you [either]* (Hebrews 13:17 AMP).

Make the jobs of your leaders as easy as possible because one day you may be the leader. *Agape* will make you leadable. What a gift to the Body of Christ!

Thoughts and Questions

🌱 Why does the complexity of *Eros* and darkness require exercise of our conscience?

🌱 Why are spiritual issues a priority over external rules?

🌱 In what ways does godly leadership need and deserve your support?

READING 89

Exercises in Father's Gym—Functions for the Spirit

Dividing asunder of soul and spirit (Hebrews 4:12 KJV).

A S WE BEGIN TO live in Kingdom reality, the skill of discerning between soul and spirit becomes a necessity.

☙ *Three-dimensional reality.*

> *"Jesus Christ (the Messiah) is [always] the same, yesterday, today, [yes] and forever (to the ages)"* (Heb. 13:8 AMP).

We have been given existential reality through Christ so that we know where we came from, where we are now, and where we are going. We are in possession of the most wonderful philosophy of life. If we follow Jesus we won't walk in darkness. As we learn to see through every situation, past, present, future, rather than look at circumstances, we begin to live in Kingdom reality.

☙ *Bearing His shame.*

> *"Let us then go forth [from all that would prevent us] to Him outside the camp [at Calvary], bearing the contempt and abuse and shame with Him"* (Heb. 13:13 AMP).

Christ bore the shame simply by despising and ignoring it. There will be times when we will be ashamed. If it is time to embrace the shame, just do it. Do not act like some strange thing is going on. I did not want to speak up in that philosophy class; I wanted to fit in as one of the brilliant philosophy students. However,

I ignored the shame and spoke up anyway. Instead of being part of academia, they ended up perceiving me as a weirdo from the Jesus world. If this happens, just eat it. This is called the selfless witness.

☙ *Praise and worship.*

> *"Through Him, therefore, let us constantly and at all times offer up to God a sacrifice of praise, which is the fruit of lips that thankfully acknowledge and confess and glorify His name"* (Hebrews 13:15 AMP).

Hosea 14:2 KJV says, *"Take with you words, and turn to the Lord: say unto him, Take away all iniquity, and receive us graciously: so will we render the calves of our lips."* While the two Scriptures above both speak of praise and worship, the Hebrew word "calves" in Hosea 14:2 literally means "a young bull, bullock, or steer." (This word is translated "fruit" in some versions.) The calves or fruit of our lips under the New Covenant is the new sacrificial system. Instead of animals, the sacrifice is praise and worship coming out of the deepest part of our being. When Jesus says the Father seeks those to worship Him in spirit and truth, He is not suggesting the Holy Spirit, but rather the deep, inward part of our being identified as our human spirit as contrasted to our mind, emotions, or will. Praise is an expression or gratitude for God's goodness. Worship is coming to know Who He is.

Practice. Lift the weights. Do the exercises. In this we are doing what Jesus did—doing good and releasing those held captive by evil.

Thoughts and Questions

☙ Where have you come from? Where are you now? Where are you going? (see John 8:12).

☙ In what ways have you endured shame in Christ's behalf? What was the result?

☙ What is the difference between praise and worship?

PART IX

The Joys of Freedom

READING 90

Abiding

*Let us therefore be zealous and exert ourselves and strive diligently to
enter that rest [of God, to know and experience it for ourselves], that
no one may fall or perish by the same kind of unbelief and disobedience
[into which those in the wilderness fell]* (Hebrews 4:11 AMP).

IN CHRIST, THE FATHER is restored to His Creation and Creation is
restored to the Father. Living in the Kingdom of God involves abiding
or posturing ourselves in Christ so that we do not waver. However, we can
only abide if we understand and embrace the wedding garment, which is
a symbol of the Bride putting on the righteousness of Christ—the passive
righteousness that was provided for us. Even when we are resting or abiding,
we continue to experience pressures that try and move us away from this
posture. Our job is to remain in a place of rest in God where our striving
ceases, our pride has been addressed, and the downward plunge has been
stopped while He works in our behalf. Abiding requires effort and involves
a form of suffering because it entails repentance and relinquishing our personal preferences. Like Jesus, we learn obedience through suffering (see
Heb. 5:8). Staying unmovable in spite of these shifting pressures is critical.
Paul gave us the tools to withstand the pressures:

> *But He said to me, My grace* (My favor and loving-kindness
> and mercy) *is enough for you [sufficient against any danger and
> enables you to bear the trouble manfully]; for My strength and
> power are made perfect* (fulfilled and completed) *and show
> themselves most effective in [your] weakness. Therefore, I will
> all the more gladly glory in my weaknesses and infirmities, that
> the strength and power of Christ* (the Messiah) *may rest* (yes,

may pitch a tent over and dwell) *upon me!* (2 Corinthians 12:9 AMP).

When we learn to abide, we bring glory to our Father because it is through believing and abiding that our Father's nature can be worked into us and revealed through us. Our objective in abiding is to establish a mature Kingdom thought pattern that is capable of encountering and embracing the complexity and crises that life presents us.

Thoughts and Questions

🐝 Explain how the wedding garment allows you to abide.

🐝 In what ways have you had to work to enter rest?

🐝 What are some of the tools you have been given to remain in an abiding position?

READING 91

Abiding—The Exact Location
of the Kingdom of God

Apart from Me you can do nothing (John 15:5).

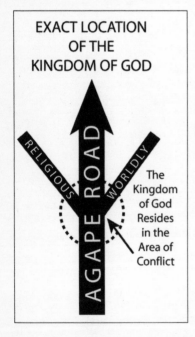

**EXACT LOCATION
OF THE
KINGDOM OF GOD**

RELIGIOUS

AGAPE ROAD

WORLDLY

The Kingdom of God Resides in the Area of Conflict

O N THE *AGAPE* ROAD, the area of conflict is where, as fallen sovereign kings over our own lives, circumstances and problems make us want to veer off onto a religious or sensual road rather than abide on the road to the Father. The exact location of the Kingdom of God on the earth is right smack in the center of the area of conflict. Staying on the *Agape* road inevitably brings conflict because it disallows our ability to continue to acquire, possess, or control. *"Apart from Me you can do nothing"* can only be experienced in a position of abiding. His promise is that He is the way, the truth, and the life, and that He will take us to the Father. Because we live in a fallen world, if we don't learn to abide, we can be sure that persecution, affliction, crazies, and unpredictable pressures will move us off the *Agape* road. When we abide in and through the conflict, we are living in the unshakable Kingdom of God and can enjoy righteousness, peace, and joy in the Holy Spirit—no matter what circumstances come our way.

The Church is called to proclaim Christ's Kingdom to the world. Evangelism is being faced with God's sovereignty: *"Repent, for the Kingdom of God is at hand!"* (see Mark 1:15). Unfortunately, the Church is not always Kingdom-oriented. In the exact location of the Kingdom of God—the area of conflict—we will find an absence of striving and confusion. Abiding means that we have learned to live for the audience of one.

Abiding is both passive and active righteousness. We never do anything to be seen or to be the center of attention, nor do we refuse to do anything because we will be seen or be the center of attention. We have a cessation of movement up and down (what I call the "yo-yo" Christian). Because we are in Christ, we are wise as serpents in understanding the manner in which the seven giants work, their power, and their reward mechanisms. We are also harmless as doves because we refuse to employ the seven giants for personal goals or revenge. We have no choice but to forgive and release others because we are governed by *Agape*.

Thoughts and Questions

- Why do you think that *"apart from* [Jesus] *you can do nothing"* can only be experienced in a position of abiding?

- What are some of the signs that you are living in the Kingdom of God?

- Why do you think the Kingdom of God on earth resides in the area of conflict?

READING 92

Abiding in Declining Prosperity

Yet it has no real root in him, but is temporary (inconstant, lasts
but a little while)*; and when affliction or trouble or persecution
comes on account of the Word, at once he is caused to stumble [he is
repelled and begins to distrust and desert Him Whom he ought to
trust and obey] and he falls away* (Matthew 13:21 AMP).

IN ORDER TO REMAIN in the exact location of the Kingdom of God, it is
important to learn to abide in seven specific areas, so that affliction or
persecution cannot shake us off our foundation. In the next two sessions,
we will look at each of these areas.

* *Declining prosperity.* God is still God even when finances are
tight and we live paycheck to paycheck. Many people have lived
there so long they are unable to see themselves living in prosperity. When finances are not an issue, our true personality tends to
be concealed in the glitter of materialism. It is in the diminishment of prosperity that our character is revealed, and we begin to
see circumstances and events in their spiritual reality.

* *Economic uncertainty.* In a manner similar to declining prosperity,
we simply are not capable of seeing ourselves as in Christ when the
economy continues to improve. The implications of an economic
bubble are clear. There are, in a similar vein, personality bubbles and spiritual bubbles, none of which are rooted in existential
Kingdom reality. That is global, even if the stock market crash-
es. Illegal desires take us out of the Father's purpose for our lives.

* *Outright danger.* Danger includes disease, hurricanes, biological or
nuclear warfare. The Scriptures are full of testimonies regarding

the faithfulness of God in the midst of natural and man-made disasters. The psalmist declared his faith and abiding confidence in the midst of danger when he said, *"For by You I can run upon a troop; and by my God I can leap over a wall"* (Ps. 18:29). Over the years this very verse has literally served me in the presence of serious and unmanageable danger. It is not based on false confidence but in the very DNA of God.

❦ *Unexpected happenings.* If we thought that Father was the kind of person who would forsake us every time we became angry, we would be living in bondage, not freedom. If we feel pressed to make serious decisions when we are euphoric or depressed, they are nearly *guaranteed* to be wrong. It is frightening to try and find guidance on an issue when the guidance system upon which we depend is a little bit crazy. It is also very difficult to hear the word of the Lord if we are depressed. When we discover ourselves in some euphoric, prideful state—whether emotional, religious, or financial—we do come short of the glory of God. Likewise, when we feel depression or rage, we injure our capacity to reveal God's glory. The moment we insist on acquiring, possessing, or controlling, we are injuring that for which we were chosen. *"If any man's work is burned up, he will suffer loss; but he himself will be saved, yet so as through fire"* (1 Cor. 3:15). If we are always up or always down, or, God forbid, are spending most of our time journeying to one or the other, chances are that everything we are seeking to build will be burned, but we ourselves will be saved.

Thoughts and Questions

❦ Which of these four areas has been the most problematic place to abide?

❦ Why is our character revealed in the diminishment of prosperity?

❦ What unexpected happenings have tried to shake you from your foundation of abiding?

Reading 93

Abiding in Specific Crises

But one who looks intently at the perfect law, the law of liberty, and abides by it, not having become a forgetful hearer but an effectual doer, this man will be blessed in what he does (James 1:25).

CONTINUING FROM OUR LAST session, following are the last three areas that we need to learn to abide in so that we can remain in the exact location of the Kingdom of God.

- *Spiritual warfare.* This involves direct demonic or satanic attack. Excessive focus on deliverance and fighting the devil are almost always counterproductive because it distracts us from our position of abiding. I knew a man who encountered a demonic being each night when he got up to go to the bathroom. He rebuked the spirit, cleansed the house, and did everything he knew to do. When he told me about it, I knew that he had come to expect the demonic, so I encouraged him to simply ignore it and abide. The next night he walked right past the spirit and it never appeared again. The demonic is often a tar baby!

- *Past failures and habit patterns.* This is one of the most effective of all strategies to keep us from freedom and usefulness. We must learn to abide when the old tape starts playing. We can either choose to live present-past, or to live present-future. The fruit in your life reveals your intention in this area.

- *Unfulfilled promises and expectations.* There are many reasons for unfulfilled promises. We must learn to live by the Kingdom principle of building our lives with gold, silver, and precious stones rather than with wood, hay, and stubble. Many expectations and unfulfilled promises have come as a result of *talking to ourselves in God's Name*. We must never build our hope or place our ultimate confidence in anything other than God's own nature, His DNA, knowing that

- God is *Agape* in whom there is no *Eros*.
- God is Light in whom there is no darkness or shadow.
- God is Spirit in whom there is not animus.

We must filter everything, including every promise, through the aspects of His nature. Receive and rely only on that which originates from His person. When a promise given is to your own advantage, check it three times, not just once!

The area of conflict is where decisions are made. When we hold our position of abiding in the exact center of the Kingdom of God, even in the midst of pressures or people's up and down reactions, we will not be moved or make so many wrong choices. If we don't know which way to go, we are instructed to abide until the *Agape* road becomes clear. Under the most severe temptations, Christ's response was to abide. He did nothing, said nothing, and refused to engage the tempter in debate. We know our Father's love is true, and that we can do nothing to bring it to pass. It is on faith alone that we can rest in the completed work of Christ until we are able to follow Him again. This is the law of liberty.

Thoughts and Questions

- Explain why the demonic is often a tar baby.
- In what ways have past failures kept you from abiding?
- Why is it important to filter everything through the aspects of God's nature?

READING 94

Responding to Our Freedom

Abide in Me, and I in you (John 15:4).

ABIDING ENABLES GOD TO answer our prayers. If we are not puffed up in pride or cast down in depression or rage, we are free to ask Him for things, and He can answer our prayers without injuring us. When we keep going up or down, Father's glory is injured, but when we are able to hold our abiding position, the Father's nature and glory shine through us as a reflection of His Light. It is when we come to some degree of godly normalcy that we find freedom.

We can see from the following Scriptures that freedom is the issue and goal of the Kingdom:

> *It was for freedom that Christ set us free; therefore keep standing firm and do not be subject again to a yoke of slavery* (Galatians 5:1).

> *For you were called to freedom, brethren; only do not turn your freedom into an opportunity for the flesh, but through love serve one another* (Galatians 5:13).

> *Act as free men, and do not use your freedom as a covering for evil, but use it as bondslaves of God"* (1 Peter 2:16).

God *wants* to set us *free*. Unfortunately, *freedom* scares most leaders because they are sure you are immature and will abuse it. And we have! While in seminary, I was a hot-blooded, tongues-speaking, law-abiding Charismatic. Then God sent me to an Episcopal seminary, and I was sure He had sent me there to straighten things out. As I was sitting in a Hebrew class, the professor made an unqualified statement that rocked me: "Saint Augustine said, 'Love God and do as you please.'" I had never heard such insanity in all my life. But in that instant, the Seed of God penetrated my person, and it has taken me almost 50 years to understand that radical statement. Jesus states plainly that freedom is the New Testament goal. "If you love Me (governing)...you will (freedom)" (see John 14:15). Like a loving Father, God is saying that if we will *receive* His love, it will both govern us and set us free. This is the essence of Saint Augustine's words.

When we *Agape* God with our entire heart, soul, mind, and strength, we are free men and women. We are governed from within by *Agape* so we cannot and will not injure or use others for our own purposes. When we are free, we can influence others to find freedom, even if it threatens them.

Thoughts and Questions

🍂 In what ways does abiding allow God to answer our prayers?

🍂 Why do you think freedom is an issue and goal of the Kingdom?

🍂 How have you experienced Saint Augustine's statement to "love God and do as you please"?

READING 95

Freedom

In Him we also were made [God's] heritage (portion) *and we obtained an inheritance; for we had been foreordained* (chosen and appointed beforehand) *in accordance with His purpose, Who works out everything in agreement with the counsel and design of His [own] will* (Ephesians 1:11 AMP).

OUT OF A RENEWED vision of *Agape*, there emerges *freedom, grace,* and *destiny*. These are part of the Kingdom inheritance to which we have been called. In the next sessions we will see that with the presence of one of these, the other two will follow.

Freedom is that to which we have been called: Our freedom is the result of redemptive, restorative, and Fatherly care. It was lost in Adam but given back to us in Christ.

In over 50 years in ministry, I have watched the yo-yo phenomenon in Christians. I can personally identify with this because I am an emotional man and feel deeply about things. I move in highs and lows that sometimes frustrate me. Everyone knows that we teach and speak out of our own needs and weakness. However, Jesus set us free, so you and I are set free from the necessity of having to go up or down. Because we are free, we can stop running, hiding, and shifting blame. We can be increasingly addressable and accountable. It is freedom that leads to usefulness. Freedom comes from the increase of spiritual stability. The condition of freedom involves being free of external restraints; release from slavery, oppression, and incarceration; political independence; possession of civil rights; immunity from the arbitrary exercise of authority; the capacity to exercise choice; free will;

the right to enjoy all the privileges of membership or citizenship. Freedom is not a quality of man or a possession; it is a state of being.

Abiding on the *Agape* road allows us to act as free men and not to misuse our freedom. Often, we are not free for the simple reason that we do not know, nor have we been taught the purpose and value of that freedom. A parable in Fyodor Dostoyevsky's novel, *The Brothers Karamazov*, called "The Grand Inquisitor," identifies freedom as "that terrible gift." It provides us an insight into the manner and expense of rising to freedom and using it in a proper Kingdom manner.

Freedom is a simple, four-step process: abide, become true and intentional disciples, love Truth *as* a person, and follow Jesus. These four steps lead to quantity and quality of freedom that is more than we can ask or think!

Thoughts and Questions

🕊 Why do you think freedom comes from the increase of spiritual stability?

🕊 In what ways does abiding help us not to misuse our freedom?

🕊 In your own words, explain how freedom is a four-step process.

READING 96

Grace and Destiny

The grace of God has appeared, bringing salvation to all men (Titus 2:11).

T HE SECOND ASPECT OF the inheritance given to us in the person of Christ is *grace*. Grace is a person, not primarily a doctrine that we acknowledge or disavow. Followers of Christ are usually surprised to discover that His grace is an aspect of His person in the same manner as truth. He *is* truth; He does not *have* truth. He *is* grace, He does not *have* grace. He gives us of Himself, and that is what leads to spiritual stability and fruitfulness.

We discussed earlier how grace is given to us in the rubber room. *Grace* is what teaches us. It is an attribute of Christ, the Son of the living God, who reveals the inner nature of the Father. It is a disposition to be generous or helpful; clemency; a favor rendered by one who need not do so; indulgence; a temporary immunity or exemption; a reprieve; divine love and protection bestowed freely upon mankind. Grace is the state of being protected or sanctified by the favor of God, and it involves an excellence or power granted by Him. God's image—His DNA attributes—being restored in man releases the climate and conditions for God to express His own love to a hurting world through you and me. Grace appeared in the person of Christ and in His anointing, which is given to us. *Grace* is the only way we can expand our capacity for God. The more we understand the grace of God, the more our capacity for Him increases.

The last of these three aspects of our inheritance is the concept of destiny. *Destiny* is to reveal God's glory. It is the inevitable or necessary end to which a particular person or thing is destined—our lot or inheritance. It is the predetermined or inevitable course of events considered beyond the

THE JOYS OF FREEDOM

power or control of man. It is an inner conviction to live our lives in such a way that the will of God would not or could not be neglected or ignored.

We must see ourselves as increasingly mature, free, and godly problem-solvers in a world of increasingly complex problems. Amazingly, God uses us as co-workers in His Kingdom. His purposes are given to us in Christ, and they override our failings and limitations. Paul said that

> *we are fellow workmen* (joint promoters, laborers together) *with and for God; you are God's garden and vineyard and field under cultivation, [you are] God's building* (1 Corinthians 3:9 AMP).

In light of this, what were we called to be? What were we called to do? Paul clearly identifies our destiny: *"I press on in order to lay hold of THAT for which also I was laid hold of by Christ Jesus"* (Phil. 3:12). THAT is our destiny. We were not called to be successful; we were called to be faithful. Faithfulness is THAT, and it does take us to our destiny. Praying for THAT in our lives takes us out of the sandlot and into the professional league! It can be both exciting and frightening to learn the spiritual reality of God's *Agape* nature being revealed through us. But *Agape* casts out all fear, allowing us to pray for THAT and to risk pursuing our destiny with freedom and grace.

Destiny enlarges our Kingdom usefulness. As we begin to experience freedom in spiritual stability and increase our capacity for God through His grace, we begin asking Him to make us useful in His Kingdom.

Thoughts and Questions

🌱 In what ways has God revealed grace as a person to you personally?

🌱 Explain why THAT is our destiny.

🌱 How has destiny enlarged your Kingdom usefulness?

READING 97

Autonomous Freedom

*Creation waits eagerly ...[to] be set free from its slavery to corruption
into the freedom of the glory of the children of God* (Romans 8:19-21).

ALL CREATION WAITS FOR us to mature as free men and women. It is
the kind of freedom that means we are not *required* to floss all our
teeth—just the ones we want to keep. A fish is free in water; but if it jumps
out of the water, it will eventually die. A train is free when running on the
railroad tracks for which it was designed. That which seems restrictive is
often the thing that gives us life. *Autonomous freedom is a deception.* We are
instructed to use our freedom in a Kingdom manner rather than to misuse
it, but we must understand the issues. We are called to freedom; so our goal
should be to love others, those whom God puts in our life, as Christ loves
us. Jesus set us free so that we could love those to whom He was sending us.

Freedom means that we are being restored to the sovereign call of God
on our lives. World systems—including natural family; economic systems
that perpetuate systemic poverty; school systems that have lost their com-
missioning and become tyrannical; governmental entities that have learned
to skillfully possess, acquire and control; and religious systems that have
lost their Kingdom mandate and function as a Mother and not a Father—
want to see us in eternal childhood because they can manage us better. If
we grow up, we might threaten them. But if we do not grow up, we end
up abusing our freedom by turning it into a self-serving opportunity. God
gave us freedom, even the freedom to choose to abuse and use it wrongly.
One would think that an authentic, free believer would not do this, but we
do it all the time. We abuse our freedom when we refuse to repent or apol-
ogize. If we don't learn to *retract, restrain, and renounce,* we cannot govern

our freedom. This could cause us to injure our inheritance by insisting on going further *up* into pride or further *down* into rage or depression. We would be effectively trading our personal inheritance of freedom and liberty that Christ purchased for us by using that freedom in a nonbiblical manner.

All parents have gone through frightening experiences when their children start finding their freedom. Some parents are not capable of giving their children that much freedom, so they resort to manipulation, domination and control: "Where have you been? What did you drink? What was the address? Who were you with?" Their child gets defensive, and thinks, "Back off!" On the other hand, there are parents who abuse their children's freedom because they don't care at all. All parents have experienced tremendous difficulty in knowing how much *autonomy* to give their children so that they can assist them in the unpredictable process of growing up and learning to function in true freedom. This is particularly difficult for parents who were not free or healthy in their own growing-up process. For many of us, childhood was that period of life we spend the rest of our years getting over!

Learning to walk in real freedom is applicable to individuals as well as to all types of leaders in our society. As parents and leaders, it is often a complex and not-so-thankful occupation. The fact is, we must duplicate these principles within the Church if we are motivated to bring forth mature sons and daughters who will know and live in their own freedom. More rules simply will not do it. Only *Agape* will bring us to freedom.

Thoughts and Questions

🐝 How would you define freedom in your own life?

🐝 What is the goal of a free man?

🐝 In what ways does it take freedom to accomplish this goal?

READING 98

Misusing Our Freedom

*That nature (creation) itself will be set free from its bondage to
decay and corruption [and gain an entrance] into the glorious
freedom of God's children (Romans 8:21 AMP).*

MISUSING OUR FREEDOM CAUSES us to injure or increase the possibility
of losing the inheritance Christ gave us. Christ died to set us free.
Our freedom is Christ's gift to us without effort or work. Paul stated,

> *Exercise your freedom by serving God, not by breaking the
> rules. Treat everyone you meet with dignity. Love your spiri-
> tual family. Revere God. Respect the government (1 Peter
> 2:16-17 MSG).*

People who are truly free don't have to prove that they are free. When
we walk in real Kingdom freedom, we seldom have the need to impress
anyone. We can simply be who God designed us to be. Misusing our
Kingdom inheritance of freedom inexorably leads to an *Eros* prison. This
happens in three ways:

Our inability to embrace the Kingdom. If we use our freedom wrongly,
we fill ourselves with all kinds of things that are not Kingdom priorities
for us. Simply stated, there is no longer room in the inn for the Christ and
His Kingdom.

Our absence of capacity for the Kingdom. When we are filled with all kinds
of possessions that are not focused on the Kingdom, our *capacity* for Christ
and His Kingdom is displaced—instead of fruit we get thorns.

Our ignorance of the issues of the Kingdom. When Jesus said the Kingdom
is like a treasure or a precious pearl and to sell everything you have and buy

242

it, He was stating in parable form a truth that the Kingdom of God is the single answer for a deeply hurting world. It is only when the Kingdom is preached that the true Church is formed.

We were called to freedom—it is our destiny. *When the fullness of the Kingdom comes, it won't be different, there will just be more of it.* It is important that we understand and walk in our freedom because we are inviting people out of the world system into the Kingdom freedom that has been provided by the King of that Kingdom. I have been in situations that were so devoid of righteousness, peace, and joy that it would have been wrong to invite anyone out of their own confusion into mine. Our destiny is to know such a degree of freedom that we are eager to invite people into all that we have discovered.

Paul stood in the court before Felix with chains on his hands and feet after being beaten and said, *"I would to God that not only you, but also all who are listening to me today, might become such as I am, except for these chains"* (Acts 26:29 AMP). Even though physically imprisoned, he was free in his person, in his circumstance, and in his future. Like Paul, little by little, we should become aware that we, too, are learning to choose freedom in spite of and in the presence of any chains. It is important that we learn how to properly use our freedom, but we have to first experience our freedom before we can use it.

Thoughts and Questions

- ⚜ What are some of the results of misusing or abusing our freedom?

- ⚜ Explain why Kingdom people don't have to prove their freedom.

- ⚜ In what ways have you found freedom in spite of any chains?

Freedom from Systems

When God is personally present, a living Spirit, that
old, constricting legislation is recognized as obsolete.
We're free of it! (2 Corinthians 3:17 MSG).

FREEDOM IS MORE OF an issue than present-day believers have ever considered. Since the Tower of Babel, man has continued to erect systems to try to prevent God from interfering and thus be "free." By nature, however, freedom does not lend itself to systems. Freedom can only be understood in relationship to the living God because it originates in Him. Created freedom is a gift of the Creator and cannot be *possessed* by man. Freedom can be lived, enjoyed, and imparted to others but never *owned* as some commodity or entity that is for sale.

Dietrich Bonhoeffer succinctly defined freedom:

> Freedom is not a quality of man, nor is it an ability, a capacity, a kind of being that somehow flares up in him. Anyone investigating man to discover freedom finds nothing of it. Why? Because freedom is not a quality which can be revealed—it is not a *possession*, an object, nor is it a form of existence—but a relationship and nothing else. The Fall of Man thrust him into the new status of *unfreedom*. For Bonhoeffer, rediscovery of this lost freedom is the special function of Christianity. He labored to clarify the concept of freedom, yet still refused to present it as a closed system, knowing that men and circumstances change, while fixed systems remain unmovable and quickly become tyrannical.[1]

Bonhoeffer carefully and wonderfully defines Christ's vicarious role in restoring original freedom. Christ brings us full freedom by means of incarnation, humiliation, and Resurrection. God's incarnation is incomprehensible and impossible and can only be seen as an act of God's freedom. His humiliation in becoming one with us is the very thing that makes belief in Christ possible because it shows that Christ identifies with us and is for us. His Resurrection from the dead also brought us freedom; for there is absolutely no transition or continuity between the dead and the resurrected Christ except the freedom of God, which, in the beginning, created His work out of nothing. Christ was resurrected for one simple reason: Father willed it so.

Freedom is restored to man by identifying with Christ who is being formed within us. We were designed by the Creator to be free for others and free for God. It is a freedom over which man has no *control*. Freedom is what makes our relationship to God and to fellow humans possible. If we are not free, we are being ruled by one of the alternate forces of the fallen world—religious, economic, political, or others. This is the logic behind the words of our Lord Jesus about calling Him Lord: when alternate forces that are not of Him rule over us (see Isa. 26:13).

What this means for man is that creaturely freedom has been restored to him by Christ. By conforming to the living and present Christ, a person is now *free* to be a person before God and before other people. This is the purpose of the redemptive act.

Thoughts and Questions

- ǂ Explain why freedom does not lend itself to systems.

- ǂ In what ways would rediscovery of our lost freedom be the special function of Christianity?

- ǂ How is freedom restored to you?

ENDNOTE

1. A.J. Klassen, *A Bonhoeffer Legacy: Essays in Understanding.* (Grand Rapids: Eerdmans Publishing, 1981) 333.

God Limits His Freedom

What if some did not believe and were without faith? Does their lack of faith and their faithlessness nullify and make ineffective and void the faithfulness of God and His fidelity [to His Word]? (Romans 3:3 AMP).

A T 12 YEARS OLD, I was sweaty, little Bobby Mumford from the other side of the tracks. If you knew me then, you may not have liked me because I was an intense *fallen* king. But God came to me and placed His love within me and upon me. Within three weeks, I refused His love and, as most of you know, lapsed in my relationship with Him until I was 24 years old. Even when under the *alcolfluence of incohol*, I somehow instinctively understood what He meant when He said, "*I will never desert you nor will I ever forsake you*" (Heb. 13:5). That's when I first understood—this phrase is not an actual promise, it's a veiled threat. He intends to stay with us, even on our most wild rides. God, in His own freedom, makes a choice to limit His freedom by never, ever leaving us.

In the act of marriage, we are exercising our freedom by choosing to *limit* (retract, restrain, renounce) ourselves to one woman or man to the exclusion of all others. Freedom requires us to be able to *exclude* things as well as *include* them.

Many people are convinced or have been taught that the moment we fail in our relationship with God, His presence leaves us. This is not how God's *covenantal faithfulness* works. Some years ago, I knew a young man who was heavy into parties, drugs, and sex but had a real destiny on his life. His parents were praying that God would not relax His hold on their son. At a drug party one night, the power of God struck him without warning, hitting him directly in the chest, literally driving him across the room.

When he hit the wall, he slid down to the floor. Like the prodigal, he said, "What am I doing in this place?" He got up and went home and from that day he never turned his back on God. His parents were overwhelmed with gratitude because God did what He promised. God limits His freedom by allowing us to make choices, even when they are not in our own best interest. He also honors His promise to never leave us or forsake us.

Thoughts and Questions

* In what ways have you experienced God never leaving or forsaking you?

* Explain what it means to exercise freedom by excluding or including some things.

* In what ways has God limited His freedom by allowing you to make choices that were not in your own best interest?

READING 101

White Knuckle Club

So, what do you think? With God on our side like this, how can
we lose? If God didn't hesitate to put everything on the line for
us, embracing our condition and exposing himself to the worst
by sending his own Son, is there anything else he wouldn't
gladly and freely do for us? (Romans 8:31-32 MSG).

GOD IS NOT MAD at you. God is a Father and He is not angry at you. Grieved? Maybe. Somewhat disappointed? Possibly. But not angry. He *chose* to give His *Agape* to a hurting world; consequently, He loves you. In order to keep covenantal faithfulness, He was determined to pour all His wrath on Christ for the purpose of giving you His pleasure and acceptance. We can *abide* in Christ's love in spite of all our failures or things we do or don't do.

He asks us, actually commands us, to love others, knowing that we cannot love on command. As a wise Father, He still asks this of us because He knows that our attempts to do so will press us into Him. Trying to love out of our own reserves is what I call the White Knuckle Club because it sets us up for inevitable failure. The members of the White Knuckle Club will all recognize the following statements: "Tomorrow I'm going to do better." "I *am* going to love that annoying person in the office." We must learn to drop back to confidence in the wedding garment—Christ's righteousness on our behalf—because that is where we will find grace for the situation. When we love, it must be and can only be His Love (*Agape*) flowing through us as an expression of His own person.

In order to cancel our membership in the White Knuckle Club we must freely admit, "God, I can't do this!" When we open ourselves to Him and abide in Him, His love can and does flow through us to others without religious games or pretending. Even though walking in reality requires time in the rubber room, walking in *unreality* can be more painful.

Freedom, grace, and destiny give us the ability to abide rather than repeatedly become a member of one White Knuckle Club after another. On our gravestone, we don't want written: "He was clubbed to death"!

Thoughts and Questions

🌱 In what ways do you think God is mad at you? Explain why He is not.

🌱 Describe your involvement in the White Knuckle Club over the years.

🌱 How can you cancel your membership in the White Knuckle Club?

READING 102

Freedom from the White Knuckle Club

How much more will the blood of Christ, who through the eternal Spirit offered Himself without blemish to God, cleanse your conscience from dead works to serve the living God? (Hebrews 9:14).

ABIDING GIVES US FREEDOM from the White Knuckle Club through growth in the following positive actions and responses. Each of these aspects of abiding reveal intentionality and freedom:

- We allow grace to teach us in the rubber room and we are actually learning. When guilt and false expectations have been removed, the rubber room can be joyful and exciting. Like a waterslide, we know where it is taking us and enjoy the wild ride. Fear departs and joy takes its place.

- We are *following Jesus* in spite of circumstances. If everyone is going back to Egypt, we don't have to go with them. If the crowd is going right or left, we can stay on the *Agape* road. Abiding gives us the strength and courage to not yield to peer pressure and false expectations. It is a real victory when we first break out of the social and religious expectations that do not take us to the Father.

- Whatever we do, we do for God's glory. We live our life (work, home, business, and social) so that the seven aspects of God's glory—His DNA—can be revealed in a non- compartmentalized life. May the Father of our Lord Jesus Christ be our audience of one.

- Failure has lost its power over us. Of course, we are going to fail, but Father has already planned for quite a few of these failures so that we are not caught in the snare of unbroken success. Failures are part of our learning and maturing process.

- We are abiding and have ceased from striving. We are now living from Heaven to earth rather than from earth to Heaven. God is coming to us in the form of His New Jerusalem. His government is being formed in us. We are beginning to love Him, creation, our enemies, and, strangely enough, ourselves.

- Christ's nature is being formed in us. We are beginning to touch the freedom that Jesus talked about. Remember the four-step process to freedom from our earlier session. Our freedom is a determined purpose of God as our Father. He will not let up until we are free.

- We are at rest just as God entered His rest. We must discern what or who disturbs our rest and bring it under His governmental control so that we can once again abide.

- All is quiet within us and our conscience is at rest. A clean conscience is only possible by means of the wedding garment and abiding.

- God's hidden attributes are revealed in us when we are free from the White Knuckle Club. God is a Spirit and can only be known when He chooses to reveal Himself to us by the person of Christ or in the realm of the Holy Spirit.

Little by little, we are being set free from the White Knuckle Club and are being conformed to the image of Christ. Before long, people will begin to ask, "There is something different about you! Who are you and where did you come from?" And we can say, "I thought you would never ask." Abiding allows our testimony to come out of the nature of God being revealed in us. This is the definition of the selfless witness.

Thoughts and Questions

- 🐛 To which of the White Knuckle clubs do you belong?

- 🐛 Which of these points are you still struggling with? In which can you see growth?

- 🐛 In what ways has the strength of failure lost its power over you?

PART X

Freedom and Mental Health

READING 103

Legalism and Mental Health

And this is His order (His command, His injunction)*: that we should
believe in* (put our faith and trust in and adhere to and rely on) *the
name of His Son Jesus Christ* (the Messiah), *and that we should love one
another, just as He has commanded us. All who keep His commandments
[who obey His orders and follow His plan, live and continue to live, to stay
and] abide in Him, and He in them. [They let Christ be a home to them
and they are the home of Christ.] And by this we know and understand
and have the proof that He [really] lives and makes His home in us: by
the [Holy] Spirit Whom He has given us* (1 John 3:23-24 AMP).

HEBREW SCHOLARS OF THE Old Testament managed to take the Ten
Commandments and turn them into 613 legalistic "commandments
of reason" for the purpose of seeking the approval of God. There were 365
prohibitions, 65 of which involved the whole community. The longer we
live under the 613 commandments, the more we struggle with a clean conscience, forcing us to lengthen the list with new commands to cover all the
issues. The latent fear is that we have missed the one that will take us down.
The hard thing about legalism is that while the list continues to get longer,
our mental health becomes increasingly feeble.

My father-in-law fasted every Wednesday. He was miserable and if he
had to be miserable, he knew how to include the entire family. When he
came home from work he would immediately feel the television. If it was
warm, he would physically chastise all three of the children; no one was
allowed to watch television on *his* fast days. This is reminiscent of Martin
Luther who wrote about spending three hours every day repenting but never
finding any relief.

Jesus knew how worn out we would get from trying to keep all those commandments; and He told us that if we would take His yoke and learn of Him, He would give us rest (see Matt. 11:28-29). He reduced all the commands to one: love one another. *"For the whole Law is fulfilled in one word, in the statement, "You shall love your neighbor as yourself"* (Gal. 5:14). That is a pretty good deal! Every law is fulfilled when we love others without a hook. The reason we can abide is because the Father's commandments were completed in Christ. Jesus kept the Father's commandments for us and gave us a robe of righteousness—the wedding garment. We find spiritual and mental balance when we understand and accept the wedding garment. Without it, we cannot find relief from struggles with our conscience. If we don't understand that Christ (plus nothing) is our righteousness, we will never find relief or mental or emotional stability because we will just keep pressing into legalism, and the list will continue to grow longer.

Thoughts and Questions

- Why were the 12 commandments turned into 613 laws?

- What two commandments did Jesus reduce the 12 commandments to? Why?

- In what ways does the wedding garment give us mental health?

Freedom and Mental Health

Who can know the Lord's thoughts? Who knows enough to teach him? But we understand these things, for we have the mind of Christ
(1 Corinthians 2:16 NLT).

ONE OF THE MOST damaging and dangerous of all human emotions is *self-pity* because it is a deadly withdrawal into ourselves. When we turn in upon ourselves, there inevitably follows a disruption in our emotions and thought processes. The moment we are overly emotional or self-referential we become a little bit crazy!

Consider the triumph of the therapeutic, i.e., the psychological categories, ideas, and terminology that have nearly displaced plain and workable biblical categories. Pastors and Bible teachers now think and teach in psychological terms, placing unintended interpretation on various biblical concepts such as sin, failure, and anxiety. This leaves us thinking *we* can or should do something about these issues. There is a tenuous balance between human responsibility and God-given release and freedom. We must always see God as a Father whose revealed heart is to do us good.

There are several categories to address and own if we are to be successful in our journey out of bondage into biblical freedom. Here are five presuppositions to consider:

- Man as the created is addressable and answerable.

- Man is accountable and has the innate ability to respond.

- What we *believe* makes us act a certain way.

- Inferiority, insecurity, and rejection are old tapes replaying.

❦ Paranoia, whether secular or religious, is a frightening prison.

For our mental health's sake, we must remember the words of Jesus: *"Man shall not live by bread alone"* (Luke 4:4). When we are in the *Eros* pit of self-pity, we have an urgent and unqualified need for the mind of Christ and the life that comes from the Word of His mouth. As our Creator and Father, He knows what we need.

Thoughts and Questions

❦ Why do you think self-pity is one of the most danger-ous emotions?

❦ Which of the five presuppositions stands out to you the most? Why?

❦ In what ways have you needed the mind of Christ and the Word of His mouth when in a state of mental unhealthiness?

Sources of Emotional Disturbance

When I kept silence [before I confessed], my bones wasted away
through my groaning all the day long. For day and night Your
hand [of displeasure] was heavy upon me; my moisture was
turned into the drought of summer (Psalms 32:3-4 AMP).

THERE ARE FIVE MAIN sources of mental and emotional disturbance that keep us from walking in freedom and joy in our Kingdom lives. Each of them has to do with the insidious nature of the seven giants.

Hiding. Refusing to acknowledge and/or confess sin and failure results in psychological and physical pressures that we were not designed to handle. If someone has been hiding an abortion since they were sixteen, they need to tell someone about it and get it out in the sunshine. If they continue to hide, they will experience emotional instability. It is dangerous to live a lie in hiding because our light begins to become darkness when we begin to believe the lies.

Striving. Paul identifies striving as one of the Christian sins: *"Let us not become vainglorious and self-conceited, competitive and challenging and pro- voking and irritating to one another, envying and being jealous of one another"* (Gal. 5:26 AMP).

Striving is the result of an absence of security, identity, and belonging due to ignorance of the wedding garment and the gift of God's righteousness. Failing to abide makes us competitive and jealous because we have to fight to attain some real or imaginary goal at the expense of others. Rest is entered by faith, not works. Striving is unhealthy, so be normal, be real, and let God be supernatural.

Controlling. This is one of the three biggies: acquire, possess, and *control.* Control is the most neglected and powerful factor in the realm of disturbed mental health. Fear of the future causes us to feel the need to be in control. It does not take long to discover that we are unable to do so and it quickly affects our demeanor. The more we lose control, demeanor we get! We must recognize our tendency and propensity to control people, circumstances, and situations. Deal with control without condemnation by use of the wedding garment and abiding. Cessation of attempts to control life and people will result in unexpected freedom.

Rationalizing. One of the more vague aspects of our surrendering to Christ and seeking to follow Him is in the realm of the mind, will, and intellect. Add to this Paul's admonition that our mind be "transformed" (see Rom. 12:2), and we are able to see what intellectual sacrifice means—yielding our thought processes to the guidance of the Scriptures and God's purpose. We do have the mind of Christ. Rather than excusing ourselves from situations and making everything someone else's fault, we must take personal responsibility. Remember, man as the created is addressable and answerable. This means that we cannot run, hide, or shift blame.

Ignorance. People perish for lack of knowledge. We must break the cycle of ignorance. If we walk in Light while we have the Light, darkness, which includes ignorance, will have no place in us.

When we are under the domination of the seven giants, we are governed by that which is demanding and irrational. *Eros*, in its essence, makes us a little bit crazy!

Thoughts and Questions

- In what ways can you see hiding as producing emotional instability?

- What role does control play in the realm of disturbed mental health?

- Why is striving a result of the lack of security, identity, and belonging?

Expectation and Emotional Stability

We do not boast therefore, beyond our proper limit, over other men's labors; but we have the hope and confident expectation that as your faith continues to grow, our field among you may be greatly enlarged, still within the limits of our commission (2 Corinthians 10:15 AMP).

NOW THAT WE HAVE examined several aspects of mental health and emotional stability, we can make an application of the principles. Expectations—what we think may happen or what we want to happen—are powerful motivations. They can be healthy and strengthening, but they can also be frightening and excessively damaging. Consider the following three aspects of expectation and take some time to read their descriptions in the Scriptures. Expectation is fearful and dreadful as well as joyful and confident (see Luke 21:26, 2 Cor. 10:15). Expectation is what enables us to effectively respond to the realities of life. When we love God with all our heart, soul, mind, and strength, our expectations are true and biblical. However, discovery and recovery from false or imposed expectations (those we place upon ourselves or others) can be exceedingly complex.

The person who does not figure sin and failure into his equation of life is in for great disappointment. Human failure is the main source of false expectation. In a euphoric atmosphere of religious activity, we may find ourselves increasing our expectation of what God intends to do. This builds false expectation and sets us up for deception and disaster. The person who lives in fresh and wholesome expectation is mentally balanced and hopeful.

Maturity is a process or a journey. On the diagram, the first expectation is to move from D to E to F, which is a natural and biblical growth mode.

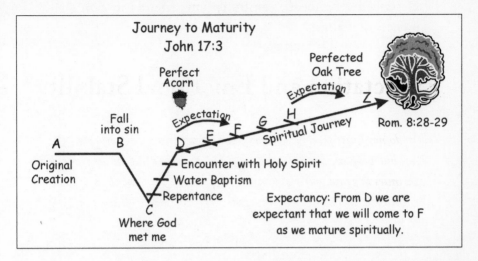

The second eexpectation, moving from H and jumping to Z, is an attempt to move into spheres or responsibilities that we have not naturally grown into and that are not normal. A teenager can hardly wait for the natural progression of time and maturity before he or she can drive a car. We often find ourselves trying to force God's hand or pressing Him for that which He knows we are not ready to receive.

Those who understand false expectancy soon discover they have *decreasing* expectations from people, including officers, educators, politicians, scientists, philosophers, and particularly religious leaders. The fact is, we are all fallen and have all come short of the glory of God (see Rom. 3:23). To be consistent with what we believe, we should not expect too much from anyone, including ourselves. Our response should be, "Of course they will act in a self-referential and sinful manner. We could not expect anything else." This is biblical reality that will keep us mentally healthy, lessen our shock, and maintain our emotional balance.

Thoughts and Questions

🦌 What stood out to you in the Scripture reading about the three descriptions of expectation?

🦌 What happens if we do not figure sin and failure into our equation of life? Why?

🌱 Describe how someone can try to jump from H to Z in the process of maturity.

Security, Identity, and Belonging

*But as many as received Him, to them He gave the right to become
children of God, even to those who believe in His name* (John 1:12).

SECURITY, IDENTITY, AND BELONGING may be the three most scarce,
expensive, and needed items for any human. Even at my age, I continually discover my own need for one or more of these to be reaffirmed by God
my Father. When Father had nothing else to give to His Son who was so
pleasing to Him, Father spoke from Heaven words that seem to sink into
the deepest longing of the human psyche: You (security) are My (identity)
beloved (belonging) Son in Whom I am well-pleased (see Matt. 3:17).

Security, identity, and belonging (SIB) result in mental health because
these can only come from above. SIB cannot be manufactured, self-gener-
ated, or earned. Because of God's love in the person of Christ, Father has
provided each of us SIB as His gift. It is what Christ accomplished, and it
is not present or absent due to our success or failure.

Security is such an important factor in our journey that Jesus makes a
special effort and gives a direct teaching to assure us that we are, without
question, within the confines of His care and love. Note the two repetitions
Jesus uses to lock us into the idea that we are as safe on our journey to the
Father as we are when we get there.

> *The sheep that are My own hear and are listening to My voice;
> and I know them, and they follow Me. And I give them eternal
> life, and they shall never lose it or perish throughout the ages.
> [To all eternity they shall never by any means be destroyed.] And
> no one is able to snatch them out of My hand. My Father, Who
> has given them to Me, is greater and mightier than all [else];*

*and no one is able to snatch [them] out of the Father's hand. I
and the Father are One* (John 10:27-30 AMP).

To place our *security* into the hands of the person who gave Himself so
freely and so painfully to purchase us as His Bride *is not a false expectation.*
We are safe, protected, and locked in His love, no matter what.

Our *identity* is in Christ, irrespective of immediate conduct, whether it
positive or negative. Our behavior is in Christ for the simple reason that we
received Christ by faith alone. Consequently, He has given us the identity
of Father and His family.

Belonging comes out of security and identity in Christ; I am His and He
is mine. Father completes His heart response by saying of the Son, "*in You
I am well pleased.*" It is God's pleasure that we belong to Him alone. Our
belonging is motivation to become a Father pleaser.

Abiding reinforces these realities until they become foundation stones
upon which we can build our lives and endure the storms so that our house
doesn't get washed away. Each of us can say: I am *secure* in God's love. My
identity is that I'm a child of God, and no one can take that from me. My
belonging is in the family of God; therefore, I can abide and rest.

Thoughts and Questions

- What is the one thing you know for sure?

- Why does security, identity, and belonging (SIB) result in
  mental health?

- Why is security not a false expectation?

Reading 108

Providence and Mental Health

We are assured and know that [God being a partner in their labor] all things work together and are [fitting into a plan] for good to and for those who love God and are called according to [His] design and purpose (Romans 8:28 AMP).

PROVIDENCE, OR DIVINE INTERVENTION, is something that God, as Father, reserves for Himself alone. It is His preferential choice whereby He is able to make *all things* work out for good in our lives. This includes our sinful nature, inclination to refuse and rebel, mistakes, and repeated dumb choices. It also includes our striving on some occasions and wanting to quit on others. Providence is able to make every circumstance serve His purpose of conforming us to the image of His Son.

The Scriptures make a distinction between Father's sovereignty and His providence. Sovereignty means that He, as Creator, has the ultimate right and unquestioned authority to do as He pleases in the earth and no one can say to Him, "What are You doing?" Providence, on the other hand, is much more personal and could be more perfectly defined as Father's care for His own. There is a difference between relating to the Creator (sovereignty) or to a Father (providence). In both cases, God is able to accomplish what is in His heart, but He most often chooses to reveal providence to His family: I will be their Father and they shall be My own. Father's care, then, takes on a filial or family dimension that is very considerate and tender.

Those who have taken the Scriptures alone, Christ alone, and faith alone as their refuge can have confidence or mental stability that God's purposes are being accomplished, even in dark circumstances. Mental rest comes out of confidence that the Creator is our Father and He knows what

He's doing. He is neither partial nor capricious. His *Agape* allows us to know His nature and mentally rest in His intentions toward us. The sovereign overview or philosophy of life is not as comforting as knowing Him in providence.

Providence is God's special care for His own children. John Knox, head of the Presbyterian Church, had a fascia board in his home in Chester, England inscribed with the words, "God's providence is mine inheritance." While ministering in that very city, my wife, Judith, and I made the effort to go to the house and see the inscription. We made it our life's message, and later had it carved into our own fireplace mantle.

Jesus' intention is for us to believe and lean into Father's providence as our inheritance. He lived His life like that and asks us to imitate Him in so doing. Providence, for the maturing believer, is embraced as an increasing desire to bow our knee, will, emotions, and intentions to the inexorable law of providence, knowing that His nature and faithfulness can be relied upon. God is our Father.

Thoughts and Questions

- In your own words, describe the difference between sovereignty and providence.

- What are some of the family dimensions of providence?

- What is the result of having confidence that the Creator is our Father and that He knows what He's doing?

PART XI

Unshakable

READING 109

Being Established

After you have suffered for a little while, the God of all grace,
who called you to His eternal glory in Christ, will Himself
perfect, confirm, strengthen and establish you (1 Peter 5:10).

NOTICE THE SEQUENCE OF the four words that Peter uses: perfect,
confirm, strengthen, and establish. To be established gives us the idea
of being unvarying, settled, or turning in one given direction. It is a spiritual quality that is lacking in those who are hesitant and divided; they are
unable to discover a quiet and permanent peace. The Aucca Indians' translation for *peace* means "sitting down in your heart." Abiding is especially
important during physical, moral, or doctrinal crises. Jesus steadfastly set
His face toward Jerusalem—He was constant and unequivocal about what
He had to do. As Kingdom priests, our commission is to remain unshaken,
so that others who are shaken can draw strength from us in their crisis.

Paul summarized his teaching to the Roman believers by saying, *"Now*
to Him who is able to establish you...according to the revelation of the mystery
which has been kept secret for long ages past" (Rom. 16:25). This constancy is
reinforced in several Scriptures:

> *I have prayed for you, that your faith may not fail; and you,*
> *when once you have turned again, strengthen your brothers*
> (Luke 22:32).

> *We sent Timothy...to strengthen and encourage you as to your*
> *faith...so that He may establish your hearts without blame* (1
> Thessalonians 3:2,13).

Comfort and strengthen your hearts in every good work and word (2 Thessalonians 2:17).

But the Lord is faithful, and He will strengthen and protect you from the evil one (2 Thessalonians 3:3).

You too be patient; strengthen your hearts, for the coming of the Lord is near (James 5:8).

Rouse yourselves and keep awake, and strengthen and invigorate what remains and is on the point of dying; for I have not found a thing that you have done [any work of yours] meeting the requirements of My God or perfect in His sight (Revelation 3:2 AMP).

Some of our best-laid plans have a tendency to die on us; these Scriptures show that being established keeps us from immoral and crazy behavior in the midst of unpredictable circumstances.

In a parable Jesus compares someone who does not act on His words with the foolish man who built his house on the sand and the floods and winds made the house fall. He compared someone who hears His words and acts upon them with the wise man who built his house on the rock and his house withstood the fierce storms (see Matt. 7:24-27). Everything and everyone that is divided and unstable must be exposed and introduced to the Kingdom, which seeks to establish us as part of the answer rather than part of the problem.

Thoughts and Questions

- In your own words, what does being established mean?

- Why would the Aucca Indians translate *peace* as "sitting down in your heart"?

- In your experience, why is it important to be established in the midst of unpredictable circumstances?

READING 110

Jesus' Example of Being Unshakable

For we have become fellows with Christ (the Messiah) *and share in all He has for us, if only we hold our first newborn confidence and original assured expectation [in virtue of which we are believers] firm and unshaken to the end* (Hebrews 3:14 AMP).

THE FOLLOWING PRINCIPLES ARE literal lifesavers. Remaining unshaken demands that we abide in *reality* with unambiguous clarity and a heart reverence for truth. Jesus exhibited being unshaken in several notable examples:

- *His thorough naturalness as a leader.* He was so real that even the prostitutes, children, and sick people came to Him; they loved Him because He was natural and real. He did not love titles, degrees, or other accoutrements of leadership. The less we seek to add to that which is natural, the more effective the Kingdom message.

- *His fearless directness.* His directness in facing the actual facts of circumstance disallowed all denial and false expectation. Jesus always stayed with the truth of the situation; He was never distracted by circumstances or wishful thinking.

- *His steadfast determination.* He was a Father pleaser. His ability to hold to the fundamental call to do the will and wishes of His Father was uncompromised. He never went off into other things seeking to accomplish or prove anything.

- *His unworldly standard of personal worth.* He touched people as they were; He never measured them by their fancy clothes or their station in life. He was not partial, so He could see and speak into any human situation.

- *His perfect candor.* Rather than being circuitous, He was clean and clear in the bestowal of appreciation or reproof. We always know what He meant and why it was being said.

- *His forthrightness in dealing with popular expectation.* The disciples were waiting for a natural rather than a spiritual Kingdom, and Jesus confronted them without ambiguity—just as he confronted the people and the Jewish religious leaders. This distinction is what cost Him His life. Dealing with popular error is never easy.

- *His reverent sobriety amid popular enthusiasm.* He was never puffed up and He was never cast down; He was always stable, established, in control of Himself and His emotions. He was the Son of Man and the Son of God whom we are able to follow.

- *His scrupulous honesty regarding the cost of discipleship.* He said simply, *"If it were not so, I would have told you"* (John 14:2). Putting the difficult cost up front is a very important model for every person, parent, leader, and follower.

- *His consistent devotion to an unselfish purpose.* Christ was the ultimate giver. His sole divine commission was to serve the will of God and to do good to all mankind.

- *His calm resoluteness in facing the consequences of His teaching and work.* False expectation as to the rewards and acclaim we would receive from following Jesus cannot be exaggerated; we will pay a price for following Jesus Christ.

These ten examples are so important; we should tape them to our bathroom mirrors and read them each morning until they are engraved upon our mind and emotions. An embrace of Kingdom reality in our walk with God and relationships with others will serve us all our days upon earth.

Thoughts and Questions

❦ In what ways can you see these ten points as lifesavers?

❦ How do they exhibit Jesus' ability to remain unshaken?

❦ Which of the ten stand out to you the most? Why?

READING 111

Principles of Abiding

[God] raised us up with Him, and seated us with Him in the heavenly places in Christ Jesus (Ephesians 2:6).

THE KINGDOM IS ABOUT abiding—being seated with Christ and seeing life's events from His perspective. One godly businessman had a rather bold sign on his desk that said: "Keep Looking Down." Those who read it thought it should say "Keep Looking Up" and wanted to question his logic; but he explained that your perspective depended on your position in Christ. "From where I am seated," he said, "I am required to keep looking down!"

Remember that abiding and being seated with Christ are both *relational* and are not simply some doctrinal position. If they do not become existentially real, you will discover the inability to do either. Truth is not enough; we must also have Life!

- Abiding forces us to embrace the Cross in daily life. We are not free to attempt to possess, acquire, or control. Abiding requires a certain kind of suffering because we are not free to extend our sovereignty and presence in all situations. We must learn to contract ourselves, refusing to engage anything that is not within our own sphere or responsibility.

- Abiding creates a field of freedom that is the result of courage and faith. This freedom needs to be guarded. We can sense when people illegally penetrate that field or get in our space, and we can then take the necessary precautions.

- Abiding preserves the real spiritual person—the one God whom others are seeking to know. Being real in an unreal world of flatterers and hidden agendas is not easy, but Jesus' ten examples from the last session will help us abide in the midst of circumstances.

- Abiding releases us to the Father. We are unafraid, comfortable, and open in His presence. When we sense sin or error going on in us we can say, "Father, I know I shouldn't be angry, but I am. Help me." When we are open to the Lord, He is able to deal with root causes.

- Abiding cultivates real freedom in the human will, spiritual growth, increased discernment, a clear conscience, and our response-ability.

- Abiding requires risk. When you cease risking, you are no longer living in the Kingdom because Kingdom life is always out on the living edge. Risk involves becoming more comfortable with uncertainties.

- Abiding is the route to the supernatural. It is the condition to answered prayer (see John 15:7). If we are puffed up and God answers our prayers, our tendency is to continue to go up into a sphere where there simply is no oxygen. If we're cast down and He doesn't answer them, we tend to exhibit the tendency to go even further into the pit.

- Abiding is a skill—a delicate balance between God's grace and personal freedom. Like snow skiing, it is a skill we must gain.

Everything works together to contribute to our freedom and to reveal God's glory (see Rom. 8:28). Abiding causes us to be safe, but it does not mean the absence of perplexities. It means an inner knowing and confidence that our Father is at work, even if we are not fully aware of all that is happening. We need to learn to see life from a *theomorphic* perspective—like we are out in space looking back at the world from God's perspective.

Thoughts and Questions

❦ In what ways are you seeing things from Christ's perspective in your current circumstances?

❦ Explain why abiding creates a field of freedom and preserves the real person.

❦ In what ways have you experienced that abiding requires risk?

READING 112

Abiding Without Condemnation

Therefore there is now no condemnation for those
who are in Christ Jesus (Romans 8:1).

AITH ONLY IN THE sufficiency of Christ's redemptive act is the working
presupposition of an abiding posture, which in the New Testament is
called "in Christ." Abiding should be without condemnation even in the
presence of failure, fear, reluctance, and/or disobedience. When Father asks
for obedience, it is for the simple reason of teaching us how to walk in the
Spirit. Failure, refusal, or outright fear to try it is rather normal and, from
Father's perspective, is almost expected.

I remember teaching each of our four children to dive head first rather
than to jump into the pool. Depending on the amount of risk—balking,
anger, and fear can all be part of the process of moving into a more mature
sphere and gaining confidence. No one who is unwilling to embrace failure
can possibly learn something new. When we fail, we need to simply forget
the embarrassment and soreness, get up, and try again. The next time we
fail—and there will be a next time, because failure is inevitable, practice
failing without condemnation. Don't run, hide or shift blame. Learn to
accept it and repent without guilt or condemnation because Christ carries
the guilt, and in Christ there is an absence of condemnation. We will never
learn to walk in the Spirit until and unless we can fail, get up again, and
move into the skill with new determination.

Abiding is the only known antidote to both pride and anger; it keeps
us steady. Both are vacuums that force us *up* if possible and *down* if that is
more effective and circumstantial. The enemy doesn't care whether you go
up or down, all he wants to do is get you out of the abiding posture. The

skill of abiding must be learned individually, then corporately as a couple, a family, a church, a group or a team.

We can only abide in God's *Agape*. Whenever it gets through to us that the Father loves us in the same manner that He loves Christ, we can actually be at rest. We are being trained in Father's gymnasium, and failure is part of the package. When we learn to abide in the living room rather than the attic or basement, it allows us to know a deep intimacy with God. The Kingdom is about abiding—being seated with Christ and seeing life's events from His perspective. It is about bringing each of us, and ultimately, all creation, to a place of freedom.

Thoughts and Questions

❦ Why does God want to set us free from guilt and condemnation?

❦ Why do you think another failure is inevitable?

❦ In what ways is abiding the antidote to both pride and anger?

Paradox of Hedonism and Legalism

By the works of the Law no flesh will be justified in His sight; for through the Law comes the knowledge of sin (Romans 3:20).

THE PARADOX OF HEDONISM. Hedonism is living for pleasure or enjoyment—happiness is the goal. The focus of hedonism is me and the object of hedonism is the third million, the third house, the third luxury automobile, none of which have the capacity to bring happiness. Hedonism, which those who live this way do not seem to understand, is based on the law of diminishing returns: the more we get of anything, the less it satisfies.

Suppose I tell you that you can look in any pocket of my jacket except the left one. Most of us are not interested in any other pocket but that one. *This is a law of life: prohibition awakens desire.* When we know we can't have something, desire is awakened, resulting in ungoverned behavior (see Rom. 7:7-8). It is what we cannot have that attracts us. The unconquered or the unavailable becomes the object of our ungoverned desire. This is the motivation in most cases of rape, addiction, or pornography. It is even evident in materialism because it is the promise that attracts and then denies. The law of diminishing returns is a hard taskmaster.

Adam and Eve were given access to all the trees in the Garden but one. The prohibited tree was the only one in which they became interested. Desires are awakened in us the moment someone says we can't have it. The alcoholic who repeatedly says, "I will never drink again!" will likely be opening his next bottle before long because his focus is on the alcohol and all the reasons he should not have it. The same is true of other obsessive-compulsive issues.

The paradox of legalism is similar to that of hedonism. Hedonism is the positive pole and legalism is the negative pole of the same circuit. With legalism, the focus is me and the object is doing things right. Have you ever made lists of what you thought you should do to please God? I have. It was something like this—read more of the Scriptures, pray longer and earlier, fast more often. My list kept growing, and every time I failed, I would start beating myself up and would end up cast down in condemnation. If I succeeded, I was puffed up in pride. The basic problem was that my entire focus was wrong. As long as we are focusing on ourselves, whether it is sensual or religious, the object of our focus expands, and our whole world is taken over by it. Oh, yes, religion can become obsessive-compulsive. All of us who have walked out of legalism will testify to how addictive it really is. After all, God gave ten commands and legalism turned them into 613 rules.

Thoughts and Questions

- In what ways have you experienced hedonism and legalism?

- Why do you think prohibition awakens desire?

- Explain how hedonism is the positive pole and legalism the negative pole of the same circuit.

READING 114

Paradox of Grace

And God is able to make all grace abound to you, so that
always having all sufficiency in everything, you may have
an abundance for every good deed (2 Corinthians 9:8).

THE PARADOX OF GRACE is God's gift to us. In grace, our focus is Christ, and the object is the Father. Jesus said that He was the way, truth, and life, and that no one could come to the Father except by Him (see John 14:6). John Baille explains this paradox well:

A far greater and deeper paradox than those which we have been considering lies at the very heart of the Christian life and vitally effects every part of it. It is what we may call the paradox of grace. Its essence lies in the conviction which a Christian man possesses, that every good thing in him, every good thing he does, is somehow not wrought by himself but by God. This is a highly paradoxical conviction, for in ascribing all to God it does not abrogate human personality nor disclaim personal responsibility. Never is human action more truly and fully personal, never does the agent feel more perfectly free, than in those moments of which he can say as a Christian that whatever good was in them was not his but God's. The paradox of grace requires less repentance and more believing. It is inevitable that we are going to fail. When we fail on the religious road, we start focusing on ourselves, which causes the failure to expand, and leads to our unavoidable embrace of guilt and condemnation.[1]

When Luther sinned, he repented for four hours without stopping, until his spiritual director said to him, "You're forgiven! You're forgiven!" What was Luther's problem? Self focus. If our focus is on Christ and His righteousness, we get more of Him and can say, "Thank You for what You have done for me. I bless You for Your goodness, Your faithfulness, and Your grace!"

Take care to see where your focus lands in your next failure. If the focus is on Christ and the awareness of Jesus taking all things in us to the Father, including the failure itself, our object becomes the Father and grace and peace become ours. Stability and usefulness will follow.

Thoughts and Questions

- Explain the paradox of grace.

- Why do you think the paradox of grace would allow you to abide when hedonism and legalism would not?

- Why is it important where our focus is?

ENDNOTE

1. John Baillie, *A Diary of Private Prayer,* "Walking in Light" Reading 225, 114. New York: Charles Scriber's Sons, 1949, 1977, 1996.

Roots and Fruits of Abiding

As for what was sown on thin (rocky) *soil, this is he who hears the Word and at once welcomes and accepts it with joy; Yet it has no real root in him, but is temporary* (inconstant, lasts but a little while); *and when affliction or trouble or persecution comes on account of the Word, at once he is caused to stumble [he is repelled and begins to distrust and desert Him Whom he ought to trust and obey] and he falls away* (Matthew 13:20-21 AMP).

ABIDING MEANS HAVING A firm root in the Kingdom, which produces an abundance of fruit in our lives. Movement away from our state of abiding (up into God's space or down into rage or depression) is precipitated by either success or affliction/persecution. And, as Matthew shows us, affliction and persecution come because of the Word of the Kingdom. When events of persecution or affliction present themselves, we are forced to respond. Our choices are three: First, we can abide, unmoved, unshaken; second, we can attempt, in pride and egoism, to enter God's sphere, trying to control everything or everyone; third, we can go down in depression. While in the basement, we are sure that even God cannot do anything about this situation! We are as deceived when we think we can do it as we are when we think we can't. Deception comes from both sides of the paradigm.

Every experienced pastor dreads a certain phenomenon—when Frank comes back from the hospital, and he has just prayed for someone who was sick and he or she got healed. As a result of this one healing, spiritual pride suggests that Frank now has the gift of healing and should travel around healing people. So he begins making plans to get an RV, buy a tent, and start a magazine. The spiritual vacuum of pride seems to suck him up into a realm that is not his. God uses persecution and affliction to get Frank back down into his own sphere. This is spiritual warfare but in a different context than most of us has been taught.

The euphoric feeling that takes us into realms of unreality is just as dangerous as feelings of depression, which cast us down and causes us to be cynical. If you have ever had serious doubts or outright cynicism about whether or not Christianity was real, you were probably engulfed in the downward vacuum force field. It sucks us in like a magnet. Either way, the result is lack of fruit.

Irrespective of whether the forces take us up or down, we are moved from the Kingdom posture of abiding and fruitfulness.

Thoughts and Questions

❦ Explain why abiding requires roots in the Kingdom.

❦ In what ways have you experienced the deception of euphoria and/or depression?

❦ Which do you think is more dangerous—euphoria or depression?

PART XII

Reality and Unreality

READING 116

Unreality

For the anxious longing of the creation waits eagerly for the revealing of the sons of God. For the creation was subjected to futility, not willingly, but because of Him who subjected it, in hope that the creation itself also will be set free from its slavery to corruption into the freedom of the glory of the children of God (Romans 8:19-21).

UNREALITY IS BOTH SECULAR and religious. Religious unreality is clearly expressed when the Jews argued with Jesus about how free they were by stating, *"We are Abraham's descendents, and have never yet been enslaved to anyone; how is it that you say, 'You shall become free'?"* (John 8:33).

It never ceases to amaze me that while they were speaking, the Roman soldier standing guard was in full sight. The bondage of Judah to Rome was more real than one could imagine. Unreality persists. Denial prevails. Popular error remains. Secular unreality is equally obvious. As Paul clearly stated:

> *Because when they knew and recognized Him as God, they did not honor and glorify Him as God or give Him thanks. But instead they became futile and godless in their thinking [with vain imaginings, foolish reasoning, and stupid speculations] and their senseless minds were darkened* (Romans 1:21 AMP).

The knowledge of freedom becomes cyclical frustration. Freedom cries out for release in each of us, while internal and external circumstances dictate our bondage. Paul stated it well: *"Wretched man that I am! Who will set me free from the body of this death?"* (Rom. 7:24). Note the cry was *"Who will set me free,"* not *"what* will set me free." Freedom cannot be attained by assumed unreality, which is exceedingly futile. In order to be free from unreality, we must surrender to Christ who is ultimate reality. Freedom is relational. We must identify and release all illegal attractions that compete with our undivided affections for God Himself. He insists that we set our affections upon Him, taking them away from all that is both worldly and religious. He wants us to love Him with all of our heart, soul, mind and strength because He knows this is reality and will bring us freedom. The simple fact is that once we move in this direction, there is little room left for self-focus and unreality.

Eros is ultimate unreality—it promises freedom when it itself is held in bondage. Nothing demonstrates unreality more forcibly than Peter's words about false teachers: *"promising them freedom while they themselves are slaves of corruption; for by what a man is overcome, by this he is enslaved"* (2 Pet. 2:19). Unreality must give way to reality. Faith must become *Agape* substance, but faith that is *"activated and energized and expressed and working through love"* (see Gal. 5:6 AMP). Luther said that God's indwelling Word *creates* that which is experiential. We are not suggesting ungoverned subjective religious experience or emotionalism. Reality results in freedom because God is ultimate reality. The closer we are to God, the closer we are to pure Kingdom reality.

Thoughts and Questions

- In what ways is unreality both secular and religious?

- How can we get free from unreality?

- How does faith become *Agape* substance?

READING 117

Kingdom Reality

You will know (the true) *God and He will*
set you free (John 8:31-32 UBS).

LIKE PILATE, WE ARE sometimes forced to make decisions we would
rather avoid or delay; and we find ourselves pressed to ask, *"What is
Truth?"* (John 18:38 AMP). Jesus had already spelled out to the Jews, "If you
obey My teaching you will be My disciples; you will know the truth and the
truth will make you free" (see John 8:31-32). *Truth takes us from unreality to
reality and consequently, to freedom.* For Jesus, truth is not simply that which
is opposed to what is false; neither does truth suggest the accumulation of
facts. Truth is used to identify ultimate reality, which is nothing less than
God Himself. Christ does not have truth, He *is* truth.

When Paul expounded on the Kingdom in Romans Chapter 8, he used
two unusual Greek terms: *vanity* and *unreality.* The hurting world is held
captive in these two concepts. Baptism in water literally takes us out of four
bondages: shadow, vanity, unreality, and darkness. John's Epistle picks up
this theme by stating that the whole world lies in the lap of the evil one,
that is, shadow, vanity, unreality, and darkness. Baptism is our preferential
response to Christ's love: it buries all that would keep us from knowing
Him and walking in His governmental Kingdom of substance and reality,
or *Agape* and Light.

The *kairos* moment occurs when we enter the waters of baptism. Like
a bride expressing her single desire for her bridegroom, our baptism illus-
trates that all that keeps us from knowing and loving Him is to be buried
in the waters of death, both us to the world and the world to us. In this
light, water baptism can be seen as the prophetic perfect (the now and

not yet, or both present and future reality). God declares the end (omega) before the beginning (alpha) and then brings it to pass. When we come up from the waters of baptism, we are His alone. His purpose and providence begin to fulfill all that is included in the promise of the Father. Going from shadow to substance is more than monotheism or a clearer doctrine of God's attributes.

Reality can be seen in this diagram in Paul's three choices, as set forth in the *Agape Road*:

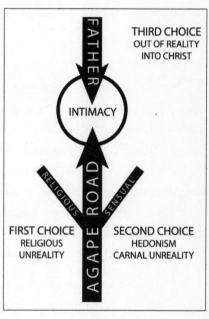

- First choice: Return to legal obedience by means of Moses' law: religious unreality.

- Second choice: Sensual freedom and false liberty: hedonism and carnal unreality.

- Third choice: Led by the Spirit on the *Agape* road to the Father: out of unreality into Christ.

Kingdom reality faces us with some hard questions and Jesus put the cost up front: Are we willing to be used by God in the manner demonstrated by His life? Are we ready to be treated wrongly or sinned against without reacting?

Thoughts and Questions

- Explain your interpretation of: *"You will know the truth and the truth will make you free."*

- How does water baptism take us to Kingdom reality?

- In what other ways does Kingdom reality face us with hard questions?

Kingdom Reality—Paradox and Tension

But as many as received Him, to them He gave the right to become
children of God, even to those who believe in His name (John 1:12).

T HE *Agape* ROAD IS the road to uncreated reality because it alone takes
us to the Father. It is a journey of discovery that progresses into a
more mature and enlightened sense of our security, identity, and belonging in Christ. These were given to us in the prophetic perfect, which stands
for both now and not yet. What we have now is the real thing. When the
Kingdom comes in fullness, it will not be different; there will just be more
of it! Like any child, we are learning to be that which we already are—sons
and daughters of our Father.

The prophetic perfect calls and urges us to

> *know Him, and the power of His resurrection and the fellow-*
> *ship of His sufferings, being conformed to His death; in order*
> *that I may attain to the resurrection from the dead. Not that I*
> *have already obtained it, or have already become perfect, but I*
> *press on in order that I may lay hold of that for which also I was*
> *laid hold of by Christ Jesus* (Philippians 3:10-12).

The paradox concerns the person of Christ, whom we seek to discover
and walk with in the prophetic perfect as Father's own sons and daughters. This paradox increases our determination and unwavering desire
to discover that true self—the one who lives in reality, allowing us to
become conformed to the image of Christ. The prophetic perfect brings
the two faith postures together: *We are now all that God wants us to be in*
Christ. This means that in Christ we are now perfect and fully pleasing

to the Father; there is nothing more that we can do to make ourselves more righteous.

The paradox, which must be held in tension, is the second part: *We are not yet all He wants us to be.* We are still in need of Father's love to mature and function within our person. In order for this to be fulfilled, He uses all things in this life to bring *Agape* to perfection within us. His intention is to replicate His own love in each of us, no matter how long it takes. This is why He said "Follow Me" and is leading us on a journey of *Agape*.

All Kingdom truth must be held in the tension of now and not yet. Biblical truth is remarkably self-correcting and organic, which means that it does not disturb other truth.

Thoughts and Questions

🐝 What is the end result of the *Agape* road?

🐝 Describe the two faith postures of the prophetic perfect.

🐝 Why do you think all Kingdom truth needs to be in tension?

READING 119

Surrender and the Cross

*Again, the kingdom of heaven is like a man who is a dealer in search of
fine and precious pearls, who, on finding a single pearl of great price,
went and sold all he had and bought it* (Matthew 13:45-46 AMP).

A FEW SESSIONS AGO, WE learned that in order to be free from unreality, we must surrender. Surrender involves discovering truth that is so valuable that we are eager and willing to sell or trade everything to which we are illegally attached for greater insight and an entrance into the Kingdom. In order to be free to follow truth, we must break out of our *Eros* prisons in both our mental thought processes as well as our emotional and behavioral processes. This is what it means to sell it all. Jesus instructed us about the manner in which we are to buy and trade when He said,

> *I counsel you to purchase from Me gold refined and tested by fire,
> that you may be [truly] wealthy, and white clothes to clothe you
> and to keep the shame of your nudity from being seen, and salve
> to put on your eyes, that you may see* (Revelation 3:18 AMP).

The Father wants us to be clothed, unashamed, and have eyes to see spiritual things. This starts with an *Agape* conversion from being a taker to a giver and is the Father's route to our inheritance and usefulness in His Kingdom. However, if we do not let go or surrender, our attempts to buy truth are often lost, confused, or rejected because of the uncertainty created by mixture. *Eros* thinks it will surely lose. *Agape* knows that it is the Father who is asking for our surrender, so it will surely be for our good. The book of James says that the divided or double-minded person should not expect to receive from the Lord (see James 1:7-8). Failure or ignorance of the necessity to yield our inner desire to Him who is ultimate reality leaves us double-minded. This allows confusion to enter.

"Follow Me" can only mean that Jesus intends to take us somewhere for our sake as well as for His, but we cannot be double-minded in following Him. Our journey of discovery is severely limited if we do not follow Him to where He wants to take us. Failure or refusal to follow signifies that we are double-minded. The painful cost of failing to follow is described as *the eternal childhood of the believer* and is clearly described in the Book of Hebrews. The word *infant* is used to describe a believer who, by the time and experience of his journey, should have grown up but remains unprofitable and essentially useless for the work of the Kingdom even though fully loved (see Heb. 5:12-13). Only by means of repeated surrenders, by selling and trading all that holds us back from following, and by buying truth and refusing to sell it are we able to enter the Kingdom and walk in the governmental purpose of the Father and His Son, our Lord Jesus Christ. Be assured that God will providentially use all things to get us there. On this journey it is the Cross alone that disarms and defeats the seven giants (unreality). It is the Cross alone that precipitates our surrender. Apart from the Cross, our inheritance remains in the realm of the prophetic perfect. Even though the Cross has been purchased and paid for by the Lord Jesus, if we have a fear of surrender or refuse to follow Him, we remain infants because it is experientially unrealized in our life. His Kingdom waits for our preferential choice.

Thoughts and Questions

- 🦌 Describe your understanding of what it means to surrender.

- 🦌 What are some results of not surrendering?

- 🦌 What is involved in growing out of our infant stage?

READING 120

The Joy of Growing Up

The kingdom of God is like a man who scatters seed upon
the ground, and then continues sleeping and rising night
and day while the seed sprouts and grows and increases—
he knows not how (Mark 4:26-27 AMP).

JESUS WORDS "FOLLOW ME" assume that we are *addressable*; i.e., God can speak to us and we are capable of understanding His purpose and meaning. It also assumes that we are *accountable,* signifying that we are to be held responsible for that choice that is evidenced by repeatedly *surrendering* to the Cross whatever hinders us from being followers. This requires *maturity.* As we saw in the last session, it is fully possible to not grow up and still be loved by the Father. Father, however, is not able to address an infant and expect a proper response and full accountability!

Christ deposits His *Agape* in us as the incorruptible Seed in the new birth, and He then addresses the Seed in the person, asking us to follow Him. As we mature and the Seed grows in us, our capacity to hear His voice also grows. He imparted the capacity for *Agape*, knowing that it is *Agape* speaking to *Agape* which calls us to a journey that is essentially against ourselves. Because our love for Christ supersedes our love for ourselves, it allows us to *surrender* whatever hinders us in our journey.

The Lord sincerely loved the rich young ruler (see Mark 10:17-27). When asked to follow Jesus, *he simply could not do it* because he was attached to too many things. He was addressable and he was accountable; however, he could not surrender. Every one of us has responded in a similar way at some point in our journey. Because we don't know what eventually happened to the rich young ruler, but we do know Father's nature, consider the possibility that Jesus approached this dear man at a later time, expecting a positive response. I know He has done that for me.

When Father addresses us, expecting a proper response in the form of a preferential choice, He often accompanies it with a moment of discovery. When we have discovered the treasure in the field, it would be quite difficult to just keep plowing and pretend nothing had changed. The discovery asks for our *surrender* of all that we have owned, known, or understood in our natural or spiritual lives. It is Father who has provoked us to respond for the purpose of *owning* what He has allowed us to discover. This is what it means to seek first the Kingdom of God.

The encounter with the treasure in the field (see Matt. 13:44) imparts faith. It also results in the expectation that we will abandon our religious confidence (both positive and negative) in ourselves. When we see the Kingdom purpose, we can fling ourselves with reckless faith upon that which Christ has done in our behalf. This requires maturity and was Paul's response to the Kingdom when he saw the glory of God in the face of Christ.

Thoughts and Questions

❦ What are the three assumptions that precede our response to His call "Follow Me," and what do they mean to you?

❦ In what ways have your responded like the rich young ruler?

❦ In what ways have you abandoned without caution your religious confidence?

READING 121

Freedom From Playing Religious Games

Be free men, and yet do not make your freedom an excuse for base conduct, but be God's bondservants (1 Peter 2:16 WNT).

Without the surrender required by the Cross, the guaranteed presence of the seven giants allows *Eros* to turn our freedom into religion and our joy into an unbearable burden. We do so by rationalization. In the absence of the Cross, freedom is biblically true but experientially unrealized. We can and do use our freedom in a wrong and injurious manner.

In my years of walking with the Lord in many nations and denominations, I discovered that outright religious and philosophical game playing disallows our journey down the *Agape* road—the journey from unreality to reality. Religious games, like philosophical ones, cannot and will not bring

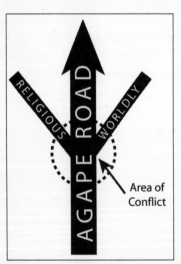

us to know God the Father. Both God the Father and Jesus Christ His Son *are Agape*; they do not *have Agape*. Their very DNA nature *is Agape*. Therefore, avoiding the alternate roads is more than game playing; it is the ultimate issue of all of life.

The dotted line on this diagram represents the area of conflict, which always involves something either religious or worldly. The alternative choice is to stay on the *Agape* road. When we are in the midst of temptation, crisis, or conflict of interest within the area of conflict, we may be hindered from following Him, but we are not hindered from *believing* in Him. This alternate posture of believing is what it means to abide, and we are instructed to do so until the *Agape* road comes clear. A strange and unknown willingness emerges from deep within, and we are then enabled, capacitated, and encouraged to follow. That willingness is *Agape* calling to *Agape*, Christ calling from eternity to eternity. He is asking to be our priority—to be loved with all of our heart, soul, mind, and strength.

Abiding is our response to the severe pressure of temptation. Jesus taught us to abide by instruction and example. Under the most severe temptations, Christ's response was to abide in that which was written. *He did nothing, said nothing, and refused to engage the tempter in debate or conflict.* He waited expectantly for the fog to clear. When He could see the road, He walked. When He could not see the road, He waited.

The proper response to the prophetic perfect is this: "I know Father's love is true. I can do nothing to bring it to pass or to make it happen. My faith allows me to rest in this completed work of Christ until I am able to follow Him once again." With this posture, we can make this journey without missing it so many times. Abiding allows us to exchange our unreality for Kingdom reality, the shakable for the unshakable. This glorifies the Father, results in Kingdom usefulness, and takes us into the knowledge of God and of His Son, our Lord Jesus Christ.

Thoughts and Questions

- Describe the end result of religious and philosophical game playing.

- What can we do when circumstances hinder us from following Jesus?

- What do we do when we cannot see the road?

The Kingdom as the Treasure and the Pearl

The kingdom of heaven is like something precious buried in a field, which a man found and hid again; again the kingdom of heaven is like a man who is a dealer in search of fine and precious pearls (Matthew 13:44-45 AMP).

IN ORDER FOR THE existential reality of the treasure and pearl to become our own, we must take hold of three words with our heart and mind: *discovery, surrender, possession*. First, we *discover* the Kingdom as the treasure. Second, we begin to *surrender* to that which we discovered. Third, the pearl is our own *possession*.

Abiding and a daily commitment to follow Jesus with wholehearted dependence upon His righteousness alone will disallow us from buying into other unreality, however appealing. This is true whether the appeal is secular or religious. Holding God's righteousness as the Kingdom treasure and the pearl means that we have sold or traded all that we have understood about life and religion for God's gift discovered in the person of Christ. This is the good news. It is radical and different and results in freedom. We soon discover that there is little up either of the two alternate roads that possesses the capacity to awaken our desire and there is even less for which we would trade. There is nothing that could profitably add anything to our being complete in the person of Christ. Seeing this truth allows us to enter the Kingdom of relational reality for which Christ came and into which He brought us by means of the new birth.

People in the religious and world systems may think the Kingdom person has entered total *unreality*. However, the upside-down Kingdom declares that we have discovered *ultimate reality* and that selling everything is not only the right thing to do, but it should be done with alacrity and joy. Both the religious and the secular systems lose their control over us when we have in our possession *by faith* the treasure and the pearl. The intimidation and envy of those in the systems of this world come from our not seeming to need or be dependent upon that which is temporal. Christ is sufficient; He will take us to the Father. This is the freedom that Christ spoke of when He said,

> *If you abide in My word [hold fast to My teachings and live in accordance with them], you are truly My disciples. And you will know the Truth, and the Truth will set you free* (John 8:31–32 AMP).

Freedom, as Christ has defined and applied it, must never be seen or presented as rank individualism or as anti-establishment but according to the Kingdom norm by which all churches should be measured. Luke explained Christ's authority over the world systems:

> *Because He has fixed a day when He will judge the world righteously* (justly) *by a Man Whom He has destined and appointed for that task, and He has made this credible and given conviction and assurance and evidence to everyone by raising Him from the dead* (Acts 17:31 AMP).

If, for any reason, we give in to the temptation to sell our treasure or trade our Kingdom pearl for something the religious or secular system offers, we will have again chosen to travel the *Eros* road of unreality. Jesus knows both the road and the end result, and He said quite plainly, "Do not seek to save your life or you will lose it!" (See Matt. 16:25.)

Thoughts and Questions

- Describe your experience with *discovery, surrender,* and *possession.*

- What keeps us from buying into unreality, however appealing?

❦ What happens when we have in our possession *by faith* the treasure and the pearl?

READING 123

Opening Ourselves to Father's Pathos

Saul, why are you persecuting Me? (Acts 9:4).

FOR MANY YEARS BIBLE scholars thought that God, because He was God, could not and did not suffer with His creation. Not only do I believe that God suffers in and through His own people, but He also suffers in the context of being a Father without impinging on the perfection of His Godhead. If you can enter into Father's heart and continue cultivating yourself as a Father pleaser, you will experience some of the light edges of His own suffering for a cosmic creation that waits for the purpose of its Creator.

A Greek word for "suffering" is *pathema* (see 1 Pet. 1:11), a derivative of the word *pathos*. It is a real and necessary experience for all of us, but it needs a fresh, new emphasis within the larger Body of Christ. In the following Scripture, Peter quite freely uses a verb related to pathos: "*He who has suffered* [pathonto] *in the flesh has ceased from sin*" (1 Pet. 4:1). He then introduces the mystery of physical suffering as related to moral behavior. Few things could be more important.

First, God suffered *for us* through Christ so that we might be His sons and daughters. Surely, one cannot think that it was anything less than genuine pain to give His own Son to the betrayal!

Second, when the Body of Christ is suffering, He actually enters into the suffering *with us* (see Isa. 63:9). Jesus, in asking why Saul was persecuting Him, identified Himself with His people in a very intimate manner.

Third, He suffers *in us*. As parents, we can fully identify with God in fatherhood when He is required to embrace and suffer through the traumas and failures of our lives just because He lives in us. He chose us to be His dwelling, and when we take Him places He doesn't want to go, He endures a certain kind of suffering. He is, however, covenantally faithful to us even when we cause Him difficulty and pain. Think of Christ identifying with Judas, whom He sought to cover and give comfort to until the final act of betrayal.

Fourth, He suffers *because of us*. As a pastor, there was a widow in my church who had suffered from just about everything you could think of: childhood incest, an alcoholic and physically abusive husband, deep rejection, and consummate insecurity. She was one of the most beat-up people I had ever known. I was convinced that the Lord had given her to me to care for and love. She went to a meeting where a big name prophet was speaking, seeking to make a name for himself. Seeing this little waif of a woman, undefended and vulnerable, sitting in the second or third row, he said to her in a loud, authoritative voice: "You there, stand up." Trembling, she stood up, and in the presence of more than a thousand people he said to her, "The Lord shows me that you are a hypocrite, disobedient in the sight of God." She was so thoroughly crushed that she became increasingly ill from that day as the poisonous arrow did its work. For three years I visited, prayed, and watched her atrophy inside. At the end, her death seemed like a gift. Because it was *a man of God* who spoke those words, I was unable to break the power of that curse. She died believing that God the Father had told her she was a hypocrite. I am sure God suffered being so grossly misrepresented.

God really does suffer for us, with us, in us, and because of us.

Thoughts and Questions

- ☥ Describe an experience when you suffered on behalf of someone you loved.

- ☥ Why would Peter say, *"He who has suffered* [pathos] *in the flesh has ceased from sin"*?

- ☥ In what ways do you think God suffers on behalf of the Body of Christ?

READING 124

There Is Another King

There is another king, Jesus (Acts 17:7).

T HIS KING ESSENTIALLY CONFRONTS and challenges our personal sovereignty without apology. Simply stated, when His Kingdom comes, our kingdom goes. It is an understatement to say that this is complex and difficult. This is the the tribulation that Paul stated we needed: *"strengthening the souls of the disciples, encouraging them to continue in the faith, and saying, "Through many tribulations we must enter the kingdom of God""* (Acts 14:22).

It is the nature of all spiritual warfare. Oswald Chambers asked, "Do I want to be identified with His death, to be killed right out to all interest in sin, in worldliness, in self—to be so identified with Jesus that I am spoilt for everything else but Him?"[1] Repentance is the surrender of our fallen personal sovereignty, rather than the surrender of the external demands of drugs, alcohol, or illicit sex. Our response to this uninvited King and His obtrusive entrance into our sphere, as well as the overt confrontation with His Kingship in our life causes several reactions.

The first is outright *denial* that there is any problem. In denial we choose to run, hide, and shift blame. Second, we don't really want to deal with the problem, so we *avoid* it. Third, we *endure* the problem and go right on through it

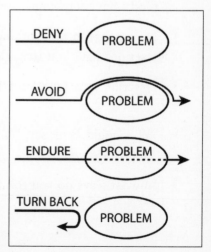

without changing. Enduring reveals itself most plainly in anger, refusal, or even threats, as we are determined to preserve our personal sovereignty. Fourth, we *turn back*. This is what backsliding is all about.

The fifth possible response is to acknowledge that there is another King of kings: one who fully intends to invade our space. Our proper response to His invasion is eagerness to discover what it is He is wanting and to surrender our personal sovereignty to Him. This is the Bent Knee Society (see Eph. 3:14). Once we are secure in Christ, the Lord loves us enough to show us to us, allowing us to see what we are actually like apart from Him.

When the eternal, sovereign King decides to invade our space, it is called the coming of the Kingdom. When we pray, "Thy Kingdom come," we better know what we're praying for because in order for Him to answer that prayer, it will require His invasion of our space. Thy Kingdom come—and my kingdom goes. In the occupation of this conquered territory, He is expecting us to surrender all seven giants to Him. We are not permitted to give Him five of the giants, preserving *Stay in Control* and *Remain Undisturbed* at our own comfort level. In exchange for our surrender of *Eros* control over our lives, another King reigns and brings with Him freedom and reality in every area of our lives.

Thoughts & Questions

- In what ways have you experienced the principle that when God's Kingdom comes, our kingdom goes?

- In response to His entrance into our sphere which of the four reactions have you struggled with the most?

- Describe your understanding of the Bent Knee Society.

ENDNOTE

1. Chambers, Oswald, *My Utmost for His Highest*, December 23.

PART XIII

A Vision for the Future

Reading 125

Crystal Clear River

*Then he showed me a river of the water of life, clear as crystal, coming
from the throne of God and of the Lamb…and the leaves of the tree were
for the healing of the nations. There will no longer be any curse…they will
see His face, and His name will be on their foreheads* (Revelation 22:1-4).

Y EARS AGO, I WAS traveling from Lima, Peru up to a high mountain
town called Huancayo, Peru with a family in a Volvo station wagon.
The mountain went up to almost 14,000 feet, and we were crossing the
peak at around 11,000 feet. As we crossed over the peak of the Andes and
began our decent down the other side, I saw pure, snowcapped mountains.
The snow was just beginning to melt. We stopped to let the car cool off and
to take a break. Hanging off the edge of a cliff was a large icicle that was
melting. One drop at a time, it joined many other drips that formed little
rivulets, and then streams that cascaded down the mountain, eventually
joining the mighty Amazon River that flowed into the Atlantic Ocean. The
river began at the top of the mountain. I understand that it is possible to
find fresh water several miles out at sea. This is how God's river—the Body
of Christ—is formed: one drip at a time. Your life really does matter.

John the revelator was called one of the Sons of Thunder (see Mark
3:17) because he was not exactly slow to anger. At about 97 years old and
exiled on the island of Patmos, he wrote an epistle addressing believers as
"little children." He said that we should "love one another" (see 1 John 4:7)
and repeated this six times. Then, in Revelation 22, John gave us a vision
for the future—a river of the water of life.

The crystal clear river of life is God's love without mixture being released
to the world. It comes to us as pure *Agape* without any *Eros* mixture. Some

rivers are so contaminated with doctrine, church fights, manipulation, and control that the nations of the world have difficulty drinking the water. A river, amazingly enough, has the capacity of self-cleansing provided there is not too much contamination. It throws the contaminated items up on the banks and continues to run.

The river of God is clear as crystal because it originates from the throne of God—the very center of the Kingdom. The nations of the world should be able to drink freely without having to ingest all the religious, *Eros* contamination. This river is designed to reach out with the *Agape* of God—compassion, grace, slow to anger, mercy, truth, faithful, and forgiving so that the nations can be healed.

John also talked about the Tree of Life, which brings healing to the nations (see Rev. 22:2). He then says these significant words: *"They shall see His face and His name will be on their foreheads"* (Rev. 22:4). There is no greater intimacy offered in the whole Bible than this. When we have truly yielded our lives to God, our whole way of looking at life undergoes a tremendous transformation and our minds are so renewed that the reality of Father's very name can be written on our foreheads. This is the impartation of the mind of Christ, which has become ours because of the incorruptible, Eternal Seed.

Thoughts and Questions

🎺 At 97 years old, why would John reduce the focus of his Epistle to *"Little children, love one another"*?

🎺 What is the crystal clear river of life?

🎺 Why is transformation required so that God can write His name on your forehead?

READING 126

Three Rivers

If anyone is thirsty, let him come to Me and drink (John 7:37).

RIVERS PROVIDE NOURISHMENT AND moisture that is needed for life. In the Scriptures there are three significant rivers.

The first is Ezekiel's river. This is the same river John saw. It's a river of God's purposes increasing in the earth. Ezekiel was led through water *"reaching the ankles...[then] reaching the knees...[then] the loins...[then] it was a river that I could not ford, for the water had risen, enough water to swim in, a river that could not be forded"* (Ezekiel 47:3-5). Ezekiel is prophesying about the next two rivers that were to come.

The second river is Jesus' river. If we are thirsty, He calls us to come and drink. He adds: *"He who believes in Me [who cleaves to and trusts in and relies on Me]...from his innermost being shall flow [continuously] springs and rivers of living water"* (John 7:38 AMP). Jesus was speaking of the river of the Holy Spirit that was to come; it would be an increasing river. There is a difference between something flowing out of us and us being immersed in something. There should be a river of life flowing out from the innermost being of each of us; we should not be just damp sponges.

The third is the river of the Holy Spirit. Jesus' river merges into the power and presence of the Holy Spirit. This river is also ever-increasing.

> *But this He spoke of the Spirit, whom those who believed in Him were to receive; for the Spirit was not yet given, because Jesus was not yet glorified* (John 7:39).

Scholars and staticians say that there are more than 500 million plus people in the earth who have had a meaningful encounter with the Holy

Spirit. Others make the count closer to 1 billion if we include what is happening in China. In spite of institutional opposition, the river of the Holy Spirit continues to increase and flow.

Each of us is just a drip! Many times, we do not think our life really matters. But, if our own single drip could be free from hidden agendas or trying to acquire, possess, or illegally attempting to control others, we could add to the *purity* (rather than the contamination) of the crystal clear river of God. Being a drip without mixture means we have been conformed to the image of Jesus Christ. If it can happen to one drip, it can happen to ten, to a thousand, to ten thousand, etc. Hurting people are looking for a clear drop of water.

> *For I was hungry, and you gave Me something to eat; I was thirsty, and you gave Me something to drink; I was a stranger, and you invited Me in; naked, and you clothed Me; I was sick, and you visited Me; I was in prison, and you came to Me* (Matthew 25:35-36).

Allow God to work His *Agape* into your own person so that you find yourself conformed to the image of Christ with His characteristics flowing out of your innermost being like a river that brings life to the nations.

Thoughts and Questions

- What is the difference between a river flowing out of us, and being immersed in a river?

- In what ways does your single drip count?

- Who do you know who is looking for a clear drop of water? What can you do to satisfy them?

Reading 127

Love What He Loves

*You have loved righteousness [You have delighted in integrity, virtue,
and uprightness in purpose, thought, and action] and You have hated
lawlessness (injustice and iniquity). Therefore God, [even] Your
God (Godhead), has anointed You with the oil of exultant joy and
gladness above and beyond Your companions* (Hebrews 1:9 AMP).

THE KINGDOM IS TOTALLY relational. Father is seeking those who will worship Him in spirit and truth, not on a mountain or in Jerusalem. He is looking for Father pleasers. This statement is quite significant. Concepts of the Kingdom are being used to teach us how to love what He loves and refuse what He refuses. When Jesus says, *"I and the Father are One,"* (John 10:30), it is not one person of which He speaks, but one purpose, one mind, one heart and one single affection. To become one with the Father is to embrace His purpose in the earth. The entire redemptive plan begins and ends with the most famous words: "Love God with all of your heart, soul, mind and strength." What could be more relational than this request?

John states this most succinctly: *"We, though, are going to love—love and be loved. First, we were loved, now we love. He loved us first"* (1 John 4:19 MSG). Sons and daughters who have come into a working intimacy and union with God their Father literally learn to love what He loves and refuse what He refuses. Spiritual maturity involves returning to God, in as pure a form as possible, the love that He first gave us. This is a reciprocal or symbiotic relationship. As we continue to allow God to take up His residence within us, and His DNA is formed in us, we are instructed, encouraged, and released to love as He loves. The single most important concept of the New Testament is the clear statement that Father expects us to replicate His own love. This is not self-compulsion or religious activity. We love because of who we are, His own children. When the center of our being has been changed, we will actually begin to love God and our neighbor, to love righteousness and hate iniquity. Keeping ourselves in the exact center of God's love allows us to learn to love what He loves; then our own priesthood starts to take form. We can look into the human garbage pit for men and women just like ourselves, properly respond to them without playing sheriff, and carry the burden of the Lord for them.

When our focus changes from religious activity to learning to love the person of Christ as Lord and King, seeking to love what He loves and refuse what He refuses, then behavior, which is the true essence of *Agape*, becomes workable. Simply stated, *Agape* is the only route to freedom.

Loving what He loves involves making God's personal preference our own. This is the Cross in its most simple form. *Agape* chooses God's preference; *Eros* chooses our own preference. *Agape*, Christ's very love that He imparted to us at the new birth, has now been cultivated and brought to maturity. In this we are being conformed to His image as pleasing sons and daughters coming to glory.

Thoughts and Questions

- ❦ Explain the meaning of the statement: The Kingdom is relational.

- ❦ What did Jesus mean when He said: "*I and the Father are one*"?

- ❦ How do we come to love what Father loves and hate what He hates?

READING 128

Contentment in Success and Failure

*But You remain the same, and Your years will never
end nor come to failure* (Hebrews 1:12 AMP).

O NE OF THE MORE basic lessons we must learn is that neither unbroken
success nor unlimited prosperity are normal. We are in need of two
skills, not one: learning to live centered on *Agape*—whether we are prosper-
ing or failing. Both are discovered in the purpose of the Father.

A Kingdom philosophy of life involves seeing our Christian life and
work as one complete unit rather than being compartmentalized. There
should be a conscious unity about our life and existence, a concept that
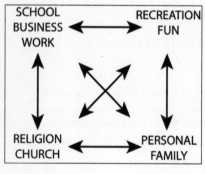 has essentially been lost in the Western
world. Compartmentalization means
having one life that involves school or
work, another that involves religion or
church, a third one that involves family
and personal life, and yet another for
recreation and fun. This means that
when we go on vacation, we put religion
and work aside. In the Kingdom of God
we don't have a business life and a spiritual life—we have one complete life
that we live for Christ. *Agape* shows up in our business and in our recreation, at home and in church, making us one whole person.

Jesus as well as the New Testament writers presented this new life with
Christ as filled with joy *in the midst of* and *in the presence of* all events and/
or worldly loss. Our ability to respond properly to both success and failure,
and to gain and loss, is one of the essential skills that seems to have been

lost in our culture. In the midst of all experiences, we have to learn how to abide in Christ. The psalmist said *"If riches increase, do not set your heart upon them"* (Ps. 62:10). Paul developed the essential skill of learning how to abide whether he was living in abundance or going hungry (see Phil. 4:12). We are able to abide with joy in all situations because being in Christ alone allows us to properly interpret both our successes and our failures. If we understand that it is Christ at work in the situation, then our successes have less opportunity to puff us up, and our failures have less opportunity to drag us into depression.

I prayed for a man for a long time, and when he did not get healed, I struggled with guilt and condemnation. Then the Lord said, "If you don't take the credit when he gets healed, why should you take the blame when he doesn't?" The Lord is the Lord both in our failures as well as in our successes. Nothing can separate us from the *Agape* of God.

Thoughts and Questions

- Why do you think that neither unbroken success nor unlimited prosperity are normal?

- In what ways is your life compartmentalized? Why?

- Why is abiding in Christ important in both success and failure?

Conclusion

That they may all be one; even as Thou, Father, art in Me, and I in Thee,
that they also may be in Us; that the world may believe that Thou didst
send Me. And the glory which Thou hast given Me I have given to them;
that they may be one, just as We are one; I in them, and Thou in Me,
that they may be perfected in unity, that the world may know that Thou
didst send Me, and didst love them, even as Thou didst love Me. Father,
I desire that they also, whom Thou hast given Me, be with Me where I
am, in order that they may behold My glory, which Thou hast given Me;
for Thou didst love Me before the foundation of the world. O righteous
Father, although the world has not known Thee, yet I have known Thee;
and these have known that Thou didst send Me; and I have made Thy
name known to them, and will make it known; that the love wherewith
Thou didst love Me may be in them, and I in them (John 17:21-26).

WE ARE UNABLE MAKE this journey alone. As the Body of Christ, we must make this Kingdom journey together, watering and nourishing the Eternal Seed within ourselves and in each other. My prayer is that you and I would sufficiently mature and allow the Lord Jesus to use us to bring about a serious reformation. May He allow us to see the beginnings of the communal restoration of all creation. In this we become synergistic, i.e., workers together with God.

> *Then comes the end, when He delivers up the kingdom to the*
> *God and Father, when He has abolished all rule and all author-*
> *ity and power. For He must reign until He has put all His*
> *enemies under His feet. The last enemy that will be abolished*
> *is death. For He has put all things in subjection under His*

feet. But when He says, "All things are put in subjection," it is evident that He is excepted who put all things in subjection to Him. And when all things are subjected to Him, then the Son Himself also will be subjected to the One who subjected all things to Him, that God may be all in all (1 Corinthians 15:24-28).

Agape is the clear, definable, and measurable Kingdom principle that is the governing force of the universe. When Paul says *Agape* controls him (see 2 Cor. 5:13-15), he gives us the universal picture that includes every tribe, tongue, people, and nation. *Agape* alone takes us to the answer that is as big as the need. *Agape* contains the inherent power to shake the thrones of kings and popes. *Agape* is reformational and transformational because God *is Agape*. God's eternal purpose is immutable and inexorable. Paul said that

in Him we also were made [God's] heritage (portion) *and we obtained an inheritance; for we had been foreordained* (chosen and appointed beforehand) *in accordance with His purpose, Who works out everything in agreement with the counsel and design of His [own] will* (Ephesians 1:11 AMP).

I can therefore say with total confidence that apart from the restoration of *Agape* as the absolute of God, we *will not* arrive at the goal predetermined in the Bible as the redemptive purpose of God as Father.

Agape is the quintessence of the Kingdom of God. It *is* the glory revealed. It *is* the absolute by which everything and everyone shall be measured. All Kingdom reality must be birthed from Christ, centered in Christ, and returned to Christ. Christ is *Agape* incarnate as Immanuel, God with us. I AM has come, and *Agape* never disappears.

About Bob Mumford

BOB MUMFORD IS A dynamic Bible teacher with a unique and powerful gift for imparting the Word of God. His anointed messages are
remembered for years afterwards because he captivates his audiences with
humor in the form of word pictures, which penetrate deep into hearts with
incredible authority, clarity, and personal application. Since 1954, thousands
of Christians worldwide have attributed their spiritual growth and determination to follow Jesus Christ to his prophetic teaching, helping them understand Father God and His Kingdom.

Bob has written for major Christian periodicals both in the United
States and abroad and published several books, including *Agape Road,
Take Another Look at Guidance, The King & You, Fifteen Steps Out, Living
Happily Ever After,* and *The Purpose of Temptation.* He has also published

numerous booklets called *Plumblines*, including *Renegade Male* and a series on *Inheritance*

Bob has a heart for backsliders, having come to the Lord at age 12 only to stray from God a few months later. During this time, when he was 13, his parents divorced, creating the need for him to quit school and work to help support his mother and five sisters. At 20 years old, he joined the US Navy as a medic. Bob would go with his Navy buddies to the bar and end up preaching to those in the bar about the necessity to repent of their sins and come to Christ. Even then, Father God was pursuing him!

While on leave from the Navy, Bob attended a church service one evening where he was overcome by the conviction of the Holy Spirit and literally ran to the altar. After being away from God for 12 years, the Lord cleaned up his heart and gave him a new purpose and direction, calling him specifically to "Feed My people".

After completing his high school education in the Navy and then graduating with a Bachelor of Science degree from Valley Forge Christian College, Bob attended the University of Delaware and then received his Masters of Divinity degree from Reformed Episcopal Seminary in Philadelphia. Over the years, he has served as pastor and as a Dean and Professor of New Testament and Missions at Elim Bible Institute. In 1972 he founded Lifechangers, and today his teaching materials are distributed all over the world and have been translated into more than 20 different languages.

Bob has traveled extensively to some 50 nations as an international conference speaker, and today he is considered to be a spiritual "Papa" to thousands of Christians. His ministry has been to prophetically proclaim and teach the sufficiency of Christ Jesus and His Kingdom in a manner which promotes reconciliation and unity in the Body of Christ. Bob seeks to bring about personal spiritual change and growth in the lives of believers, regardless of denominational persuasion. His unique style of humor is designed to keep you smiling so it isn't too painful when the truth of his teaching hits home. Such high intensity in the Holy Spirit, accompanied by his pointed and colorful delivery, enables him to impact his audiences with an unforgettable and life-changing experience.

Bob and his wife, Judith, live in Raleigh, North Carolina and can be reached through Lifechangers.

If you would like to receive information about Lifechangers, or a catalog of materials, you can write Bob at:

Lifechangers

PO Box 3709, Cookeville, TN 38502 U.S.A.

800.521.5676 🐝 931.520.3730

lc@lifechangers.org 🐝 www.lifechangers.org

Books

Fifteen Steps Out

Take Another Look at Guidance

The King & You

The Purpose of Temptation

Dr. Frankenstein & World Systems

Giving and Receiving Offense

Bible Studies:

The Agape Road

Breaking Out (also in Spanish)

Knowing, Loving & Following Jesus

Leading Leaders in Agape

Unshared Love

Booklets:

Below the Bottom Line

Church of My Dreams

Correction Not Rejection

The Difference Between the Church and the Kingdom

Forever Change

Grace: God's Rubber Room

The Implications of Following Jesus

On Being Scandalized

Prison of Resentment

Psalm for Living

Renegade Male

Riddle of the Painful Earth

Standing in the Whirlwind

Three Dimensional Reality

Water Baptism

Why God?

(and many others)

Book Recommendations

Enthusiasm by Ronald Knox

Outlines of Theology by Archibald A. Hodge

When Religion is an Addiction by Robert Minor

Agape and Eros by Anders Nygren

The Unshakable Kingdom and the Unchanging Person by E. Stanley Jones

The Eclipse of Christ in Eschatology by Adrio König

A Theology of Life: Dietrich Bonhoeffer's Religionless Christianity
by Ralf Wustenberg

IN THE RIGHT HANDS, THIS BOOK WILL CHANGE LIVES!

Most of the people who need this message will not be looking for this book. To change their lives, you need to put a copy of this book in their hands.

> *But others (seeds) fell into good ground, and brought forth fruit, some a hundred-fold, some sixty-fold, some thirty-fold* (Matthew 13:8).

Our ministry is constantly seeking methods to find the good ground, the people who need this anointed message to change their lives. Will you help us reach these people?

> *Remember this—a farmer who plants only a few seeds will get a small crop. But the one who plants generously will get a generous crop* (2 Corinthians 9:6).

EXTEND THIS MINISTRY BY SOWING
3 BOOKS, 5 BOOKS, 10 BOOKS, OR MORE TODAY,
AND BECOME A LIFE CHANGER!

Thank you,

Don Nori Sr., Founder
Destiny Image
Since 1982

DESTINY IMAGE PUBLISHERS, INC.

"Promoting Inspired Lives."

VISIT OUR NEW SITE HOME AT
WWW.DESTINYIMAGE.COM

FREE SUBSCRIPTION TO DI NEWSLETTER

Receive free unpublished articles by top DI authors, exclusive discounts, and free downloads from our best and newest books.

Visit www.destinyimage.com to subscribe.

Write to: Destiny Image
                    P.O. Box 310
                    Shippensburg, PA 17257-0310

Call: 1-800-722-6774

Email: orders@destinyimage.com

For a complete list of our titles or to place an order
online, visit www.destinyimage.com.

FIND US ON FACEBOOK OR FOLLOW US ON TWITTER.

www.facebook.com/destinyimage   facebook
www.twitter.com/destinyimage   twitter